FIRST GENTLEMAN OF THE BEDCHAMBER

Also by Hubert Cole

JOSÉPHINE

FIRST GENTLEMAN
OF THE BEDCHAMBER

*The life of Louis-François-Armand,
maréchal duc de Richelieu*

BY HUBERT COLE

New York · The Viking Press

First published in 1965 by The Viking Press, Inc.
625 Madison Avenue, New York, N.Y. 10022

Library of Congress catalog card number: 65-14511

Printed in U.S.A. by The Vail-Ballou Press

To Margery

Contents

ILLUSTRATIONS

Photographic credits:
Archives Photographiques: i, iv, v, vi, ix, xi
Photographie Giraudon: vii, x, xii
Service de Documentation Photographique, Versailles: iii, viii, xiii

FIRST GENTLEMAN OF THE BEDCHAMBER

Fronsac

When Anne-Marguerite d'Acigné, the daughter of an ancient and prosperous Breton family, married Armand-Jean, duc de Richelieu, as his second wife, in 1684, she was thirty-one and he fifty-five. She bore him three daughters in the first five years of their marriage, and then, because of differences in age and interests and his insupportable temper, their lives diverged, the testy, gouty duc grumbling the days away in the ornate palace on his estate at Richelieu, avoiding his creditors and the gaming tables at which he had lost a fortune, while his wife remained at court, where she had official duties as *dame d'honneur* to the Dauphine. The break between them was not open or accompanied by bitterness; they lived together in reasonable harmony during the short periods when they were in the same place, and, on hearing at the end of August 1695 that his wife intended to spend a few days at Richelieu, the duc very civilly went to meet her half-way on the rather exhausting journey of nearly two hundred miles.

They put up at the château of a friend who, having no reason to do otherwise, set only one bedroom and one bed at their disposal. In the morning, they continued on to Richelieu, where they remained for a month or so before returning together to Paris and Versailles for the winter. But to the duc, life in the fashionable world was a torment if he had no money to burn. He moved restlessly between his apartments in the palace of Versailles and his great mansion in the place Royale and then, very early in the new year, went back to the rustic grandeur of Richelieu, once more leaving behind him his wife, who, to his delight and her surprise, was pregnant again after a lapse of seven years.

A little after midnight on Saturday, 3 March 1696, the duchesse gave birth, very prematurely, to a boy, in the presence of two hurriedly summoned witnesses, a Roman gentleman named Francesco Mario Pompeo Colonna and his friend, the abbé Nicolas Laurent, both of whom were guests in the town house. Soon after daybreak, the abbé was sent off in the post-chaise to Richelieu, and within a few days the duc was back in Paris, overjoyed with the discovery that, at the age of sixty-five and after a total of forty-six years of marriage, he had at last achieved a son and heir to whom he could pass on his titles of duc de Richelieu in Poitou and Fronsac in Guienne, peer of France, comte de Cosnac, prince de Mortagne, baron de Barbezieu, de Coze, de Sangeon, and d'Albret.

Much less pleased was the duc's cousin, who, as the years had gone by, had increasingly counted on inheriting these titles and the entailed estates. He promptly started the rumour that the child's true father was the duchesse's friend, Hennequin de Charmont, and, for good measure, that the three girls who had preceded him were the children of the duchesse's own cousin, Charles de Bellay. There seems to have been no foundation for these allegations. The child himself, fifty years later, mentioned doubts about his legitimacy to Voltaire, but the thought arose more probably from distaste for his father than from distrust of his mother, who was regarded as a woman of impregnable virtue by everybody except the envious cousin. But it was pleasantly appropriate that the new arrival, who was in time to gain the reputation of having cuckolded half the men of quality in France, should be greeted as a by-blow at his own birth.

He was born two months before his time and did not look as if he would survive; small and sickly, he squealed feebly in a bed of cotton-wool. On one occasion, he was set aside as dead, until a maidservant, noticing some tiny movement, picked him up, placed him inside her shift against her warm, bare breast, and cuddled him back to life: thus making such an impression on his infant mind that it was said he could never thereafter set eyes on a woman without wishing to re-enact this childhood experience with her. When the baby was ten days old, a priest came in from the parish church of Saint-Paul to sprinkle him with holy water, but it was not until he was nearly three that he was formally baptized as Louis-François-Armand du Plessis and given the courtesy use of his father's second title, duc de Fronsac.

This second christening took place at Versailles, after mass on 15 February 1699 in the chapel of the vast palace that Louis XIV was still constructing around his father's former hunting lodge among the sandy woodlands a dozen miles south-west of Paris. The duchesse de Richelieu had died six months before, and the child was held at the font by the Dauphin's daughter-in-law, the duchesse de Bourgogne, and by the stern, sixty-year-old Louis, the Sun King himself—a great honour which the duc de Richelieu owed partly to the King's respect for the great Cardinal from whom he had inherited his title, but even more to his claims on the gratitude of Madame de Maintenon.

Richelieu and his first wife, whom he married for her money when he was a little over twenty and she twice his age, and her brother-in-law, the duc d'Albret, had befriended Madame de Maintenon when her husband, the dramatist Scarron, died and left her penniless. D'Albret's cousin, Montespan, had recently received the signal honour of having his wife become the King's mistress, and the fruit of this royal passion was a series of semi-royal bastards for whom the Richelieus and d'Albrets suggested that their friend, the widow Scarron, would make a discreet and intelligent governess and foster mother. In the course of time, Louis made her acquaintance and was at first repelled and then fascinated by the air of devout humility with which she cloaked the voluptuous appeal of her richly endowed figure and large, dark, lustrous eyes. So compelling were her religious sentiments, and so strong the hold that she established over the King, that she turned him from sin with his mistresses and back to the outward forms of conjugal bliss with his poor, squat, neglected queen, Maria Teresa of Spain. Then, receiving the unusual blessing of an earthly reward for these acts of simple piety, Madame Scarron found herself somehow wafted with downcast eyes into the royal

bed, where she was raised to the nobility as Madame de Maintenon and, after Maria Teresa's death in 1683, became Louis's second wife in a secret marriage.

She did not forget the kindnesses and the opportunities that
her former benefactors had placed in her way. Richelieu was given
the post of *chevalier d'honneur* to the Dauphine, which he sold
almost immediately for 500,000 livres, and his wife became *dame
d'honneur*, first to the Queen and then to the Dauphine. Madame
de Maintenon was equally gracious to his second wife, and she
lavished on the young Fronsac almost as much love as she had
given to her two favourites among the illegitimate children, the
duc du Maine and the comte de Toulouse. As soon as the boy
was old enough, Richelieu prudently posted him outside the
chapel every morning at 7 a.m., summer and winter, to offer his
hand to their patroness as she came down the steps and got into
her carriage to be off on a day of determined devotion at her
convent school at Saint-Cyr.

It was a strange society in which young Fronsac spent his childhood: mannered, intricate, brutal. It was the age of the enormous
three-cornered beaver hat and the long brocaded *justaucorps*,
tight-fitting and reaching almost to the knees, midway between
the medieval jerkin and the modern waistcoat; an age of wide-
skirted, buckram-stiffened coats, with vast cuffs pinned back with
gold and silver and precious stones; an age of high-heeled shoes,
brightly varnished (the King had a pair with pictures of his victories painted on them). Above all, it was the age of the wig, in
all its cumbersome glory before it dwindled into queues or bags or
bobs, and made preferably from a Flemish girl's hair, crimped and
curled and stitched on to crape, costing as much as 3,000 livres,
and provided in so many sizes and fashions that there was none
who could not be suited—even down to wigs with false tonsures
for those in holy orders.

It was significant that, while his subjects had their heads shaved
to offset the heat of their wigs and wore felt caps to absorb the
sweat by day and woollen bonnets to protect their naked pates at
night, the King retained his own hair, having his wigs specially
constructed with slits through which the royal locks were threaded

and then curled, thus remaining the only hairy-headed man in a nation of the bald. He reigned with a splendour and supremacy unequalled in any other country of Europe. Cardinal Richelieu had tamed the nobility at the beginning of the seventeenth century, and Louis XIV had constructed at Versailles the menagerie in which they were confined at its end. By the dawn of the eighteenth century, they had been stripped of their duties and left with their privileges: they held the towel while the King washed his hands, they helped him off with his boots or on with his nightshirt, they stood eternally waiting with well-bred, vacuous, inexpressibly bored faces turned to the royal presence like flowers to the sun.

In the richest, most fertile countryside of Europe, peasants lived on gruel and hid their grain and poultry in cellars for fear that these, too, might be taxed away from them. In the towns, a new class of bankers and lawyers awaited the chance to stretch out their hands towards the levers of power and to strike up their own clamour for privilege. In the greatest of royal palaces, the dregs of an ancient chivalry scrambled and crawled for favour and ached for the moment when they could withdraw from the ornate, piercingly draughty state apartments and huddle in the warmth of their attic-rooms, tiny, dusky and redolent of the eighteenth century's distinctive smells: ineffective sanitation and the latest cure for the pox.

For the first six years of his life, the boy Fronsac lived at the hôtel de Richelieu, the great family mansion in the north-west corner of the place Royale,* where the Cardinal had lived before he built the Palais Cardinal facing the Louvre. The houses that ranged shoulder to shoulder round the square, arcaded on the ground floor and rising to four stories of white stone and russet brick, were identical except for the depth of a set of windows on one, the decoration of an ironwork balcony on another, and broken only by the taller *pavillon du roi* and *pavillon de la reine*. From the windows in the front of the house, he looked out on the gilt equestrian statue of Louis XIII, erected by the Cardinal, and

---

* Now the place des Vosges.

the live horsemen curvetting around the broad, dusty space that surrounded it and was enclosed by a double-railed fence. In the house diagonally opposite lived the prince de Guémenée, a member of the powerful Rohan family, and next to the *pavillon du roi* on the south side, Madame de Sévigné had spent her childhood. By the year in which she died (and Fronsac was born) many of the former residents were following the fashionable drift westwards towards the faubourg Saint-Honoré, or across the river to the faubourg Saint-Germain, or to the middle of the river, where the Ile des Vaches and the Ile Sainte-Marie had been linked and furnished with embankments. The faintest air of shabbiness hung over the square and over the hôtel de Richelieu, despite the money that was lavished on its upkeep and its horde of servants.

The old duc passed much of his time sulking at Richelieu, unable to sell any more of his estates and allowed only half of the income from those that remained by the board of trustees set up by his creditors. When he came to Paris or went to Versailles, to pay his respects to the King or to complain to Madame de Maintenon that Madame d'Acigné, his mother-in-law, was trying to take his children from him, his tired angry eyes darted from side to side in search of an heiress willing to barter her ready cash for the title of duchesse. He had held the great office of General of the Galleys but had fought only one naval action, and that without any great distinction. In a moderately long and spendthrift career, he had done nothing to add lustre to the name of Richelieu, and the young boy growing up in the loneliness of the great house soon discovered that his was a name which many of his fellow noblemen considered to be in need of illumination—if indeed, they were willing to grant him the name of Richelieu at all.

Since the Cardinal had left no legitimate children, his titles and estates passed to the descendants of his sister, Françoise, who in 1603 had married an obscure squireen named René de Vignerot, seigneur of Pontcourlay in Poitou. Their son, François, adding his mother's maiden name to his father's, called himself Vignerot du Plessis and inherited the duchies of Richelieu and Fronsac. These, together with the governorship of Le Havre and the Generalship of the Galleys, he passed on to his son, Armand-

Jean, born in 1629. Those who envied Armand-Jean's position at
court and the protection he received from Madame de Maintenon, referred to him always as "Vignerot" and spread the story
that his grandfather, the Cardinal's brother-in-law, had begun his
career as the Cardinal's lute-player. Young Fronsac, pursued
throughout his early life by these jibes about his ancestry, was
plagued with doubts and with the desire to outdo those who
jeered at him.

Having scarcely known his true mother, he was confronted with
a stepmother when he was six; for in March 1702, Madame de
Maintenon found a third wife for the debauched old duc among
the Noailles family, into which she had married her niece. The
chosen bride was the widowed marquise de Noailles, daughter of
a rich financier and mother of two girls, aged eleven and eight.
She was prepared to share her life with the testy septuagenarian
and even to give him 100,000 livres towards paying off his debts,
in return for the most coveted of worldly prizes: the *tabouret*. The
tabouret would be the symbol of her rank, as the small square of
carpet, the *carreau*, was that of a duc's. In the presence of the
King, all women were obliged to stand, with the exception of
princesses of the blood, who were given armchairs, and duchesses,
who were entitled to the folding stools called *tabourets*. And just
as grown men would squabble all their lives with venom and bile
and desperation for the right to have a little piece of carpet under
their knees when they went to church with the King, so the summit of a well-bred woman's ambition was reached when, under the
gaze of other women green and rigid with envy, she ceremonially
placed her posterior on one of these small, collapsible stools.

To ensure that this right should pass to her descendants, the
marquise stipulated that the duc's son should become engaged to
her elder daughter, and, in the event of her death, to the younger
one. The bride would have a dowry of 200,000 livres in cash and
the inheritance of the magnificent new mansion that the marquise, then living in the rue de Vaugirard, had just built in the rue
de l'Université. The arrangement, common enough at the time,
did not please young Fronsac, who, even at six, was a stubborn,
unyielding little boy. He disliked his two stepsisters and resented

being moved to the mansion in the rue de l'Université, where his father joined the new duchesse in a short-lived attempt to make some economies. Fronsac was at first on bad terms with his stepmother, who kept a tight hold on the purse strings; when his friends made fun of the rather old-fashioned and hard-wearing coat and breeches in which she dressed him, he answered, with a laugh that did not conceal the bitterness, "Yes—stepmother clothes." But as time went on, he developed respect for the duchesse, which balanced his growing contempt for his father.

Upheaval, uncertainty, and depression were the background to Fronsac's boyhood: war that had broken out again in 1701; revolt by the Protestants against relentless persecution by the church and Madame de Maintenon, flaming up in the Cévennes and flaring through Languedoc and into Guienne; famines brought on by dreadful winters such as that of 1708–9, when the frost struck people down dead in the streets. With nothing to show for his vast expenditure of blood and money, Louis tried to open negotiations for peace, but the terms he was offered were so contemptuous that he was able to publish them to his people and they proudly rallied to him yet once more. Marlborough and Prince Eugène relentlessly pressed the French armies back to their frontiers and then drove them on to their own soil. Only from the Spanish front, at the end of 1710, did there come the heartening news of a great victory at Villa Viciosa.

§ 2

"I am enraptured, my dear duc," Madame de Maintenon wrote to Richelieu "to have to inform you that M. le duc de Fronsac has been a great success. . . . Never has a young man made his début in the world more agreeably. . . ." And, to prove the extent to which she had lost her heart to the boy, and that her letter was not merely politeness to an old friend, she wrote another to the duc de Noailles: "The young duc de Fronsac is sixteen and he looks twelve. He is small, but with the neatest figure in the world, a handsome face and a beautiful head; he is one of the best dancers, very good on a horse. He is fond of music and quick in conversation; respectful, well-mannered and an agreeable quiz."

The perfection of this young paragon's manners and the maturity of his deportment had played surprising tricks with Madame de Maintenon's memory, for this was the winter of 1710 and he was not yet fifteen. But there was no doubt that all the ladies had been impressed by the lively, sharp-featured boy who was making his first formal appearance at court. "Madame la duchesse de Bourgogne takes a great interest in him," Madame de Maintenon had said in her letter to Richelieu. To be admitted to the younger set that gathered around the Dauphin's daughter-in-law was to achieve immediate success.

He was invited to join the Twelfth Night celebrations at Marly, the country mansion in which Louis liked to find relief from the self-imposed, unremitting ceremonial of Versailles, and where he discarded his usual severe majesty in favour of a rusty sort of formality, presiding at the middle of the long supper table, flanked by the princes and princesses of the blood, costumed *en grande tenue* for the ball that was to follow. The remainder of the guests stood facing them, observing the steady and prolonged champing of the royal jaws with respect but no envy, since they had taken the precaution of eating their own suppers beforehand. When the fruit had been cleared away, they applauded the arrival of the Twelfth Night cake and admired the grace with which the recently married fifteen-year-old duchesse de Berry distributed the slices. The lucky bean turned out to be in the slice that the duchesse gave to her mother, the duchesse d'Orléans, and with laughing protests, in a warm cloud of sycophantic cosiness, Madame d'Orléans, as Queen of the Revels, was escorted to the ballroom by the King.

The duchesse de Bourgogne opened the ball with the duc de Berry and then partnered the duc de Brissac in a minuet. Custom demanded that she should have the same partner in the second minuet, and she had risen from her seat when she noticed to her embarrassment that Brissac, through some absence of mind or ignorance of procedure, had led out another partner. Fronsac walked swiftly over to his youthful godmother and asked: "Madame, will you permit me to remedy the fault of my friend Brissac?"

His voice was clear and perfectly controlled and the words hung for a moment in the silence around the royal party; then the King was seen to smile, everybody laughed, and the duchesse floated gaily away on Fronsac's arm. The court had been given its first glimpse of the salient aspects of Fronsac's manner: the easy gallantry that did not shrink from boldness, the instant solution to an awkward problem, the condescending reference to "the fault of my friend Brissac," who was considerably his senior and had already seen service in the musketeers.

The duchesse de Bourgogne had been the darling of the court ever since her arrival from Savoy at the age of twelve to wed the Dauphin's eldest son. She had the prominent Stuart nose (her grandmother was Charles II's favourite sister, Henrietta) and a touch of Austrian heaviness about her mouth and chin, but her contemporaries competed with one another in praising her beauty as well as her charm. She was credited with having "the most expressive and beautiful eyes in the world"; she walked "like a goddess on the clouds"; she flitted from place to place "like a whirlwind, seeming to be in many places at the same time and bringing movement and light to all them." At a court where the King suffered from chronic halitosis, it was scarcely worthy of remark that the duchesse did not have a single sound tooth in her head.

Her first child had died in 1706, and a second one had been born in 1707. In February 1710, she gave birth to her third and last baby, the future Louis XV. She had a theatre constructed in her private apartments so that her pregnancy should not prevent her from going to the play, and she was no sooner up than she began forming her own troupe of amateur entertainers, drawn from the ranks of the younger princes and princesses and peers.

She invited her godson to join this select company, and it was among the young ladies whom he met here that Fronsac scored his first amatory successes. The fresh young matrons, petting and cossetting the handsome little boy, quickly discovered that he had adult ideas. Their motherly and big-sisterly kisses were returned with startling ardour; in the narrow service passages and twilit alcoves with which Versailles was honeycombed, his hands wandered with disconcerting intentness, and he would suddenly appear from nowhere to offer a whispered word of love or attempt a stolen embrace; he was a very forward boy indeed.

It was not long before he gained his first success: with a woman who has remained anonymous because she was the only one for whom he ever showed respect. Her name was scratched from the papers that he preserved, and the most that is known of her is that she was his senior by some years, was married, and had a château near Mantes, where she first submitted, half-willingly, half-desolately, to the passionate love-making of the naked boy whom she found hidden in her bed. But soon his boldness carried him into a much more exalted bedroom. When the duchesse de Bourgogne's young friends gathered in her room before rehearsal one day, during the stay at Marly, one of them caught sight of a foot not quite concealed under the bed valance, and, amid shrill screams, the duc de Brissac stepped forward and grabbed it. To everybody's surprise—and to Brissac's delight—it was Fronsac who was dragged from under the bed. He made his apologies so humbly yet prettily that after a quick scolding he was at once forgiven, but reports of the scandalous affair spread rapidly and, in the course of their spreading, became more interesting, so that in one version the duchesse had removed all her clothes before the intruder had been perceived, and in another he had been not under the bed but in it, and undressed.

Madame de Maintenon consulted Fronsac's father and stepmother, and all three agreed that there was only one possible prescription: the boy must have a woman of his own. Fortunately, the remedy lay ready at hand: the elder Noailles girl had died in 1703, but he had become automatically engaged to the younger one, Anne-Catherine, and on 12 January Madame de Maintenon, still full of enthusiasm, wrote to the duc de Noailles; "The duc de Fronsac is going to marry your cousin; never has a man succeeded so well at court on his first appearance; he is really a very pretty creature." The marriage document was witnessed by the most eminent company imaginable: the King, the Dauphin, the duc and duchesse de Bourgogne, the duc and duchesse de Berry from the immediate royal family; from the Orléans family, descendants of the King's brother, there were the dowager duchesse, the duc and duchesse, and their son, the duc de Chartres; and from the other princes of the blood there was a whole host of Condés and Bourbons, Contis and Charolais and Bourbon-Condés. One of the onlookers, commenting on the diminutive, youthful figure of the bridegroom among all these notabilities, remarked that "one doesn't know whether it is a marriage or a christening."

It turned out to be neither. The bride's uncle, the cardinal de Noailles, archbishop of Paris, celebrated the wedding in his private chapel on Wednesday, 11 February 1711; the reception and marriage feast were held at the family mansion in the rue de l'Université. At the end of the evening, the bride and groom were put ceremonially to bed. The seventeen-year-old bride was helped into her nightgown in one room; the bridegroom—still not quite fifteen—was handed his nightshirt in another; and he was then escorted to her. The couple got into bed; the wedding guests stood around making apposite and indelicate remarks; the curtains were at last drawn together; and the guests departed for more jollities. In the deserted bedroom, behind the closed curtains, nothing happened. Nothing at all. Fronsac, resentful at having been pushed into marriage against his will, refused to have anything to do with his bride.

A fortnight later, the bride was formally presented to the King. While he ate his supper in state, she entered the dining room and solemnly seated herself on her *tabouret*; she had been officially received as the duchesse de Fronsac, but she was still duchesse in name only. She told her mother, who rebuked the recalcitrant bridegroom with all the authority of a woman who was now not only his stepmother, but also his mother-in-law. He was growled at by his elderly father and chided by Madame de Maintenon, whose feelings towards the bride must have been compounded of as much envy as sympathy and the bitter reflection that this was yet another example of the inequality of the sexes, if men but not women were allowed to refuse the performance of such duties. The King's demands on her were as incessant as they were unwelcome. On reaching her seventies, five or six years before, she had asked her religious adviser if it was still her duty to submit to her husband's will *every* day. The problem was uncommon and involved such distinguished protagonists that the priest advised submitting it to the Pope, whose decision had been that, alas, there is no age at which a wife may cease to be obedient to her husband in this respect.

Madame de Maintenon's rebukes had no effect on the stubborn young Fronsac, and, since she still had a very soft spot for him, she soon found herself defending him against his father's querulous complaints that he was wasting his money at the gaming tables. "M. le duc de Fronsac has just left my room consumed with grief at what he has done and at having angered you," she wrote on 5 March to his father. "He assures me that he has never played on credit and that he has only once staked a thousand louis; he has given me his word several times over never to play except for ready money and at small stakes. He has spoken to me with great conviction and has shown the most encouraging sentiments." But even she was forced to add "if they are sincere," and the old duc asked her to get the King's permission for Fronsac to be excused the usual preliminary service in the musketeers and be sent off to the army.

"They're going to send you our little prodigy," she wrote on 22 March to the duc de Noailles, who was commanding the armies on the Spanish frontier, "although he is no longer prodigious; they are decrying him as much now as they were praising him during the last trip to Marly, but I really do not know anything definite, except that he walked into a trap at the tables and has lost twenty or thirty thousand francs. . . . However that may be, my dear duc, the burden is to fall on you. M. le duc de Richelieu was of the opinion after this latest escapade that he needed to be sent away, and farther than Flanders. . . . I hope that Fronsac will not embarrass you unreasonably: he is the most amiable little doll that you could wish to see."

But Fronsac never reached the southern army, for suddenly a new and much greater scandal erupted around him. Everybody talked about it, yet nobody knew precisely what had happened. The family gave out stories that he had been gambling more heavily than ever, but this problem had already been solved by getting the King's permission to send him off to the army. Alternatively, it was whispered that he was in disgrace because he refused to fulfil his duties to his wife, but that was an old complaint and not one to cause this sudden turmoil and sense of crisis. Others revived the rumour that he had been found naked in the duchesse de Bourgogne's bed, but that incident, if it had ever happened at all, had taken place before his wedding. The most likely explanation of any that were put forward was that his brashness had at last outrun itself, and he had performed in public a most improper and impertinent action that could hardly have been condoned in private: his hand had strayed under the duchesse de Bourgogne's skirt as she leaned over a balcony at Marly.

His father wrote to Madame de Maintenon, telling her he was sending a friend to explain "the attitude that I take about the outrageous conduct of a son who can be corrected only by wisdom and the authority of a master who is in a position to stamp out everything that he delights in. . . . M. de Bernaville is a good teacher." The duc de Richelieu requested the King to sign a *lettre de cachet* committing Fronsac to the Bastille, and in the afternoon of Wednesday, 22 April, he drove there with his son and handed him over to the governor, Bernaville.

The great fortress loomed dark and heavy beside the porte Saint-Antoine, a familiar and still frightening memory from the boy's childhood, for the place Royale was only a quarter of a mile away. He had heard the stories of prisoners sent there in their youth and never seen again, of men shackled in underground *cachots*, to which no light ever penetrated. Despite his self-confidence and impudence, it was a chilling prospect for a boy just turned fifteen. The doors slammed behind him and he was taken under escort from the governor's office to his cell. The key turned in the lock and the guard marched away. Without trial, and without appeal except to the King, who had put him there, he was committed during His Majesty's pleasure to this small, lonely, and iron-barred room.

For several days he was held incommunicado. Then, with Madame de Maintenon still at his elbow, Louis instructed Pontchartrain, the Minister of the Royal Household, to find a tutor willing to share the boy's captivity and to try to repair some of the gaps in his education. He found one: the abbé Saint-Rémy, a man both devout and devoted, who was to remain for the rest of his life with Fronsac, first as tutor and then as secretary. With Saint-Rémy as company for part of the day, some of the terror of being locked up in the fortress began to disappear. Other tutors came in to teach him languages and mathematics, and after a few weeks he was invited each afternoon to dine with the governor or his assistant, Launay, and then to stroll with them in the courtyard or on the terrace from which it was possible to look down into the cramped streets of Paris before returning to study in his cell at 5 p.m. "I have agreed this with M. le cardinal de Noailles, M. le duc de Richelieu and Mme. la duchesse," Bernaville wrote to Pontchartrain. "I do not think it possible for him to spend his days alone in his room without its affecting his health."

This concern must have raised Fronsac's spirits and strengthened his courage, but his stubbornness in these forbidding surroundings remains surprising. Whether he had been put in prison to keep him away from the gaming tables or from the duchesse de Bourgogne, there was still the third complaint against him: his neglect of his wife. And his submission on this point was to be the proof of his repentance. He recorded later that he was told that he would remain in prison "until his wife should become pregnant, and for that purpose she was sent to see him twice a week at the Bastille." And regularly, twice a week, he refused to have anything to do with her. "She was much older than I," he explained, "not pretty and of a shrewish disposition"; yet, others found her pleasant and attractive.

He was polite and inflexible. Several ladies of the court had made it their pleasure to continue his instruction in the fascinating mysteries of sex; he had been cut off from them for weeks, which were dragging into months; his release was dependent on a simple compliance that most men considered would be more agreeable than not; but still he turned his wife away when she made her twice-weekly visits. He did it with the utmost grace; "and for my own part," Bernaville reported to Pontchartrain, "I have nothing but praise for his attitude towards my officers and myself. Nobody could be more civil and polite; he anticipates everything that might please us; we have never heard him say anything out of place."

There was one occasion when his resolution faltered. As the days passed unmarked by anything but a fresh page in his lesson books, and as the hope of release grew more and more remote, his courage momentarily slid from him, and he asked the governor that his wife should be sent for. She entered his cell and fell into his arms, bewildered and tearful from shame and injured pride— but still the senior partner in the marriage, commenting with the wisdom and experience of her seventeen years on the follies and ineptitudes of his fifteen. "Ah, my dear," she said as he held her tightly to him, "if only you had always treated me like this, you would not be where you are today."

Fronsac blushed with rage and leaped to his feet. His wife stared at him in astonishment and then recognized defeat. She straightened her clothing and then made for the door without another word. He bowed her out with exquisite courtesy and called for the gaoler to lock him in again.

At the beginning of July, his father visited him for the first time, and Fronsac assured him that he "acknowledged all his errors, that he would never forget the King's graciousness in sending him here to repent and remedy them . . . that he was not at all impatient to leave, and that he would regard an early release as the greatest of misfortunes." That, at least, was what the tactful governor wrote to Pontchartrain, but there were still no actions to prove that the boy was as submissive as his words.

Two months later, Bernaville's earlier fears were fulfilled: Fronsac fell sick. Doctors were called in and at first took the illness to be gaol-fever, a variety of typhus from which many prisoners died. When it turned out to be smallpox, a more common but scarcely less dangerous disease, the governor put Fronsac in quarantine, and the boy asked for a priest from his former parish church of Saint-Paul to be brought in to minister to him: the last time in his life that he is known to have shown the slightest voluntary sign of piety. He asked for Communion, for Extreme Unction, for permission for one of his servants to go to the shrine of Sainte-Geneviève, patroness of Paris, to touch her statue with a handkerchief and bring back holy bread. The fever subsided and, perhaps by the miraculous intervention of Sainte-Geneviève, his face was completely unmarked. By 17 October, he was able to get out of bed, and, after his cell had been fumigated by burning gunpowder in it, he was allowed to receive visitors again. On 4 November, he was well enough to take a stroll in the garden on top of the bastion.

The very real fear that he might die had not softened his father's heart—or that of his stepmother or Madame de Maintenon or the King. Fronsac wrote to Madame de Maintenon imploring her help in obtaining his release, but she replied chiding him for his obstinacy and telling him how grieved she was to learn that the duchesse de Fronsac was still not pregnant. Throughout that winter, and through the spring and early summer of 1712, Fronsac remained in his cell; and eventually it was not he, but they, who gave way. In mid-June, the duc de Richelieu announced that he had paid off his son's smaller gambling debts and had made arrangements to settle the larger ones later; on 16 June, Fronsac wrote to Pontchartrain: "My father has graciously consented to agree to my release and commands me to beg you to be kind enough to request this from the King. I shall try to deserve all the favours that he has been good enough to show me and to demonstrate that this reclusion has effected a real change in me, because of the profound reflections that I have made."

On 19 June, after one year and two months in the Bastille, he was given his release. It may have been because his family had given up hope that he would be reconciled with his wife; it may have been because his father had forgiven him and paid his debts; it may—most likely of all—have been because the risk of further scandal with the duchesse de Bourgogne no longer existed. She had died, aged 26, earlier in the year.

§ 3

Fronsac emerged from the Bastille a free man, but still in disgrace, and it was not until August that he was granted an audience at Fontainebleau, where the King spoke in affectionate terms of his father and urged the boy to mend his ways—and then sent him off to Flanders to serve under the duc de Villars, the last survivor of the generals who had won the King his earlier victories. Although the British had come to terms, the Austrians were not willing to cease fighting and their troops under Prince Eugène still pressed forward. At the moment when Fronsac reported for duty on Villars's staff, the French court and the ministries of state were already packing and preparing to flee southward, but Villars saved the day with a brilliant victory at Denain that cut Eugène's lines of communication and forced him to retire. The Austrians refused to sign the Treaty of Utrecht in the following year and returned to the attack, but Villars drove them out of Landau, chased them across the Rhine, and brought the 1713 campaign to a triumphant close with the successful siege of Freiburg.

For Fronsac, these campaigns in Flanders and Germany provided not only an opportunity to impress his seniors with his enthusiasm and fearlessness but also a valuable lesson in generalship and how to reap the rewards of victory. At Freiburg, when the Austrian commander, von Harsch, retired to the fortress and left the town at the mercy of the French, Villars extracted a ransom of one million livres before he would agree to spare the town and its inhabitants from pillage, fire, and rape. To deplete the fortress's supplies, Villars told von Harsch that he must provide the food for the 5,000 Austrian prisoners in French hands. When von Harsch refused, Villars exposed twenty of the dying wounded men in front of the fort, with neither food nor water, until his terms were met.

Because of his distinguished conduct at Landau and Freiburg— and because Villars knew that the gesture would please Madame de Maintenon—Fronsac was given the honoured and lucrative mission of carrying back to Louis the news that with the fall of Freiburg the Austrians were soundly defeated for that year. He arrived at Marly on Tuesday, 21 November, his head still bandaged from a wound that he had received during the siege, and bearing himself like a hero when he was admitted to the King's apartments after dinner. He had quite wiped out his former disgrace by his military exploits, and Louis received him warmly and open-handedly, giving him a larger reward than usual—12,000 livres—for the news that he brought, and the additional compliment of a lodging in the château of Marly itself. Since the army was about to go into winter quarters, Louis told Fronsac not to return to the front; by the following spring, before he rejoined Villars, the war was over.

In May 1714, there was a new and melancholy mark of favour for the eighteen-year-old courtier: he was chosen to escort to Saint-Denis the heart of the duc de Berry, the third of Louis's legitimate grandsons and the last of those eligible to succeed him. The King now had no male successors in either the first or second generations: his son, the Grand Dauphin, had died in 1711; his eldest grandson, the duc de Bourgogne, had died the following year, together with the duchesse and their elder surviving son; his second grandson, Philippe, duc d'Anjou, had renounced all claims to the throne of France on becoming king of Spain. In the direct line there remained only his great-grandson, the youngest child of the duc de Bourgogne, who had narrowly escaped dying in the epidemic of scarlet fever that carried off his parents and his brother.

In an age when every sudden death was attributed to poisoning until it was proved to be natural, the death of the duc de Berry was at once considered to be the work of the King's nephew, the duc d'Orléans, who had also been suspected of murdering the duc and duchesse de Bourgogne and their son two years before. Madame de Maintenon, playing on Louis's fear that there would be nobody of his own blood to succeed him, now managed to persuade him to declare that her two foster children, the duc du Maine and comte de Toulouse—Louis's sons by Madame de Montespan—were entitled to the same rank and privileges as the princes of the blood and eligible to succeed to the throne; at the same time, the duc du Maine was given what would eventually become the most influential employment at court: the supervision of the education of the four-year-old Dauphin when he left the hands of his governess in three years' time.

Although she was triumphant in her struggle to advance the

fortunes of her foster children, Madame de Maintenon had to admit defeat in her attempts to force Fronsac to live with his wife, although they still shared the same roof; after twelve years of bickering with a wife who was as tight-fisted as she was strong-willed, Fronsac's father had gone back to the hôtel de Richelieu, briskly evicting the archbishop of Rheims, who had been renting it, and taking his son and daughter-in-law with him. And it was in the Saint-Antoine quarter, adjoining his childhood home, that Fronsac came upon Madame Michelin, the unfortunate heroine of one of the more fantastic of his adventures.

She was small and blond, and he first saw her in the rue Saint-Antoine, coming from the direction of the church in the rue Saint-Paul; he guessed that she had been to mass and the next day he went to church and managed to stand close to her. It took him a long time to strike up acquaintance, for she was devout and preoccupied in church, and, when the service was over, she hurried off to the upholstery and mirror-framing shop that she kept with her husband. Half seriously, half as a game, Fronsac rented a couple of rooms not far away and engaged Monsieur Michelin to furnish them for him. It provided an excuse to make frequent visits to the shop, and he was amused by the thought that the obsequious upholsterer was lavishing so much care on the setting in which, with any luck, Fronsac would seduce his wife.

From the way in which she blushed or looked away when he spoke to her, it was clear that his elegant manners and practised charm had impressed her. He persuaded the anonymous duchesse who had been his first mistress to offer Monsieur Michelin work in her château at Mantes, and when the husband had left, he called at the shop and declared his love for the wife. But he had underestimated the strength of Madame Michelin's moral scruples, for though she admitted that she cared for him, she refused to listen to his protestations of love and would not even let him stay to supper.

Though she did not know it, she had chosen the least likely way of discouraging him. One of his acquaintances referred to him as a *dompteur de femmes*, and it was as a *dompteur*, a tamer of wild animals, that he found most of his delights in love. "My devout little woman was frightened of damning herself and my eloquence was not persuasive enough to dispel her fears. I was not in love, but I was nettled at the thought that a little bourgeoise could hold me so long at bay. I resolved to take by assault a stronghold that would not capitulate." He sent her a note by one of his servants, purporting to come from the duchesse, saying that she had decided to furnish more rooms and asking Madame Michelin to go with the bearer to collect some samples of material from a woman who was embroidering it. The young wife went unsuspectingly with the servant to what she imagined was the embroideress's workroom, walked in and found Fronsac awaiting her on a sofa. Before she could turn and run out again, the door was locked behind her.

The impact that Fronsac's amorous exploits made on his contemporaries, and on many of his countrymen in succeeding generations, was partly due to the elements of drama that he imparted to them: sometimes comic, sometimes farcical, and sometimes, as in this case, quite melodramatic; for Madame Michelin found herself confronted with a frantic struggle, against Fronsac, against her own desires, and against her conscience. She upbraided him and pleaded with him, admitted that she loved him but only in the purest of ways; the effect was merely to make him more persistent and more determined.

"I confess that I had to deliver a long and furious assault and perhaps I should have got nothing from it but fruitless fatigue, if her emotions had not played traitor to her conscience. Those of Madame Michelin were very lively, very inflammable, and resistance for her was a real effort of virtue. Eventually the doors of Hell closed before her eyes, she could no longer see anything but the delights of Paradise—and I then obtained proof that a woman can love Man with the same fervour that she loves God."

Having once succumbed, she willingly continued the affair. Fronsac called on her in the shop and there met her friend, Madame Renaud, who lodged on the top floor, a young widow who was as forward in meeting his advances as Madame Michelin had been reluctant. One night, when Michelin was away at Mantes, Fronsac slept in the upholsterer's bed with Madame Michelin until two o'clock in the morning, and then, pretending that he had to be home before dawn, went upstairs to spend the rest of the night in the arms of the vivacious widow. He was a man of great physical resources, yet always in sad need of new refinements and mental stimulus to keep his interest alive in a woman once he had seduced her. He was quite delighted when Madame Renaud's maid left the door on the stairs open the following morning, with the result that Madame Michelin, coming up to pay an early call on her friend, found the pair of them still in bed.

Madame Renaud's embarrassment at being caught in so guilty a situation by the pious young woman from downstairs amused him immensely; but there was much greater pleasure in gradually revealing to the widow that Madame Michelin was his mistress too. He laughed away the reproaches that they threw at him, and, at the end of a long and—for the two women—painful scene, in which he played with remarkable skill on their love for him and their newly discovered rivalry for each other, he took each woman aside separately and persuaded her to visit him in the rooms that Michelin had furnished for him in the rue Saint-Antoine.

With each of them he made an appointment for the same time on the same day, so that one entered on the heels of the other. Having enjoyed the startled and icy glances that they exchanged, he seated them on either side of him on the sofa and then, with extraordinary virtuosity, begged, cajoled, and bullied them into drawing lots to decide which of them should be the first to accompany him into the adjoining bedroom and receive proof of his continued affection. Madame Michelin won and Madame Renaud had to wait; but Fronsac's virility enabled him to fulfil his promise that he would always treat each of them alike.

The cynical sensuality, the contempt for women's feelings, and the relish with which this nineteen-year-old libertine humiliated them, have led later generations to believe that the story was concocted and the characters fictitious. But Fronsac was as jealous of his own reputation as he was careless of his mistresses'; he preserved their letters as trophies, and among the collection is this sad, neatly written note from the far-from-fictitious Madame Michelin.

"You ask for news of my health. I am obliged to you, but you should know that it depends entirely on you. It is you who can make it perfect, just as it depends on you whether or not I ever enjoy it again. Please remember, my dear friend, that it is only you who can ease the hardships that I suffer every day of your absence. . . . I have so little time to myself—only enough to tell you that you have all my love, and if my absence causes you pain, then do not doubt that yours gives me a million times more."

His interest in both women had begun to fade. Once, in seducing a willing but well-guarded wife, he crawled in pitch darkness along a plank stretched from one upper window to another; when his mistress urged him to go back again just before dawn, so that he should not be discovered, he flatly refused. "But you have already crossed it once," she pleaded. "Certainly," he replied, "but that was *before*—and then one would willingly go through fire. But *afterwards*—that's a different thing altogether." So it was with the over-eager Madame Renaud and with Madame Michelin, who was still oppressed by her conscience yet unable to resist his love. He saw less of her; she grew more melancholy; he found her boring and turned elsewhere. Some months later, he learned that she had gone into a decline and died. There is no indication that the news made any great impression on him. These women led inferior lives, experienced inferior emotions; they were not so much of a different class, to him, as of a different species.

§ 4

In May 1715, his querulous old father died at the age of eighty-five, after a series of apoplectic attacks, leaving him his title, the entailed estates, and debts amounting to the staggering sum of nearly one million livres. The King received Fronsac cordially as duc de Richelieu and gave him the use of the lodgings that his father had previously enjoyed at Versailles; but Louis himself was not to reign at Versailles much longer.

The old tyrant, apparently as full of vigour as ever, reviewed his troops on the plain of Marly on 12 August 1715, impassively sitting his horse in the full rays of the summer sun. On returning to the château, he ate forty figs and gulped down three glasses of ice water and the following day, at Versailles, seemed none the worse for his outing or his gluttony. But on 15 August he broke into a feverish sweat and his legs began to swell; he felt too weak to go to chapel for mass, which was celebrated in his bedroom. His doctors recommended the mineral waters of Bourbon-l'Archimbault, for internal and external use, and two hundred horses were posted at relay stages between the spa and Versailles to bring barrels of the water, rich in salt and iodine.

A week later the medical men changed their minds. They found the water did the King no good when taken internally, and they feared that baths were likely to enfeeble him. They administered quinine as an antidote to the fever, but the King continued to decline. He had now lost so much weight that his coat and breeches had to be taken in four inches, but his determination was as strong as ever, and at 8 p.m. on 24 August, he took it into his head to appear on the balcony of his bedroom, where he raised his hat three times to the curious crowd below who dutifully shouted, "*Vive le Roi!*" Twenty-four hours later, on Saint-Louis's day, the fever had become so fierce that he was put to bed at 9 p.m. and the viaticum administered at 11:30.

The next morning he was still alive. He summoned the princes of the blood, led by the duc d'Orléans, and adjured them to forget their differences in support of his great-grandson, the five-year-old Dauphin, who would shortly be called to the throne. The illness grew more hopeless and more horrible. The gangrene that had been creeping up his leg reached the right thigh, and the surgeons began to slice away the infected flesh. During the night of 27–28 August, it seemed as if even this truly royal resistance could last no longer, and Orléans instructed the marquis d'Argenson, Lieutenant-General of the Paris police, to urge the glassmakers on with their work on the street lanterns. These, not usually hung before the first week of September, would be needed to light the way if the Dauphin had to be taken hurriedly from Versailles through the narrow streets of Paris to Vincennes—since custom forbade the new king to remain in the palace where his predecessor had died.

On 31 August, Louis, now dying upwards in great pain and

stench, said good-bye to the princesses, the ladies of the court, and Madame de Maintenon, who at once left to take refuge at Saint-Cyr from the duc d'Orléans, whom she had always opposed in favour of the duc du Maine. The King then went in grave and meticulous detail over all the arrangements that would attend his death and the succession of "the Little King," as he was now calling his great-grandson: the mourning clothes that the Little King must wear; the furnishing of the apartments that he would occupy at the château de Vincennes; the provision of billets at Montreuil for those court officials who could not be accommodated at Vincennes; the need for princes and noblemen to order the funeral trappings for their carriages immediately, lest the coachmakers and furbishers should be overwhelmed by too great a rush of business.

At 8:15 a.m. on 1 September 1715 he died, after reigning for seventy-two years.

A great sigh of relief swept through the land. There was scarcely a single person who did not feel his heart lift with a sense of new freedom. The streets of Paris rang with jeers and mocking songs as the body of the dead King, intimidating no longer, passed on its way to burial at Saint-Denis.

Regency

§ 1

On the day after the old King's death, the duc d'Orléans went down to the Palais de Justice to hear Louis's will read before the *parlement* of Paris, and to dispute it. He was a man just into his forties, once handsome but now blotchy-faced, with a keen mind that he could seldom use for intelligent thought because it was so often fuddled with the quantities of Pommard and champagne that he drank each night. He had a fine reputation as a soldier and a sinister one as citizen and scientist; in his private laboratory at the Palais Royal he was popularly supposed to have concocted poisons to murder his second cousin, the duc de Bourgogne; there were rumours that he had an incestuous relationship with his eldest daughter, the duchesse de Berry, and with his youngest, Mademoiselle de Valois; his boon companions were so dissolute that a new name had been coined to describe them: the *roués*, because their dissipated looks and infamous morals suggested that they had been, or shortly would be, broken on the wheel.

The next two years were to be dominated by the struggle for power between Orléans and the duc du Maine, a quiet studious man, who limped almost diffidently across the stage on his club-foot or was jerked into clumsy activity by the strings held by his tiny and morbidly ambitious wife, the daughter of the duc de Condé. Each wooed *parlement* in the hope of enlisting its support against the other, but it was Orléans who, in these early days, gained the advantage by having himself recognized as Regent, rather than as simply head of the Regency council—a gesture that

29

parlement was glad to make in order to assert its own authority.

One other factor characterized the beginning of the Regency: an open disregard of moral standards and the public pursuit of almost every vice and perversion. It was a society in which the new duc de Richelieu, though he faced great competition, was admirably equipped to achieve even greater distinction.

During 1715 he was paying successful court to the duchesse de Berry, the most turbulent of the Regent's daughters, a creature of unbridled passions in love and drink and arrogance, married at fifteen, widowed at nineteen, dead at twenty-four. But Richelieu was only a passing lover, sharing her favours momentarily with the captain of her guard, the comte de Riom, a stocky, pasty-faced man with a placid disposition, who whipped her regularly in the conviction, as he explained to his friends, that this was "the only sure way to make a princess amorous." More permanent was Richelieu's association with the Regent's current mistress, Madame d'Averne, who was soon willing to discard her powerful protector in favour of her prodigious young lover. "I love you more tenderly than I have ever loved before," she wrote to him. "Although my letters do not have the eloquence of yours, I fear that they be more sincere."

From the Regent's daughter and the Regent's mistress, Richelieu passed to another of the Regent's relations: Mademoiselle de Charolais, who, like the duchesse de Berry, was a granddaughter of Louis XIV, though by a different one of his illegitimate daughters. A member of the great royal house of Bourbon-Condé, she was a strikingly handsome woman of twenty, olive-skinned, with gleaming chestnut hair, and a full petulant mouth and eyes so blue and bright that it was said she was at once recognized whenever she visited the public masked balls that were becoming increasingly popular. She lived with her parents in the hôtel de Condé, but without very strict supervision, and Richelieu, having scaled the garden wall, used to join her in the bedroom of a bribed maidservant. "We are more lucky than wise in this house," she wrote to him on one occasion after he had spent the night with her, "for everybody was in such a deep sleep that it was two hours afterwards before I heard the slightest sound. I think it as unnecessary to tell you that I shall be there at the time you will indicate as it is to tell you that I adore you as long as I live, for you are as certain of the one as of the other and have very good reason not to doubt it. If only I had the same confidence in your own sentiments. . . ."

On nights when there was too much moonlight for Richelieu to enter the garden unobserved, Mademoiselle de Charolais would sometimes dress up as one of the servants and sneak out of the house with her maid, and Richelieu would pick her up in a hired carriage outside the convent of the Cordeliers (which Richelieu commemorated by having a portrait painted of his mistress in the robes of a Tertiary of the Order of Saint Francis). The carriage served as their agapemone. One evening, when the jolting on stiff springs over uneven cobbles had brought on a headache, Mademoiselle de Charolais decided to descend at the Pont Neuf and walk back to the Cordeliers. They had got no farther than the entrance to the rue Dauphine when a passer-by claimed that he recognized the princess as his wife and tried to pull back the hood of her cloak to prove his suspicions. Richelieu punched him on the nose and he began to shout that his wife was being kidnapped. The watch came running up, and Richelieu found himself taken to the nearest commissioner of police together with the princess, who still managed to keep her face hidden. In the police office, Richelieu whispered his identity to the commissioner. The deserted husband, who turned out to be a perfumer from the rue de Buci, was summarily clapped into the Conciergerie and, the following morning, sent to prison for six months for his impertinence.

The disturbance had attracted a great many onlookers, and Richelieu had to wait some time before the crowd dispersed from outside the police office and he could escort Mademoiselle de Charolais home. When next he heard from her, it was clear that somebody had recognized her and that her family had been alerted. Both her mother and the divertingly titled bishop of Condom questioned her closely, and she wrote to Richelieu confessing that she had been mistaken in insisting on these moonlight meetings. "I am terribly afraid that they know something here. It is no

use your thinking of seeing me for a long time. She [her mother]
has said that I am to be put into a room next to hers. . . . I have
denied everything to M. de Condom. I am very vexed now to have
committed such a folly, but the longing that I had to see you
made it appear the simplest thing in the world." It was not an
affair that could last forever, though it flattered Richelieu to
exercise his power over a woman of her rank. She was riggish and
promiscuous, proud and possessive, unwilling to share her lover
with another woman and certainly not with several; yet as early
as August 1715 one of Richelieu's mistresses, Madame de Polignac, was writing to him to ask whether it was true that he had
given up the princess in favour of the marquise de Duras. He
and the princess quarrelled, came together again, drifted apart,
continued an intermittent liaison for several years until it eventually flared into an outburst of venomous hatred that she nursed
until her death.

The winter of 1715 to 1716 was even more miserable than that
of seven years before. It was estimated that three-quarters of the
people of France had difficulty in finding enough to eat. In the
provincial towns, bandits stole from people in the streets, un-
checked by the soldiers who had not been paid for months and
were themselves reduced to begging food from the monasteries;
in Paris it was not safe to go out after dark. Fires were kept burning day and night in the Louvre to warm the building and clear
the air, ready for the King to come from Vincennes and take up
his official residence, for Orléans had disregarded another of Louis
XIV's wishes and assented to *parlement*'s request that the new
King should be lodged in Paris and not at Versailles. When he
was brought there on 30 December, the Seine had been frozen
over for three weeks, and he was carried in a sheepskin bag to keep
him warm.

The weather did not, however, interfere with the amusements
of Richelieu and his friends, and on one of these bitter winter
evenings, he attended a party at the *petite maison* of the prince
de Soubise, at which his fellow guests included the marquis and
marquise de Nesle and the comtesse de Gacé. Anne de Gacé was
a silly young woman with no head for liquor and not a great deal

of self-control even when she was sober. On this occasion, after drinking too much champagne, she took all her clothes off and was passed from hand to hand among the guests before being sent outside for the enjoyment of the servants. This story was sufficiently piquant, even by Regency standards, to gain wide circulation. It soon came to the ears of Madame de Gacé's husband.

In the six years that he had been married to her—she was his second wife—the comte had grown accustomed to his wife's scandalous conduct but not entirely resigned to it, and he was incensed to hear that it was Richelieu who had spread the story about Paris and Versailles. This may well have been true, and certainly it was known that Richelieu was a man who liked to kiss and tell. It was a necessary part of his enjoyment that his conquests should be made known to his rivals. When he called on a reigning beauty, he was usually accompanied by liveried servants and rode in his escutcheoned carriage. On occasions, he would send both carriage and servants to stand outside the lady's home all night, in the hope that others would think him more fortunate than he was. And the more he bragged about each new mistress who surrendered to him, the more he was sought after by the ladies of fashion, each of whom deluded herself that her special charms would be strong enough to hold him.

Gacé found an opportunity for revenge at the Opéra ball on 17 February. These public balls, held in the opera house that had been built into the Palais Royal by Cardinal Richelieu, were much attended by people curious to see the recently installed machinery that raised the floor of the auditorium to the level of the stage, thus providing a very large space for dancing to the music of an orchestra of thirty violins. The ball opened at 11 p.m. and continued until 4 a.m.; the entrance fee was one écu (three livres), and admission was granted to all who were suitably dressed and reasonably well behaved. At a moment when the ballroom was crowded, Gacé walked up to Richelieu and insulted him grossly and loudly. Richelieu had no choice but to challenge him on the spot, and the two men walked over to the rue Saint-Thomas du Louvre, the street that ran southwards from the place du Palais Royal. Here they drew their swords and fought by lantern-light.

Richelieu, no match for the thirty-four-year-old soldier, soon fell to the ground, seriously wounded. He was carried to the hôtel de Richelieu on an improvised stretcher while his opponent, who had been only scratched, went back to the ball to establish an alibi for both of them.

The provocation and the fight itself had been witnessed by so many people that there was little hope of hushing it up, and the next morning the *procureur-général* opened inquiries. Not only was duelling forbidden by law but this was far from being Richelieu's first infringement. He had been involved in affairs of honour with brother officers when serving under Villars, although these, occurring far from any meddling civil authorities, were easily hushed up. A week before the affair at the Opéra, he was nearly called out by the duc de Bourbon for singing scurrilous songs about the duc's father (they were something of a family affair, having been composed by the duc's mother and no doubt first sung to Richelieu by the duc's sister, Mademoiselle de Charolais); only the fact that everybody was drunk and that Bourbon, as host, felt some hesitation about trying to kill one of his own guests, prevented an immediate duel. And in the previous December, at a shooting party given by the duc de Bourbon at Chantilly, Richelieu fell out with the chevalier de Bavière and agreed to meet him in the Bois de Boulogne. The Regent heard of the proposed duel and sent officers of his guard to arrest the two men and bring them before him at the Palais Royal. There he warned them that if either of them broke the law in future, he would take their present attempt into account when punishing them.

But more serious than any punishment by the Regent was the threat of interference by *parlement*, now that the *procureur-général* had stepped in. Emboldened by the rival wooing of the Regent and the duc du Maine, the gentlemen of the robe were ready to accept every opportunity of trying their strength against the gentlemen of the sword. Claiming that Richelieu had no right of trial by the court of peers alone, since he was under twenty-five and had not yet been officially received as a peer, *parlement* ordered him and Gacé to report to the Conciergerie, to be held in custody there during the inquiry. Richelieu's fellow peers protested that his rank came to him by birth and was not dependent on recognition by *parlement*. The quarrel surged heatedly round the Regent, who could not deny that custom was on the side of the peers, but who did not at this point wish to offend *parlement*. He avoided a decision by committing both Richelieu and Gacé to the Bastille on 4 March 1716; Richelieu, who was still convalescing from his wound, missed by two days the distinction of being twice imprisoned in the fortress before reaching the age of twenty.

Parlement, however, was not to be thwarted so easily and on 21 March, unable to claim entry to the royal fortress of the Bastille, served notice at the homes of Richelieu and Gacé, ordering them to the Conciergerie within a fortnight. On the following Wednesday night, an uproar that almost ended in blows broke out at the gates of the Bastille itself; several peers who met for a conference after dinner at the duc de Chaulnes's house went on to the Bastille to consult with Richelieu and on arrival were told to remove their swords before being admitted. Their noisy protests brought Bernaville to the scene, and he eventually agreed that it was their privilege to enter armed. This decision prompted all the inferior nobility to announce their intention to exercise the same right. This constant argument over who was entitled to wear a sword, and where, was more reasonable than most of the quarrels over prerogatives or protocol, for if a man entitled to wear a sword considered himself insulted by a man not entitled to wear one, it was evidently impossible to challenge him to a duel. Thus, without loss of honour, the man who wore a sword could set his servants to cudgel and whip the other man. This was an experience that awaited Voltaire exactly ten years later when he made the mistake of quarrelling with the chevalier de Rohan.

Parlement pressed on with its inquiries, and in mid-May, to the indignation of the peers, a special commissioner was allowed into the Bastille to interrogate Richelieu and Gacé. The two men, drawn together by a common contempt for the lady who was the cause of their trouble, had become the best of friends in captivity and were often seen strolling together in the garden on top of the bastion, grateful for the chance to escape from the stifling heat of their cells, for the harsh winter had been followed by an exceptionally sunny summer. The countryside was already beginning to parch and crack, while the smells that choked the narrow city streets were more foul than ever. The duellists were naturally disinclined to discuss their affairs with the emissary of *parlement*. Their friends outside had seen to it that there was now a total lack of witnesses willing to swear that they had seen them fighting, but on 19 May surgeons were sent in to establish whether Richelieu's body bore any marks of sword thrusts. The wound was almost healed, though still strapped up in plaster; Richelieu had the plaster painted flesh colour, and the surgeons, careful not to jeopardize their future by falling foul of all the peers of the realm, obligingly reported that they saw no sign of an incision.

Even if no conviction had been obtained, *parlement* could score many points simply by bringing Richelieu to trial, and a hearing was set for mid-June. A new quarrel broke out among the princes of the blood—this time over the style in which their summonses to court had been addressed to them—and the hearing was adjourned for two months. When the court reassembled, Richelieu's offence had almost been submerged in the wrangle; he and Gacé were again remanded, but no longer in custody, and in December *parlement* declared both men not guilty.

Shortly after Richelieu's release from the Bastille, his wife died of smallpox: an incident that was of no great consequence to him since they had lived entirely separate lives and, after making unavailing efforts to win his affection, she had taken lovers of her own. Richelieu did not demand higher standards from others than he set himself and only once showed disapproval of her actions: when he discovered that she was having an affair with a social inferior. Stepping unexpectedly into her room one day, he discovered her on the sofa with his equerry in an embrace for which not even the most charitable imagination could find an innocent explanation. He bowed to the pair of them and then remarked acidly to his wife: "Consider, madame, what embarrassment you would have suffered had anybody other than myself entered this room." He bowed once more and then withdrew. But he did not forget. Almost twenty years later, just before his second marriage, the same man approached him at Versailles and asked if he had any employment for him. "Indeed, sir," said Richelieu, raising his eyebrows, "and where did you learn that I was marrying again?"

§ 2

Mademoiselle de Charolais, deprived of Richelieu's company for five months, greeted him with open arms when he was released from the Bastille, much to the disgust of her brother, the duc de Bourbon. In January 1717, there was talk of sending Richelieu to Madrid with a decoration for one of the Spanish princes just to ease the tension and get him out of Bourbon's way for a time. But in fact he had now set his aim even higher than the Condé family and had his eye on a daughter of the Regent himself. Although he had already been the lover of the duchesse de Berry, she was at the time a married woman, living in her own establishment, and conferring her favours on so many men that it would have been difficult for the Regent to direct his wrath at any one of them. Charlotte-Aglaë d'Orléans, Mademoiselle de Valois, was a very different quarry. Born in October 1700, she was the sixth and youngest daughter of the Regent. The fact that she had reached the age of sixteen without having taken a lover was attributed to the jealousy with which her father had surrounded her with a bodyguard of maids, chaperones, and ladies-in-waiting, who kept a close watch on her even in her own apartments in the Palais Royal.

A tall, well-built but ungainly girl, she had "more charm than real beauty, very pretty eyes and a beautiful mouth" but a nose that was just too long for her pleasantly chubby face; moreover, "she walked badly and neglected herself to the point of showing no real grace in anything that she did." These shortcomings were of little importance to Richelieu, who coveted her not as a beautiful young woman but as the Regent's cherished daughter. He lost no opportunity of letting her see that he admired her, and she, intrigued by the young duc's scandalous reputation and spurred on by inherited temperament, gave him as much encouragement as strict supervision would allow her.

Notes were furtively exchanged between them; Richelieu took to appearing unexpectedly in the princess's path disguised as a lackey, a shop assistant, even a galley slave begging bread. But from these tokens of burning affection to the practical expression of it was a long stride, involving the outwitting of Madame Desroches, the aged duenna who remained within a few yards of her charge day and night. Richelieu accomplished it, demonstrating, as he so often did, that he not only had a richer comic invention and vitality than most men could boast but that he was ready to make use of the oldest conventions of farce when they suited his purpose.

Mademoiselle de Valois had a personal maid named Angélique, a tall thin girl of much the same height as the slightly built Richelieu, devoted to her mistress and prepared, when Richelieu suggested it to her, to let him borrow her clothes. As the princess and Madame Desroches sat in an ante-room that evening, Richelieu minced in, dressed in Angélique's cap, gown, and apron, and carried Mademoiselle de Valois's nightclothes into her bedroom. Madame Desroches, shortsighted and noticing nothing out of the ordinary, remained quite unsuspecting when the princess rose and said that she was going into her room to write some letters and did not wish to be disturbed.

Time passed and she did not return. Madame Desroches, growing drowsy and yawning for her bed, stepped over to the closed door, tapped on it and called: "Come along, princess—get off to sleep, and finish that tomorrow." To which the princess called back: "Oh, I can't do that—just give me a few moments more and I think I shall be done."

This was a year of fruitful disguises for Richelieu. He had begun an affair with the nineteen-year-old wife of the marquis de Villeroy and was not meeting her as often as she wished, despite her offers to entertain him in her own home: "My husband . . . will not return before five in the morning. If you would like to come here at one, the *suisse* will let you up by the little staircase that you know of." He had given up the rooms in the rue Saint-Antoine and set up a discreet *petite maison* near the barrière de Vaugirard, but the occasional sorties that she made there were not always well received. "I am not used to finding such prudence in one as wild as you. And when it prevents me from having the pleasure of seeing you, I find it very misplaced. I was anticipating the greatest pleasure in the world in seeing you this evening, and I hoped that your indolence would succumb to my enthusiasm. But there has to be this miserable lackey preventing my seeing you. I thought of telling him to get himself ———, but I recalled that I had found too much pleasure in that occupation yesterday to wish it for anybody who prevents me from seeing you. You are right in wanting to be praised for your vigour, for it seemed to me yesterday to be at full strength. I have a very agreeable memory of it, particularly the last time."

One day she sent him a note saying that she had heard of the death of a nun at the Benedictine abbey at Jouarre, about forty miles east of Paris, where she had been educated, and that she proposed to tell her husband that she wanted to attend the funeral. Her cousin, another former pupil, would go with her as chaperone, and she asked Richelieu to think up some plan by which they could meet. There was a consistent streak of irreverence in Richelieu's character; he was a naughty young man, and in the course of time he grew into a naughty old man; one of the recurring aspects of his naughtiness was his delight in little blasphemies. He had had two other mistresses, besides Mademoiselle de Charolais, painted in conventual habits, and he found amusement in dressing himself up as a monk and the women he loved as nuns. He consequently had no difficulty in finding priests' clothing for himself and for his friend, the chevalier de Guémenée, who was the lover of Madame de Villeroy's cousin and had known Richelieu since their earliest youth, having grown up with him in the place Royale.

The two men drove out to Jouarre and presented themselves at the abbey on the day of the funeral, Richelieu informing the abbess that, hearing of the visit of the two distinguished ladies, he and his fellow priest had come in the hope of interesting them in their preferment. The abbess, impressed by their good manners and well aware of the difficulty a young man would encounter in making his way in the church without influence, agreed to do her best to introduce them to the marquise and her friend and asked if either of them would care to say a few words at the funeral service. Richelieu was charmed to oblige and delivered an oration whose elegant expression and devout sentiments deeply moved the abbess and the nuns. The reverend mother found it quite easy to persuade the marquise and her companion to see the two priests privately in one of the convent rooms, where each couple in turn made the most of the opportunity, while the other pair kept watch at the door.

One reason why Richelieu sometimes had his servant tell Madame de Villeroy that he was not at home or was resting, was that he was at this time carrying on affairs with three of the Regent's mistresses, past, present, or future, Mesdames de Sabran, Parabère, and Averne, as well as with the duchesse de Durfort, formerly marquise de Duras, whose son, born in 1715, was said by gossip to be Richelieu's, and still with Mademoiselle de Charolais. Despite his remarkable constitution and his practice of snatching a quick nap whenever he could, his efforts to please all these ladies were resulting in his not quite satisfying any of them. The position became more acute when, after an interval following their decision that it was too risky to continue his masquerade as Angélique, he at last found a new way of outwitting Mademoiselle de Valois's bodyguard. In the road adjoining the Palais Royal on the west—named the rue de Richelieu in honour of the Cardinal—he rented a house that backed on to Mademoiselle de Valois's apartments and made a hole from his side of the wall into the cupboard where his young mistress kept her pots of jams and preserves under lock and key (the Bourbons, Orléans, and Condés of both sexes were, without exception, gluttons, who stuffed themselves at all hours and always ensured that they had great masses of food near at hand). From that time onward they were able to meet as often as they wished.

Mademoiselle de Charolais eventually accused him bluntly of neglecting her in favour of other women, whereupon Richelieu withdrew from society and had it given out that he was seriously ill. Ten days later, he called on Mademoiselle de Charolais and explained that the reason for his apparent lack of interest was that he was suffering from venereal disease. This, in accordance with the notions of the time, she accepted as regrettable but quite normal; victims of "the wounds of love" might meet with sympathy or derision, but it would not have occurred to their friends to greet the news with disapproval. He added, as if in passing, that Mademoiselle de Valois had been showing an interest in him, and, in order that she should not do him a disservice with the Regent, he had pretended to return her affections —had even gone to the farcical length of constructing a secret entrance to her room where he would sit talking to her on occasions—but, of course, because of his unfortunate condition, he had not dared to carry the affair any further, nor had he wished to.

Mademoiselle de Charolais found the story immensely amusing but flatly refused to believe that he had a way of getting into the Palais Royal in secret. So he had the pleasure of taking her to the house in the rue de Richelieu one day and leaving her on his side of the wall, sworn to silence, while he went through the jam cupboard, locked the door behind him, and deceived her at his leisure with her young rival.

Mademoiselle de Charolais's discretion was not to be relied upon and, knowing that she was capable of revealing his secret in a fit of pique, Richelieu decided to fill up the hole in the wall. But by this time he had already found a new way of getting into his mistress's bedroom without too great a risk. He seduced one of Mademoiselle de Valois's attendants, a plain woman named Aimée Legendre, who slept in an adjoining room that could be reached by a little-frequented staircase from the floors below. In return for his occasional favours, Aimée raised no objection to his passing through her room to visit the princess.

The Regent, although annoyed with Richelieu for stealing so many of his mistresses from him, was still unaware that Richelieu had succeeded in seducing his youngest daughter, and in March 1718, he allowed him to buy the colonelcy of the Régiment de Béarn, eighth in seniority among the infantry regiments. The young colonel, just twenty-two, now gave his own name to the regiment and had command over a lieutenant-colonel, a major, thirty-four captains, two aide-majors, thirty-four lieutenants, eight second lieutenants, two ensigns, and thirty-four companies of thirty men each. Shortly afterwards, when the wearing of uniforms became general in the army, he rigged out his men in white coats, waistcoats, and breeches, with blue stitching, red collars and cross-pockets, and gold gorgets for the officers. The drummers wore Richelieu's livery, and the ensigns carried banners on which the white cross of the royal army was quartered with the regimental colours, violet and yellow.

The main body of the regiment was stationed at Bayonne, and Richelieu was in no hurry to join it; the professional officers, headed by the lieutenant-colonel, would carry out all the duties, and the colonel would take over command only in time of war or for special manoeuvres. But, although Richelieu appeared to be exclusively occupied with affairs of the boudoir, he was already making plans for his newly acquired regiment that were to lead him close to the scaffold.

§ 3

The war that the princes of the blood and the dukes and peers were conducting on two flanks against the legitimized princes grew in virulence. The princes of the blood were intent on thrusting them into a rank below them; the peers were equally intent on not having them in an intermediary rank above them. The fiery little duchesse du Maine urged her lethargic husband to retaliate, and the Regent grew more suspicious that the Du Maines were plotting a palace revolution. In February 1717, Louis XV reached his seventh birthday, and the princes, princesses, and notabilities of the court assembled in the Tuileries for the ceremony of stripping the King. The boy was undressed in their presence and, standing completely naked, examined by them to verify that he was in good health, well nourished, unblemished, and male: an examination for which his governess, Madame de Ventadour, had prepared for several weeks by putting him to bed early and washing his feet every night. The inspection finished, he was dressed in entirely new clothes and handed over to the duc du Maine, superintendent of his education, and the maréchal de Villeroy, his governor. The young King left the duchesse de Ventadour with tears in his eyes, and she, even more deeply moved, retired to console herself with his clothes, linen, all the movable furnishings of his apartment, and a pension of 40,000 livres.

Louis was a timid, impressionable child, and there was no knowing what use Du Maine might make of the control that he could now exercise over the boy's mind and affections. The Regent decided to act quickly. In July 1717, with the approval of the princes and peers, he issued an edict under which Du Maine and Toulouse were deprived of their right of succession to the throne and their children of the rank of princes. But the duchesse du Maine was far from defeated. She had plans to overthrow the Regent with help from both inside and outside the country. She hoped to persuade *parlement*, which the Regent had recently been neglecting in order to curry favour with the peers, to declare the King of age and end the Regency; she counted on the support of many of the lesser nobility who were jealous of the peers. Alternatively, she was prepared to aid Philip of Spain to expel Orléans and take over the Regency himself. In this, she had the active interest of the Spanish ambassador, the prince de Cellamare, and the probable backing of many of the older soldiers who had served under Louis XIV—Villars, Huxelles, Harcourt—who disapproved of the Regent's policy of friendship with France's former enemies, Britain and Austria.

Under the terms of the Triple Alliance between France, Britain, and Holland, engineered by the Regent's former tutor and preceptor in debauchery, the abbé Dubois, France was committed to destroying her fortifications at Mardyck and expelling the Stuart Pretender, whose invasion of Scotland she had supported not much more than a year before. To conform with George I's interests as elector of Hanover, she had to approve of the Austrian theft of the former Spanish possessions in Italy. To maintain the British monopoly of the slave trade and the clause in the Treaty of Utrecht under which British merchants had the exclusive right of trading in slaves in Spanish America, France had again to support the British against the Spanish. A Negro, captured and delivered f.o.b. for four guineas in Africa, could be sold in America for forty, and the maritime strength which the British built up from the profits of these operations was to be the deciding factor in France's loss of her colonial empire later in the century.

It was impossible to predict this chain of events, but uneasiness over the alliance with Britain increased in the summer of 1718 when the half-crazy Philip of Spain, encouraged by his wife, Elizabeth Farnese, attacked Sicily after successfully invading Sardinia. Austria at once joined the Triple Alliance while Britain seized the opportunity to wipe out the Spanish fleet. France was confronted with a war that she had not wanted and from which she had nothing to gain. Richelieu went down to Sainte-Foy-la-Grande, on the Dordogne below Bergerac, to inspect the detachment of his regiment that was quartered there and to introduce himself to the officers.

There was a great coming and going of secret messengers between the Du Maines and Cellamare and between Cellamare and Madrid. Another of the periodic shortages of food in a land that was potentially so rich inflamed discontent against the government. There was a series of irritable outbursts, particularly in the always unruly province of Brittany; the King's health was far from robust, and his death would produce turmoil in which the Du Maines or Philip might well attempt to seize power. The Regent decided that the moment had come for the decisive blow.

On 16 August 1718, he summoned an extraordinary meeting of the Regency council at the Louvre, to be followed by a *lit de justice* in the King's ante-chamber at the Tuileries. While the members gathered in the council room, Du Maine limped agitatedly up and down, halting to take Villars into a corner and whisper: "Something violent is going to happen to my brother and myself." The Regent, meanwhile, had taken the comte de Toulouse aside and told him that, in view of Du Maine's excited state of mind, it would be best if he persuaded him to leave, and assuring him that there was no plot on foot against either of them. Toulouse, a good-tempered, unsuspicious little man who had not yet become involved in the Du Maine plot, did as he was told. No sooner had the two royal bastards quit the room than Orléans convened the council and announced that they were to discuss measures to deal with the legitimized princes—adding that he would rather have a declared enemy than a hidden one. The business did not take long. Du Maine was deprived of his rank as a prince of the blood, reduced to the status of an ordinary peer—and with seniority from the date of creation of his peerage. Since this put him almost at the bottom of the list of peers, below the maréchal de Villeroy, the duc de Bourbon proposed that he should be relieved of his post as superintendent of the King's education, it being manifestly impossible for the holder of that post to be junior in rank to the King's governor. The council agreed, and Bourbon met no opposition to his supplementary proposal that he should be Du Maine's successor. The Regent, at last having to decide between the support of the princes and peers and that of *parlement*, chose the former. Measures for restricting the powers of *parlement* and ensuring the automatic registration of edicts within seven days were agreed upon, and the council rose. At the *lit de justice* that followed, the First President of the chamber was refused time to consider the measures, and all the council's decisions were registered as law.

The abbé Dubois was appointed Foreign Minister as a reward for negotiating the agreements with Britain and Austria, and shortly afterwards Villars, the cardinal de Noailles, and others who had opposed this policy were dismissed from the council. The Regent had for the moment crushed all opposition, and the only hope for the Du Maines lay in Spain. One of the few offices of which Du Maine had not been stripped was that of Grand Master of the Artillery, and it was in a little pavilion at the bottom of the Arsenal gardens beside the Seine that the duchesse du Maine held her first serious talks with Cellamare about the possibility of armed intervention from Spain. Cellamare was instructed from Madrid to encourage the duchesse, and, with her natural taste for plotting, she found this such an agreeable outlet that she enlisted conspirators on every hand—including at least two who were spying on her on behalf of Dubois.

The intrigue was conducted with childish carelessness from beginning to end. Secret papers that the chief conspirators had not had time to deal with were handed out to be copied by people who were not even in sympathy with the plot. One of them, a clerk in the *bibliothèque royale,* reported his suspicions to the shrewd, ferrety-faced Dubois and from thence forward was under instructions to report to the abbé every day. Finally a crucial piece of information came from one of the government's most reliable sources: a brothel-keeper.

The police of Paris made much use of the city's many procuresses to obtain criminal and political information. In principle, prostitution was illegal, and the laws against it were severe. The marquis and marquise de Morival had recently been stripped to the waist and whipped at the cart-tail from the Conciergerie to their house in the faubourg Saint-Martin, and then banished from Paris for nine years, for having run a *maison de débauche* and corrupted six girls aged from 17 to 20. But this, in an age when prostitution usually began at the age of 13 or 14, was an exceptional prosecution and was attributable partly to the complaint of the prince de Conti that he had caught pox in their house, and even more to their failure to cooperate with the police. So long as the bawds kept a note of their visitors, they were usually safe from fines, beatings, or banishment; the whores were unlikely to have their heads shaved or to be sent to work at the Hôpital de la Salpêtrière, provided they reported all the conversations they heard in the brothel or in the private houses to which they were sent out on call.

It was one of the most notorious of Paris procuresses, La Fillon, who reported that one of her girls had been kept waiting by a secretary from the Spanish embassy and that when he eventually arrived he explained that he had been delayed because he had had to encode urgent secret messages for a courier who was leaving that evening. It was midnight before the news reached Dubois, and he immediately sent off a party of horsemen to arrest the courier, the abbé Porto-Carrero. They caught up with him at the staging inn at Poitiers and took the papers from him, but one of his postilions managed to gallop back to Paris and warn Cellamare. Making no effort to destroy the other incriminating documents in his embassy, Cellamare went to protest to Dubois against the detention of his messenger and was promptly detained himself. Dubois put him under house arrest, searched through all his papers, and returned to the Palais Royal to report to the Regent, who had just gone to bed with Mademoiselle Emilie from the Opéra.

The papers in the Spanish embassy contained a wealth of information about the conspiracy, including the names of 150 of its leading members; Dubois and the Regent sifted and discussed them for three weeks before deciding to pounce. On 19 December, the duc du Maine was arrested and escorted to the fortress of Doullens, and the next day his wife was taken off to Dijon. The tiny, tigerish duchesse snapped and snarled all the way, but the duc was cowed and white as a sheet. "They should not be putting me in prison," he said, "but in a strait-jacket for having let my wife drag me into this."

For more than a week, the bodyguard and the two companies of musketeers slept with their boots on and their horses saddled. In the sudden storm of suspicion and arbitrary arrest, the whole court was in turmoil. Richelieu called to warn his old commander, the maréchal de Villars, that he had been told by one of the Regent's mistresses that Villars was to be arrested on New Year's Eve; the information proved to be unfounded, but there were a great many people who worried intensely about the revelations that the police might be extracting from those who had been arrested already. An attempted uprising in Brittany was quickly crushed, and a total of 1,500 people were arrested in the provinces.

On 10 January 1719, France declared war on Spain, and Richelieu received orders to be ready to march at the head of his regiment when the campaigning season opened in the spring. But before that time arrived, Paris was entertained by a new scandal involving two of Richelieu's friends: the marquise de Polignac and the marquise de Nesle. Early one March morning the two women drove to the Pré aux Clercs, a popular duelling ground on the south side of the Seine, and, leaving their servants with the carriages, walked off to talk together. Their voices were soon raised, and the servants, horrified to see the women draw knives from their skirt pockets, ran to separate them. It looked like an unequal contest, for the dark-haired, dark-eyed, dark-complexioned Madame de Polignac had the longer reach as well as the more handsomely fierce appearance; but Madame de Nesle, flaxen-haired, china-blue-eyed, pink-and-white-complexioned, enjoyed a figure of such opulence that the weight as well as the low-slung concentration of her attack almost bowled over her taller opponent. The fight was short but desperate; before their servants could drag them apart, Madame de Polignac had received a cut on the face and Madame de Nesle had been wounded in the breast. They were taken to their doctors for treatment and shortly afterwards banished to their country estates on an order signed by the King.

There were many explanations for this savage little incident. The two women, related by marriage, had been rivals in love for some time. Both had set their caps at the marquis de Nesle; Madame de Polignac, having lost that contest, became the mistress of the duc de Bourbon, only to find that Madame de Nesle had taken him from her. She became the mistress of the prince de Conti for a time but then decided to take the prince de Soubise from Madame de Nesle—and it was over Soubise, a member of the Rohan family, that the women were at first thought to have quarrelled. Others maintained that the bone of contention was the marquis d'Alincourt; and still others claimed that it was—as usual—Richelieu, who was known to have been the lover of each in turn.

This intriguing discussion was brought to a sudden halt on Tuesday, 28 March, when the news came that Richelieu had been arrested for complicity in the Cellamare plot and was locked in a cell in the Bastille.

§ 4

He had been out all night on an amorous errand, and it was not until five in the morning that he got back to the place Royale and into his own bed. Scarcely four hours later a party of *archers*, the constables of the watch, marched along the rue Neuve Sainte-Catherine into the north-west corner of the square and halted outside the hôtel de Richelieu. An officer of the royal household led the way into the mansion and up to Richelieu's bedroom before the duc could be warned. He woke up to find the constables surrounding his bed, was ordered to dress and was then taken on the short journey to the Bastille while the police put seals on his private apartments and papers. His fellow peers at once protested that the manner of his arrest was improper and an affront to their dignity, but the Regent was in no mood to listen; he had, he said, enough evidence to cut off Richelieu's head four times over. That same evening the comte de Saillant, colonel of the Dauphine Regiment that was sharing garrison duties with Richelieu's regiment in Bayonne, was also arrested and taken to the Bastille. The startling rumour ran round Paris that Richelieu had persuaded Saillant to join him in placing his troops at the disposal of Philip of Spain. The story became still more convincing when it was learned that Richelieu had recently been pestering the marquis de Biron, a member of the war council, to have him sent to take over command of his regiment at once: a surprising request from a courtier when there was no active war on.

Richelieu, who was so fond of bragging of his performances, could now lay claim to a very unenviable record: at the age of twenty-three years and a few days he was in the Bastille for the third time. And this time it was not for an affair of the heart or honour; not for a trifling, gentlemanly peccadillo; but for treason. The tiny room to which he was escorted was only one floor above the dreaded *cachots*, in which men had lingered until death; the thin beam of light that descended from the barred window high in the wall seemed to fade and dissipate before it filtered as a faint glimmer on to the rickety furniture. His visitors were not friends but inquisitors: Le Blanc, the War Minister, and Argenson, the former Lieutenant-General of the Paris police who was now *garde des sceaux* (Lord Chancellor), a frightening figure with piercing eyes under black, always-frowning eyebrows, a face so horrifyingly ugly that it was said he had never persuaded a woman to sleep with him except for money. What story Richelieu told them was never known; nor how he explained away the damning evidence against him, for it seems clear that he had at least discussed the possibility of defecting with his troops to the service of Philip of Spain.

Was Richelieu involved in the Du Maine plot to hand over the Regency to Philip? He had close ties with Madame de Maintenon, who would certainly have done her best to win his support for her favourite foster son. He had served under Villars, who was linked with the Du Maines. He was related, through his step-mother and his first wife, to the Noailles, who, like Villars, were on bad terms with the Regent. The Regent's pro-British, pro-Austrian, and anti-Spanish foreign policy was bitterly opposed by most of the people whose opinions he might be expected to re-spect, and was contrary to the policies of his own great ancestor, the Cardinal. Yet none of these arguments carries much convic-tion. Richelieu was capable of the most rash and dangerous ac-tions when prompted by pride or stubbornness, but he had not yet shown any signs of political interests. His class consciousness made it unlikely that he would enter a quarrel on the side of *parlement*, particularly since one of *parlement*'s recent pamphlets against the dukes and peers had contained the familiar and hate-ful jibe about "René Vignerot, a lute-player to the Great Cardi-nal" and was understood to have been written by the duchesse du Maine.

There was a third story in circulation at the time, and this seems to be the most likely one: that Richelieu had offered his sword and his regiment to Philip in return for the promise of the colonelcy of the guards and permission to marry a princess whose relations opposed the match. This princess was variously identi-fied as the duchesse de Berry—an improbable candidate, since her passing affair with Richelieu had ended, and she was more in love than ever with Riom and his whip; or Mademoiselle de Charolais —a possibility, for she still loved him and their association was known and frowned on by her relations; or Mademoiselle de Valois—the most likely person of all, because she was head over heels in love with Richelieu, and he would have leaped at the opportunity of marrying into the house of Orléans.

This theory is supported by the correspondence of the Regent's mother, the fat, horsy Charlotte of Bavaria, whose first comments on his arrest were: "This will cause many tears to flow in Paris, for all the ladies are taken with him. I don't understand it—he's a little toad whom I do not consider at all gentlemanly; he is not much to look at, has no courage, is impertinent, faithless, indis-creet and speaks ill of all his mistresses. Despite that, a princess of the blood is smitten with him to the point that, when he was widowed, she wanted to marry him at any cost, but neither her grandmother, her mother nor her brother would consent to it. They were very right for, apart from the fact that he and she are not equal in rank, she would have been unhappy all her life with this maniac, who is completely worthless. I call him the Gnome, since he is as like to a goblin as one drop of water to another."

In this letter, written on the morning after Richelieu's arrest, she is evidently referring to his affair with Mademoiselle de Charolais. Her hatred of him has a hysterical ring that springs from something more violent than ordinary moral disapproval and cannot be attributed to shocked innocence, for she herself was the widow of a pervert and the mother of a libertine whose alleged excursions into incest and other sexual aberrations were far more scabrous than anything that was ever charged against Richelieu. Four weeks later, the same shrill, suspect scream is there: "He is an arch-debauchee, a blackguard, a poltroon, who holds neither to God nor to his word. He has been worthless all his life and he never will be worth anything; he is false and a liar and as ambitious as the devil with it all. . . . The first time he was put in the Bastille because he falsely bragged that he had been to bed with Mme. la Dauphine and all her young ladies; the second time he went there because he himself let it be known that the chevalier de Bavière wanted to fight with him; and now this time the trick that he has played caps the lot, as they say."

The confusion and misrepresentation of the quarrels with Bavière and Gacé was no doubt a deliberate attempt to make Richelieu seem a coward who tried to hide behind the law in order to avoid a duel; but the dowager was likely to have been well informed about the inquiries that her son was having made at the Bastille and close to the truth when she wrote three days later: "The duc de Richelieu is not part of M. du Maine's conspiracy. He plotted on his own account, in the hope, they say, of making himself so important that he could bring off a brilliant marriage which has been opposed until now." It was not until the middle of May that she suddenly learned that the princess with whom Richelieu was involved was not Mademoiselle de Charolais but her own granddaughter.

"You ask me what has upset me. . . . I cannot tell you the details, but in short it is a horrible flirtation that Mlle. de Valois has had with that fiendish duc de Richelieu. He has left her letters lying about everywhere, for he loves her only out of vanity. All the young people have seen them. You can tell from them that she has been meeting him here [the dowager's home at Saint-Cloud]. Madame her mother asked me to bring her away with me again, but I have flatly refused and told her that I do not want her near me any more and that they cannot fool me more than once. And every day they keep bringing it up again. . . . I have a horror of that girl. . . . My stomach turns whenever I have to look at the little fool. May God forgive the mother, but it is she who has brought all her daughters up so badly. And this impertinent duc is brazen and laughing it all off; he knows my son's kindness of heart, puts on a bold face, and refuses to give in. If they punished him as he deserves they would make him die under the lash; he has earned it twice and three times over. I am not cruel by nature but I could see that rogue hanged without shedding a tear. I am really upset by that gnome; I hate him with all my heart."

Her noisy lamentations over the fate of her granddaughter were so indiscreet that she did more harm than any letters that Richelieu may have left lying about. The prince of Piedmont, to whom the Regent had intended to marry Mademoiselle de Valois, heard of these escapades and took fright; it was only by luck that the Regent learned during the summer that the Duke of Modena might be interested in marrying her. Mademoiselle de Valois disliked what she had heard of her proposed husband, and his abnormal tastes made him a peculiarly unsuitable spouse for a girl of her temperament. He did not even have position or wealth to recommend him, and the wits soon were reciting a piece of bad verse which punningly commented on the unfavourable bargain that Mademoiselle de Valois was being forced into:

> *On y manque de tout; la finance est petite;*
> *Quelle différence, grand Dieu,*
> *Entre ce pauvre et triste lieu*
> *Et le riche lieu que je quitte!*

However, the Regent had the means of forcing his daughter to agree. She had pleaded for leniency for her lover and had pestered her father so successfully that he had given instructions for Richelieu to be moved from his gloomy cell to a large, airy room and to be allowed to take daily strolls on the ramparts, where he became something of a local attraction, bowing, waving, and blowing kisses to the women who stopped their carriages in the streets or leaned from nearby houses. It was doubtful if his head was any longer in danger, but there was no guarantee that he would recover his liberty for many months or years. The Regent made it clear to his daughter that unless she accepted marriage to the Duke of Modena, Richelieu would stay in prison indefinitely; and her infatuation was sufficiently strong for her to sacrifice her own happiness to that of her lover.

On 30 August, Richelieu was released from the Bastille for the third time and went to stay with the cardinal de Noailles in the archbishop's official residence at Conflans, but this was too temptingly close to Paris, and he spent too many nights in the town. The Regent feared that he was again seeing Mademoiselle de Valois and, even if re-awakened passion did not cause her to go back on her word, a fresh scandal might well cause the Duke of Modena to call the marriage off. Richelieu accordingly received on 10 September a *lettre de cachet* signed by the young King "on the advice of my uncle the duc d'Orléans, Regent," ordering him to go by the shortest and most direct route to a house that he owned in Saint-Germain-en-Laye, escorted by a former lieutenant-colonel of dragoons. There he was to be permitted to see anybody that he wished, to hunt and take walks, but not to sleep away from the town.

He renewed his affair with Mademoiselle de Charolais, whose movements were not as closely watched as those of Mademoiselle de Valois, and, with his usual recklessness, was soon making clandestine trips to Paris, easily outwitting the decrepit colonel of dragoons. He was discovered, and this time threatened with banishment to his estate at Richelieu, and once again Mademoiselle de Valois came to his rescue. But in the sad letter that she sent him early in November, it is clear that she was already beginning to regret the sacrifice that she was making for this unfaithful lover:

"My marriage has just been announced. I am giving you a greater proof of my love than I have ever given you before, for, judging from the state of my affairs at present, this will be the greatest misfortune of my life. But since nothing can increase that of being separated from you, I do not fear any unhappiness sufficiently to weigh it for a moment against the chance of giving you pleasure . . . but, when I sacrifice myself for you, do not refuse to give me proof that you have broken off with Mademoiselle de Charolais in such a way that you could never be reconciled. I leave you the choice of what proof you give me. You can provide me with a proof so convincing as to make me as happy as I can ever be, far away from you, and that will be a great consolation for me: longing for you but knowing that you have deserved the love I have for you by the proof that you have given me of your own."

The threat of banishment was lifted as soon as the marriage had been announced, and he was allowed to return to Paris at the beginning of December. A fortnight later he made his bows to the King and the Regent and was officially received back into grace. In February 1719, he attended the wedding of Mademoiselle de Valois and the Duke of Modena, and onlookers remarked that he spent much of the ceremony smiling at Mademoiselle de Charolais.

For twelve months he was discreet. He got 80,000 livres by letting the mansion in the place Royale and spent much more time at Richelieu, where he entertained his friend Voltaire. Voltaire had visited him in the Bastille several times during his imprisonment in 1716 and had himself been imprisoned there in the following year, accused of writing scurrilous verses on the Regent's incestuous relations with the duchesse de Berry. Voltaire's sharp tongue and irreverent eye appealed to Richelieu, who, during the summer months, liked to have his company when he went to take the waters, the duc delighted by the fulsome flattery of the poet, and the poet enchanted to claim the friendship of a peer.

In July 1720, Paris was full of rumours that Richelieu had married Mademoiselle de Charolais at Vincennes, she having reached her twenty-fifth birthday and legal majority in June; but he was with his regiment at Oléron at the time, and the rumour seems to have been spread simply because Mademoiselle de Charolais was pregnant. Despite the fact that she never married, this was far from being an unusual experience for her, although she did not perhaps take it quite as calmly as her grandmother, the princesse de Condé, who, when told of her predicament, answered: "Well then, my girl, you'll just have to lie-in, won't you?"

In the autumn of 1720, fauteuil no. 32 at the Académie Française became vacant on the death of the marquis de Dangeau, and, more as a pious gesture to their founder than as a tribute to the literacy of his heir, the members elected Richelieu to occupy it. He was ceremonially received on 12 December with a speech of welcome that praised him for not having joined in the frenzied speculation which preceded and accompanied the collapse of John Law's credit system in the early summer; people had been crushed to death trying to get their money from the bank, and the nobility, having already withdrawn theirs by threats or force, immediately put it to use in buying up foodstuffs and holding them until prices soared. If Richelieu did not take any part in this scandalous profiteering, it was no doubt because he lacked the ready cash and not because of any scruples.

His speech of reply was well received (as it should have been, since three prominent members of the Académie had composed it) and was applauded by an audience in which many more women than usual were present. Of these, three sent him notes inviting him to call on them that evening, and, in rotation, he demonstrated to Mademoiselle de Charolais, the duchesse de Durfort, and the marquise de Villeroy that his new academic interests had in no way sapped his physical powers.

His tussle with *parlement* over their jurisdiction in the affair with Gacé, and the more recent offensive pamphlet in which mention had been made of René Vignerot, had stimulated his interest in politics. He joined the group of ultra-conservative ducs and peers who held meetings at the maréchal de Villars's house to discuss what could be done to offset the capital that *parlement* was making out of the aristocracy's involvement in the Law collapse and the subsequent profiteering. The Regent's earlier courtship of *parlement* had left it in a strong position. It could summon peers before it—as in Richelieu's own case—and the battle for the moment was over matters of etiquette and privilege: whether a peer could prevent the officers of *parlement* from searching his house, whether a president of *parlement* could be forced to remove his cap when addressing a peer.

Richelieu made an appearance before *parlement* in March 1721 to receive official recognition as a peer. On Wednesday, 3 March, he reached his twenty-fifth birthday and made formal proof of his identity to a King's Counsellor; on the 6th he took his seat for the first time on the bench of peers, dressed in a coat and breeches made of cloth of gold at 260 livres a yard, and "looking like the God of Love himself." He had, as usual, spent more than he could afford or the trustees of the estate would advance and had to pawn his diamond buckles.

In May 1721, a guest once more at a hunting party at Chantilly, he was drawn aside by his host, the duc de Bourbon. Bourbon was in the mentally disturbing situation of hating his sister, Mademoiselle de Charolais, yet bitterly resenting Richelieu's association with her. He had frequently tried to provoke him to a duel: unfairly, since provocation would not have been a sufficient excuse to save Richelieu from severe punishment if he had done serious injury to a prince of the blood. This time Bourbon ordered him to draw his sword on the spot, saying: "Richelieu, you know that I have disliked you for a long time; now you shall answer to me for it."

Richelieu protested that he had no wish to comply. "I know the respect that I owe you, Monseigneur, and I am not the man to fight you." The only reply was a lunge from the prince, and Richelieu put himself on guard. He allowed Bourbon to wound him in the hand, thinking that this might satisfy him. It did not, and in the end Richelieu was fighting in earnest, desperately trying to ward off the furious attack without inflicting too much damage on his opponent. In this he was only half successful; Bourbon was wounded in the stomach, but he had the grace to admit that he had forced the fight on Richelieu. Fortunately, he was known to be a man of violent and uncontrolled temper. As one diarist put it: "Everybody says that Monsieur le Duc's mind has been deranged for some time. Not that this makes much difference, for what he had was small and evil."

In June 1722, the court moved back to Versailles, to the great disappointment of *parlement*, which had hoped to keep the King and his ministers under its eye in Paris. The monstrous rookery that Louis XIV had not quite completed before his death had been empty for seven years, but now the struggle for lodgings began again. The height of ambition became the allotment of a section of an attic to live in; the vast palace echoed with the batter of carpenters' hammers, putting up and taking down partitions, marking out square feet of musty paradise to the fortunate, sounding sometimes literally the death-knell to the unfortunate who, unable to face the shame of losing favour, went back to their estates and pined their way into the grave. Room was found for 4,000 people, a figure that was to be more than doubled by extra building and closer crowding before the end of the reign.

In November 1722, the Regent finally dismissed Madame d'Averne because she refused to give up her association with Richelieu, which had lasted for several years; but by now Orléans's power was coming to an end. In February 1723, the thirteen-year-old King came of age and the Regency ended. Dubois remained as First Minister for a few months and then, riddled with disease, died in August. Early in December the former Regent had a stroke while sitting in his ground-floor room at Versailles, talking with his latest mistress, Madame de Phalaris; he died without recovering consciousness and the "small and evil"-minded duc de Bourbon became the young King's *premier ministre*.

His Excellency

The accession of the duc de Bourbon to the office of *premier ministre* was a turning point in Richelieu's life. A few days before cardinal Dubois died, the corrupt, crafty old priest had been discussing this wild young man and had remarked that he was "certainly intelligent and if he would only renounce the delights of pleasing the ladies he would be capable of handling affairs of state." Richelieu had come to the same conclusion, though he did not intend to neglect the ladies; instead, he saw that his talent for seduction could be used for something more than gratifying his craving to conquer women and outshine other men—it could be a means to power. His duel with Bourbon was less than three years old, and he had still not parted definitely from Mademoiselle de Charolais. Thus, he had every reason to expect that the new *premier ministre* would persecute him and try to harry him from the court. Instead, he was shown marks of favour and, in May 1724, astonishingly given the appointment of ambassador to Austria. And all of this he owed to a woman: the twenty-six-year-old Jeanne-Agnès de Berthelot, marquise de Prie.

Madame de Prie was handsome, outwardly demure, well-read, and highly intelligent: "everything about her was seductive, she was simple in vice, violent beneath an air of gentleness, libertine by temperament." Her husband was French ambassador to Savoy from 1714 to 1719; then, having exhausted his money and being unable to live on his pay, he sent his very young wife back to Paris to prepare a new career for him. She did not require any

directive on how to set about this; her good looks, quick-witted-
ness, and complete lack of moral scruples made her task an easy
one. She began with an affair with Richelieu, whom she met
through her cousin, Richelieu's former opponent and now his
friend, the comte de Gacé; she ended at just the right moment
as mistress to the treacherous, one-eyed, spindle-shanked duc de
Bourbon. Richelieu had already seen, in Madame de Maintenon,
the influence that a woman could exercise over a strong and autocratic monarch; now he was to learn how much greater that power
could be when a determined woman was dealing with a moral or
intellectual weakling. It was a lesson that would have practical
applications in the history of France for the next fifty years.

Bourbon's policy was dictated by two considerations: to
strengthen his own position and to undermine that of the House
of Orléans. From the Orléans family, he had no need to fear much
opposition, for its new head, the ex-Regent's successor, was a
mild man with a harmless and pleasing mania—he firmly believed
that death had been abolished—who presently retired to a monas-
tery. But Bourbon's attempts to win support at home did him
more harm than good; he repealed several of the more unpopular
taxes, only to find that the state was running short of money and
new taxes had to be imposed; he fell foul of the Church when
trying to collect a universal tax of 2 per cent, and stirred up more
strife when he attempted to placate the priests by launching fresh
persecutions against the Protestants.

In foreign affairs, he was guided largely by André-Hercule de
Fleury, bishop of Fréjus, a gentle, wily old man who was the
King's tutor. When Orléans and Dubois died, Fleury could have
had the post of First Minister for the asking, since he had the
King completely under his influence. But either he thought that
at seventy he was too old for the task or else his natural caution
prompted him to wait and see how things turned out. He was
now waiting and watching and preparing and not even risking
the title of Foreign Minister, which was officially held by the
comte de Morville. Certainly neither he nor Morville had any
part in the appointment of Richelieu to the Austrian embassy, a
decision that was greeted with a mixture of derision and disbelief

that the most important and thorny diplomatic post in Europe should be entrusted to an unreliable dandy with no qualifications other than the ability to leap faster than any rival from one bed to the next.

France, still recovering from the ruinous expenditure of Louis XIV and the financial chaos of the Regency and Law's System, had desperate need to stay out of wars. But the Quadruple Alliance was being severely strained, especially by Austria's decision to license the use of the port of Ostend by a new company trading with the East—a move which Britain and Holland fiercely protested was an infringement of the interests of their own East India Companies. In April the situation was aggravated by a new quarrel between France and Spain, threatening the peace that had been patched up between them after the brief war of 1719 and that the Regent had hoped to strengthen by marrying one of his daughters to the Prince of the Asturias and engaging Louis XV to marry one of the Spanish infantas, eight years his junior.

The three-year-old child was brought to Paris with her nurses and her dolls to be brought up in the country whose throne she would one day share and to be educated in the French fashion. It was agreed that the marriage should take place when she was fifteen and the bridegroom was twenty-three. Unfortunately, Louis was no sooner into his teens than he began to show signs of the lustful Bourbon temperament, and, though he was still timid with women, he exhibited a warm interest in other adolescent boys. The duc de la Trémoille, sixteen years old and with a passion for crochet and tapestry work, had to be hurriedly removed from the court in June 1724, and as a hasty temporary measure, Fleury had a set of pornographic and excessively orthodox engravings hung in a place where his pupil was sure to see them at least once every day. Madame de Prie and Bourbon, who had long been worried at the thought that the King might die and be succeeded by an Orléans, now insisted that he must be provided with a wife as soon as possible so that he could be cured of his regrettable tendencies and could beget children for the succession. There was some genuine cause for alarm, for there was a strong streak of homosexuality in the royal family, and for several successive reigns male favourites had alternated with mistresses as powers behind the throne. For Bourbon, there was the additional attraction that the rupture of the engagement would probably wreck the marriage of the Regent's daughter to the Prince of the Asturias, and the new queen would owe her choice to Bourbon and not to an Orléans.

While a hurried search was made through lists of the princesses of Europe, unmarried, nubile, and Catholic, the little infanta—who fortunately understood little of what was going on and was delighted at the prospect of seeing her parents again—was sent back to Madrid. The Queen of Spain, knowing that Bourbon had recently asked for a Spanish honour to be conferred on Madame de Prie's husband (so that it might be inherited by the bastard child that she had borne him) shrieked that "this one-eyed scoundrel has sent our daughter back because the King would not create the husband of his harlot a grandee of Spain." Meanwhile, Philip, flying into a justifiable tantrum, decided to settle his differences with Austria and form a new coalition against France. He sent a special envoy, the baron Riperda, to Vienna to sign a pact in which Spain recognized both the Austrian concession at Ostend and the Emperor's claim that his daughter Maria Theresa was the lawful heir to his throne. Moreover, Riperda was to assess the possibilities of a marriage between Maria Theresa and Philip's second son.

Richelieu, although he had been appointed twelve months before, had not yet left Paris. He had spent a great deal of time assembling a suitable staff and entourage, and Voltaire had busied himself with finding secretaries. He received instructions on the aims of his mission at the end of March 1725, and supplementary notes were given to him in May after Riperda had been sent to Vienna. He was to do everything he could to preserve the peace; he was to show no resentment at the new Austro-Spanish agreement and was to treat Riperda with the utmost courtesy while preventing him from taking precedence over him; he was to work closely with the British and Dutch emissaries and try to discover whether Austria and Spain had entered into any secret agreements; and he was to try to get the Emperor to reverse his decision over Ostend and thus bring about a reconciliation with Britain and Holland. It was a difficult task and the outlook seemed black. The Quadruple Alliance was splitting at the seams, no one partner trusting any of the others. Austria was on the point of reconstituting her alliance with Spain, thus raising the old nightmare of simultaneous attack along all France's land frontiers: across the Pyrénées, up the Rhône valley from Italy and Savoy, across the Rhine, and down from the Austrian Netherlands.

Richelieu arrived in Vienna in July 1725 and found the atmosphere tense and unfriendly. Most of the Emperor's courtiers and advisers supported the Spanish alliance; Riperda had openly proclaimed that he would not yield precedence to Richelieu nor even recognize his existence; behind him at Versailles he had left very few people who thought he could succeed and many who would be glad to see him fail. It was the sort of situation that he welcomed. The odds were so much against him that there could be no doubt about his glory if he were victorious, and he always had sufficient courage and confidence to ignore the possibility of failure. Though she may never have considered them, these qualities in his character justified Madame de Prie's apparent recklessness in procuring the post for him.

She had, meanwhile, decided on a successor for the infanta: Maria Leczynska, a pleasant, pious, undistinguished, robust girl of twenty-two, not quite seven years older than her future husband. Her father, a Polish nobleman, had been elected King of Poland and, after five years on the throne, had been chased off it by the Elector of Saxony. This brief taste of royal comforts was followed by fifteen years of comparative penury in a modest house in Wissembourg. On hearing of the marriage proposal, father, mother, and daughter fell on their knees and thanked God; there was little doubt that they would be equally grateful to Madame de Prie. In August Maria was married by proxy in the cathedral of Strasbourg, and in September she began a royal progress to her new home and the four hundred attendants, from lackeys to ladies-in-waiting, who had been appointed to her household.

Continual rains had brought famine conditions to the countryside and destroyed the roads; on occasions the Queen's escort had to drag her from her carriage to save her from drowning in unexpected water holes; at overnight stops her possessions floated about in the flooded baggage rooms. It was a dismal, seemingly unending ordeal by mud. Local government officials mustered the starving peasantry into line and forced them to march through the uncut crops to tread out new roads for the royal cortège. The carriage horses and those ridden by the escort foundered and had to be replaced by horses that were commandeered locally and were so feeble from lack of fodder that ten had to be employed to do the work of four.

Her young husband drove out to meet her and bring her back to Fontainebleau, where the marriage was to be solemnized a second time. In her dress of silver brocade she was prettier than he had expected; and when she began a curtsey, he leaped forward, raised her, and kissed her on both cheeks—and she fell head over heels in love with him. In the chapel next day, surrounded by the nobility of France, glittering with orders and decorations, she made him a brave consort, her purple velvet gown sprinkled with golden lilies chiming with his gold brocade coat and white-plumed hat adorned with an enormous diamond. There were festive illuminations in the palace grounds, but a wind sprang up and put them out and the bridegroom took his bride off to bed. Fleury's carefully chosen engravings had not been wasted on the young King; next morning he agreeably informed a member of his suite that he had demonstrated his affection to his bride seven times during the night.

In Vienna, Richelieu was in the thick of his silent, smiling war with Riperda. Usually they avoided each other, and, since Richelieu had not yet been invited to present his credentials, they did not meet on formal occasions. But already they had met by chance in the street, driving in opposite directions but on the same side of the road. Richelieu ordered his coachman to halt, and waited impassively. After a few moments' hesitation, Riperda's carriage pulled over and drove past on the other side, both envoys exchanging the deepest bows and most cordial flourishes of their hats. It was a small, though significant, victory in the struggle to establish his position in the diplomatic pecking order, but Richelieu knew that the real test would come after he had made his official entry and presented his credentials to the Emperor. He would then share with the other ambassadors the right to accompany the Emperor to church and would come face to face with Riperda in the fight for the place of honour in the row of seats reserved for them.

By November, the Austrian government could no longer postpone the moment of Richelieu's official reception. He had prepared for it with a lavishness that did credit to the nation that he represented and satisfied his own love of display. He drove through the city preceded by running footmen in velvet uniforms frogged with silver; then fifty grooms with silver swords at their sides; then a dozen *heyduques*, valets dressed in the Hungarian style, with short boots, tall plumed caps, and silver maces; a dozen pages; the ambassador himself, in a suit of cloth-of-gold, borne in a carriage encrusted with gold figures and arabesques, the horses shod with silver and the nails driven home so lightly that the shoes would be scattered in the streets for the crowds to scramble after. The Viennese were suitably impressed, and Richelieu's diamonds went into pawn again.

Next day he was presented to the Emperor and the tension mounted; throughout the court there was a sense of waiting, of high-pitched silence. Riperda had let it be known that if Richelieu tried to take the place of honour in church, he would push him out of it; the Emperor had made it clear that he would tolerate no brawling. That evening, as Richelieu was making his first formal appearance at a diplomatic reception, a German walked across the room to him and whispered in his ear the astonishing news that Riperda was believed to have left Vienna. It was true. As Richelieu triumphantly reported to the Marquis de Silly at the foreign office two days later: "I confess that I have experienced some trying moments and undergone great tribulations. However, I made my entry on the 7th of this month. I had my audience on the 8th and M. de Riperda took his leave of the King on the evening of the 7th and left on the morning of the 8th."

He had won the game of bluff. Had he lost it, his mission would have failed at the outset, but, having won it, he was still not much farther forward. The Treaty of Hanover between France, Britain, and Prussia in September had increased Austrian suspicions, and he found himself kept at arm's length whenever he tried to get information about Austria's real intentions or some indication of the way in which France could show friendship. He was dispensing bribes lavishly: regular payments to secretaries in the Austrian ministries for notification of the arrival of couriers; to an engineer for plans of fortifications; to decoders, for individual messages and for copies of the imperial codes; to the Empress's favourites; to the Emperor's doorkeepers, for news of secret audiences; to a secretary in the Ministry of War for details of troop movements. Also in the list of expenses that he sent to Versailles was an item of 200 florins for rent of a *petite maison* outside Vienna, for he made no secret of the fact that he hoped to get a great deal of information from the ladies of the court, whom he knew how to entertain better than any other.

He was spending about 7,000 florins a month; setting himself up in the embassy, with five carriages and a dozen saddle horses, had cost him 58,000 florins, to which had to be added the cost of the furniture, linen, pots and pans that he had bought, and the parties that he had given in honour of the King's marriage. He had borrowed 50,000 francs from the financier Bernard before leaving Paris, and this debt had been transferred to the royal account. Since arriving in Vienna he had received no salary, and even before his official entry he was complaining to Silly that he was running short of money. "I have been obliged to buy many extras," he wrote in mid-October 1725, "since I cannot do less than Riperda. These things have a great effect in foreign countries, and it was even more important for me to make a show at a time when people were putting around, not without some reason, stories of excessive misery in France. . . . Although I have not incurred any unnecessary expenses, it is a miracle that I have survived. . . . But nobody understands such things at our court, where they would rather give a hundred thousand francs to a whore than ten to an ambassador."

In December, Morville wrote to tell him that the King had graciously awarded him better lodgings at Versailles, but there was no mention of the money that Richelieu claimed was owed to him as salary, nor of the extra grant for which he had applied to cover the expenses of his official entry. In April 1726, he was complaining to Silly that "I expected to receive money from the King or from my own bankers but nobody has been able—or wanted—to give me any. . . . I have just been forced to pawn my silver. . . . If the tradesmen hear about it I shall not even get a chicken on credit from now on. I am owed more than forty thousand écus by the King and a considerable amount by private individuals, and I cannot get any of it. . . ." He was annoyed at having his expenses compared unfavourably with those of "that paragon Broglie," who was ambassador in London, and in the following month he was furious at being told that the 50,000 livres that he had had from Bernard, though put down to the royal account, were still to be collected from him. "As for the conjuring trick with the 50,000 livres that Bernard lent me . . . if they are going to persist in trying to deduct them from my first year's salary, then they are going to make it impossible for me to live. . . . I have written about this, by an English courier who left some time ago, to M. le duc, M. de Morville, M. Duverney, and Madame de Prie, and I have also informed M. de Fréjus [Fleury] of all the details of this affair. . . . You know that it is impossible to do anything in France at the moment and I am at the end of my resources here, having reached the point where it is all in the hands of the Jews, who have kept me afloat until now by a miracle but who will refuse me any further services at any moment."

He was raging at having heard that somebody had told the duc de Bourbon that the tightness of money in Paris was due to Richelieu's own reports of an imminent war with Austria—when instead he had reported that, though Austria was making warlike preparations, he did not believe she would take the final step. He threatened so often to resign that he was probably not greatly alarmed when the news reached him in June that the duc de Bourbon had been dismissed, though he was certainly interested to find that his own assessment of the young King's character—"dissembling and lacking in courage"—was confirmed by the circumstances of Bourbon's dismissal.

Bourbon, irritated by Fleury's constant interference and vastly overestimating his own power, determined to exclude the aged bishop from meetings of the council. Fleury no sooner heard of this than he left Versailles and wrote a letter of farewell to the King. Louis had become completely dependent on his tutor and at once ordered Bourbon to ask Fleury to return. With that, the little struggle for power seemed to be over; Fleury said nothing, Louis said nothing, Bourbon foolishly thought that all had been forgiven. And when Louis left for Rambouillet a few days later, he said very affably to Bourbon as he left: "Do not keep us waiting for supper tonight, cousin." His carriage had no sooner disappeared than the captain of his guard handed Bourbon a *lettre de cachet*, signed by the King's own hand, ordering him into exile at Chantilly. Madame de Prie was sent to her own home at Courbépine in Normandy. There, described by eyewitnesses as being so emaciated with rage and syphilis that she looked like a spider with an enormous head and spindly arms and legs, she engineered one final love affair with a hardy local priest and then poisoned herself.

The disgrace of Bourbon served to remove some of Richelieu's difficulties, for Philip of Spain had rightly held Bourbon responsible for the rejection of his daughter and was now less intent on pressing his quarrel with France. It also provided an opportunity for Richelieu to ingratiate himself with Bourbon's successor—for Fleury had openly taken over the control of the council. Fleury had long been yearning for a cardinal's hat. The Emperor's assent was necessary before the Pope would agree to confer the honour, and for years the Emperor had refused to oblige—so it was with considerable pride that Richelieu reported at the beginning of September that the Emperor had now agreed.

Winter arrived and with it an opportunity for Richelieu to get much closer to the Viennese beauties at the fashionable sleigh parties, charming them with his studied manners and titillating them with his effronteries. It was usual for the men to draw from a hat the names of their lady partners, who accompanied them not only on the sleigh ride but also at the subsequent supper and ball. Richelieu always had the name of the lady of his choice written on a slip of paper and given to him beforehand, so that he already held it when he went through the motions of fumbling in the hat. He assured other people that the contacts made in this way, and the information he derived from them, were immensely useful, but there is no reason to believe that the Emperor or his ministers were enslaved by their wives or mistresses as so many of their French equivalents were. Much more valuable was his friendship with the papal nuncio, Grimaldi, who acted as a trusted go-between in Richelieu's approaches to the Emperor and by March 1727 had helped him to persuade the Austrians to suspend the Ostend venture for seven years.

Richelieu had achieved this despite the suspicions and frequent opposition of the British and Dutch missions, who, at the beginning of April, were not allowed any direct contact with the Emperor and who suspected Richelieu of being hand in glove with the Austrians. "I cannot conceal from your Eminence," the British ambassador in Paris wrote to Fleury, "that independently of all that we have heard from M. de Saint-Saphorin [the British envoy in Vienna] we have various other reliable reports which do not leave us any doubt that for a long time M. le duc de Richelieu has made no *démarche* without having previously concerted it with the imperial ministers." Three days later, the protest was stronger still: "I have again heard from several sources that M. le duc de Richelieu is in concert with the Court of Vienna to betray us, and I consequently do not see how we can trust him in any respect nor leave anything at all in his hands." It was true that Richelieu was spending more on spying on France's allies than on her enemies, but at the moment France had more to fear from them. While Austria and Spain were inclined to come to terms, Britain and Holland were clamouring for war, and Colonel John Armstrong was already discussing with the maréchal de Berwick plans for a simultaneous attack on Austria and Spain. Fortunately, Fleury was adept at cooling passions by deferring decisions; he agreed with everybody, assured them that he would do everything in his power, and later excused himself for doing nothing because, after all, he was an old man and not always capable of controlling those who worked under him. Thus he assured the British ambassador that Richelieu was certainly not treacherous, but on the other hand he was not perhaps acting wisely, and the best thing would be to recall him—but without any dangerous precipitancy, keeping an eye open for a favourable excuse. And so the delays multiplied until, in May, agreement was reached by all parties on all points.

Richelieu had brought his mission to a successful conclusion and was repeating his requests to be recalled to France, for he was impatient in his public affairs as in his private ones, and for months past he had been asking to be replaced. His successor had not yet arrived when horrifying rumours began to circulate about Richelieu, beginning in Vienna, spreading quickly to Paris and other capitals, and then finding their way into print in Holland. Who started them was never discovered. It may have been a rival in love. It may more probably have been somebody in the British or Dutch missions in Vienna, for they were now doing their utmost to prevent him from leading the French delegation to the conference at Soissons, where the definitive treaty was to be drawn up. Wherever it may have originated, the rumour was grave and widespread, as he learned from a letter in cipher that he received in the middle of August 1727 from the French minister in Ratisbon:

"Several days ago I heard whispers of a vexatious affair involving the Graf von Westerloo. Some people have alleged that you were partially involved in the story that they are telling about him. . . . There is something else, which merits more of your attention and of mine. I chanced to see in the hands of a third party a news-leaflet printed in Amsterdam that is sold under the name of *La Quintessence*. The story about you is there in full and, although they set it in the court of the Khan of Tartary, they have been at great pains to describe you and your name can easily be recognized by transposing the letters of the one that they have given you. . . . The story is not badly written. It can only come from somebody who understands our language perfectly and who takes a great interest in injuring and disparaging you."

The story, which varied in detail from one version to another, was that Richelieu had been dabbling in black magic and had been caught performing ceremonies that were blasphemous and perhaps murderous. In an attempt to summon up the devil he had fed consecrated wafers to two goats—one white and one black —in a quarry at midnight and then sacrificially slaughtered them by the light of the full moon. Another version had it that two Franciscan friars had made the sacrifice in Richelieu's presence; and another that it was a Franciscan who had been sacrificed. Certainly it was true that the Viennese police had arrested a Spanish priest on a charge of black magic, and Richelieu had made attempts to have him released.

Many of Richelieu's acquaintances believed that the rumours were well founded. He was known to be interested in the occult and given to minor—though not major—blasphemies; and one of his friends, the duc de Levis, said many years later that he believed him to have sacrificed a white horse to the moon. Nobody, luckily for Richelieu, linked the rumours with an event that was reported just a year before, when two old gentlemen were found burned to death in their beds in the rue Saint-Anastase, a stone's throw from the hôtel de Richelieu. One of them had published a set of treatises on alchemical subjects: the philosopher's stone, transcendental medicine, the art of extracting seminal essences from the three realms of nature, and so on. The fire had occurred on Shrove Tuesday, a detail that would have impressed the superstitious, particularly in conjunction with the fact that "the remains of their bodies were no larger than those of a newborn child."

What devilish rites had resulted in this fiery rebirth for two lifelong friends of Richelieu? For the two gentlemen were no others than the signor Colonna and the abbé Laurent, who had been present at his birth and had given evidence before the commission that established his claim to the peerage in 1721. Which of his parents introduced them to the hôtel de Richelieu is not clear; his mother may have had the common Breton interest in necromancy; his father could have seen a solution to all his difficulties in the transmutation of metals, which was one of their particular fields of study. The young duc certainly encouraged their inquiries and set up a laboratory in the place Royale where Colonna conducted many experiments on oil of vitriol with a "philosopher" named Girard, or Diesbach, and his pupil, Dumas —both of them claiming to be adepts in transmuting gold, silver, and mercury. The Regent had encouraged the fashion for chemical and alchemical experiment, and diabolism had been common in France for centuries. Like many others, Richelieu rejected the mysteries of religion but was childishly credulous towards the mumbo-jumbo of science; he firmly believed that he had second sight and, when a very old man, told friends that he *knew* that Louis XIV's elder son would never succeed to the throne.

The court of Vienna had every reason to hush up the affair, since Richelieu's alleged companions in the exploit were Westerloo, a captain in the Imperial Halberdiers, and Sinzendorf, son of the Austrian Chancellor. No proceedings were taken against them, though Westerloo resigned his commission and retired to the country, apparently in disgrace. But the incident remained in people's minds (particularly those of doctors, who resented Richelieu's habitual assumption that he knew more about medicine than they did), and the accusation of sorcery was revived against him from time to time. But in this instance, at least, it seems to have been unfounded, for his papers show quite clearly that he had never met the Spanish priest—whose name was Père Montoya —until a few days before the man was arrested. Montoya arrived in Vienna in the early days of June with a letter of introduction from the comte de Bonneval, a soldier who was later converted to Islam and with whom he had lived for four years. When Montoya was arrested, Bonneval implored Richelieu to do what he could for "le pauvre révérendissime" (a title suggesting that he was an abbot). Richelieu obligingly did so but discovered that, when questioned by the police, the abbot had made statements incriminating Richelieu, Sinzendorf, and Westerloo. He wrote in code to Bonneval to tell him what had happened, and Bonneval replied with imprecations against "that rascally monk" and apologies for having involved Richelieu in the affair. Whether Bonneval and Montoya were addicted to evil practices is not clear, but there is nothing to show that Richelieu was guilty of anything more sinister than trying to protect a man who had been recommended to him by a friend—and in whom he may have had a special interest because of the monk's claims to occult knowledge.

The scandal did nothing to impair his relations with Fleury, and on New Year's Day 1728, at the annual chapter of the orders of Saint Michael and the Holy Ghost, he was appointed in his absence to this highest of French chivalric dignities, with a special dispensation because he was still three years short of the required age of thirty-five—a dispensation usually reserved for princes of the blood. In the same month the gossips predicted that he would be recalled because the Emperor had complained of his attempts to seduce the Empress. But he remained in Vienna to complete the arrangements for the peace conference at Soissons in June and was very well received by the King when he returned to Versailles in July after more than three years' absence. Elated by his success, he at first considered asking for the ambassadorship to Spain, but he changed his mind and decided to stay at home, partly because his health was poor and was to give him great trouble during the next two years, but principally because he believed that by staying at court he could now achieve a high place in politics.

The old cardinal was seventy-five, and it appeared unlikely that he would last much longer (a false conclusion that many others besides Richelieu jumped to); and the young King had already revealed his essential qualities. He was a weakling behind whose handsome exterior lay a mean and devious personality, confused by lust and timidity. He admired Richelieu and envied in him those qualities which he lacked himself: courage, confidence, elegance, and a way with women. Richelieu had shrewdly assessed this while in Vienna and had remarked that until the King "has taken a mistress or a true friend," he would be most influenced by the First Gentleman of the Bedchamber. Since it was unlikely that he would be made First Gentleman of the Bedchamber, an office normally reserved for the ancient nobility, he resolved to try to become that "true friend" and alternatively to look for an intelligent woman to be his accomplice and the King's mistress—though this might have to wait a while, for he also knew that Mademoiselle de Charolais had recently offered herself and been rejected.

In this new phase of his career he was encouraged by one of the most remarkable women of the time: Claudine-Alexandre Guérin de Tencin. Madame de Tencin, who had had children but had never married, was a dozen years Richelieu's senior. The "long, well-shaped neck, rather large but fresh mouth, scarcely perceptible bosom and eyes that were more witty than agreeable" that had been a little less than enthusiastically described by an earlier admirer were now cushioned with the plumpness of middle age. She was conscious of the fact that it was for her intellect that most of her lovers had wooed her (with the exception of the Regent, who discarded her after a brief affair with the comment that "I don't like tarts who talk politics between the blankets") but her former relentlessly vivacious expression had mellowed to one of bright-eyed smugness. Her ruthless, uncompromising ambition was concealed beneath an apparent sweetness of manner on which one of her friends once commented that "if she had any reason to poison you, she would choose the least painful."

She was a brilliant conversationalist and an incorrigible schemer, but she had never achieved real political influence. Her life was now devoted to one end: the advancement of her somewhat flabby brother, the bishop of Embrun, and his eventual succession to Fleury. She saw a useful ally or tool in Richelieu and urged him to continue his plans for a political career either in the council or behind the throne.

§ 2

In Paris, Richelieu found many of his former mistresses eagerly waiting for him and, having disposed of his *petite maison* near the barrière de Vaugirard, he rented a new one in the rue Cadet, just off the road that led northwards out of Paris and up towards Montmartre. It was not long before the town was buzzing with more scandalous stories of his exploits: of a dinner party in the summer when it was so hot that he proposed first that his guests should dine in the nude and then that they should change partners for the dessert; of the stupid coachman who brought him the marquise de Goesbriant instead of Madame de Sabran, so that, Madame de Sabran arriving some time later, the marquise was hustled into a neighbouring room to allow Richelieu to make love to her rival—a scene reminiscent of his adventures with Mesdames Michelin and Renaud twelve years before. As usual, he showed no gratitude for his mistresses' forbearance, and, when Madame de Goesbriant wrote to protest at his unkindness and concluded "If you are well and would like to see me, let me know where you wish it to be—if it is with you, send your carriage to me in the Kitchen Court," Richelieu scribbled at the bottom: "I recommend you, Madame, to remain in that court and delight the scullions for whom you are made. Farewell, dear child." But he seldom quarrelled unnecessarily with his women friends; and on second thoughts he filed the letter away with the rest of his trophies.

Towards the end of 1728, there are indications that his thoughts had turned towards matrimony: a hostess would have been useful to him if he entered politics, and a letter from Mademoiselle de Charolais at this time says that she does not wish him to marry a relation of Madame de Villeroy, of whom she is jealous, but she will accept the situation if he promises to spend his nights with her. And his stepmother, making her will soon after his return from Vienna, stipulated that the large sum of money and the two houses on the Ile Saint-Louis which she left him should be held in trust for his younger son—an odd bequest unless he had told her that he intended to take a wife, for as yet he had no legitimate children at all.

These plans were not fulfilled. He was preoccupied with his health and in August 1728 went off to take the waters with Voltaire, who had secretly joined him in Paris in March after slipping over from London, where he had been in exile for two years after his beating by the chevalier de Rohan's servants and his subsequent imprisonment in the Bastille. This time they went eastwards to Plombières instead of to Forges, which they had favoured before the Vienna mission, and in September Richelieu returned to Paris to accompany the King to Notre Dame for the *Te Deum* in honour of the birth of a Dauphin. In 1730 he went to Holland to consult the famous physician Boerhaave as well as making the usual trip to Plombières, and in 1731 he spent six weeks in Belgium, trying the waters at Spa. He seemed quite to have forgotten the schemes he had discussed with Madame de Tencin for gaining power in the council or behind the throne. Louis, delighted with the birth of a Dauphin, showed no signs of deserting Maria Leczynska, and Richelieu spent a boring two or three years in miserable health, traipsing around his various houses and mansions at Paris and Fontainebleau and Richelieu and Saint-Germain, often with Voltaire as his guest. The poet, who was small and sharp-featured and enjoyed describing himself as the "ugly model" of Richelieu, always claimed to have been the man who first introduced Richelieu to the princesse de Guise, but this is unlikely since her mother had been a friend of Madame de Prie and the two would have had many occasions to meet. It may be that he helped to promote the romance, for Richelieu had now found the woman whom he was to make his second wife. Elisabeth-Sophie de Lorraine was the younger daughter of the prince de Guise, almost the last of an impoverished family that traced itself back to Charlemagne. She was a tall, quiet, gentle-mannered woman, "with beautiful eyes but a plain face." Richelieu was pressed for money, as he always was, and it might have been expected that he would look for an heiress to repair his fortunes, as his father had done. But the princesse de Guise had no handsome dowry to offer. It was her imposing lineage that dazzled Richelieu; and one can only suppose that it was his extraordinary charm that fascinated her, for there is no doubt that, on her side, this was a love match.

They were married in the chapel of her mother's estate at Montjeu, in April 1734. Many of the guests on the bride's side failed to appear, thus registering their silent disapproval and their conviction that marriage between a Guise and a Vignerot was a grave *mésalliance*. But Voltaire wrote a sprightly epithalamium which he managed to find time to recite to the bride and groom before hurrying from the scene, hotly pursued by royal functionaries bearing *lettres de cachet* issued against him because of his recently published *Lettres philosophiques*. Voltaire left behind him the marquise du Châtelet, with whom he had been living for the past year and who had previously been Richelieu's mistress. A plain but kindly-faced woman with deep brown eyes and a nose that took too long to reach its point, Gabrielle-Emilie du Châtelet was one of those most daunting of creatures, a highly sexed bluestocking, and she was deeply grieved when Voltaire had to leave her. She recorded that "Madame de Richelieu provides my only consolation. She is a charming woman; her heart is capable of friendship and gratitude. She is, if that is possible, more affected than I am; she owes him her marriage, the happiness of her life. We share our affliction and our consolation."

It did not seem to occur to Madame du Châtelet that the new duchesse de Richelieu's affliction might have been on account of her husband's absence, for Richelieu too had had to leave—to rejoin the army on the Rhine. France had stumbled into war with Austria in the previous year because of Louis's half-hearted attempt to put his father-in-law back on the throne of Poland. The Polish venture was never pursued with any determination, but Fleury took the opportunity to try to annex Lorraine and to drive the Austrians out of Italy. Richelieu, who had been promoted brigadier in February, joined the army of the maréchal de Berwick, which had crossed the Rhine and was preparing to besiege Philippsburg, taking with him a vast retinue of servants, seventy-two mules to transport his baggage, and thirty horses for his personal use.

The French army, with its left and right wings on the Rhine above and below the beleaguered fortress, was strung out in a great semicircle where 100 men from each battalion worked with the 7,000 pioneers to throw up earthworks and bastions, cut brushwood for fascines and gabions, dig approach trenches and divert streams, since they had to prepare not only for their attack on the fortress but also for defence against a relieving Austrian army. On 2 June, when the approach trenches were closing in and the working parties had to be protected against frequent sorties from the fortress, Richelieu was invited to take supper with the prince de Conti. Either because the prince had forgotten or because he thought that differences would be overlooked on active service, he had been rash enough to invite at the same time two of the new duchesse de Richelieu's relations who had refused to attend the wedding: the prince de Pons, colonel of one of the regiments in

Richelieu's sector, and his brother, the prince de Lixin. Both were arrogant and still seething with rage at the upstart Richelieu's impertinence in marrying into their family.

Richelieu was delayed in the trenches, and dusk was falling by the time that he reached Conti's tent. His two reluctant relations had already arrived, and they greeted him coldly. As they sat down to eat, the prince de Lixin noticed flecks of dust on Richelieu's coat and sweat on his forehead and, sneering, remarked that he had had to get himself cleaned up to marry Mademoiselle de Guise, and it was a pity that he had relapsed into his natural filth. The insult was unforgivable as well as peculiarly inappropriate, for in an age of general uncleanliness, Richelieu was noteworthy for his finicky addiction to washing and his lavish use of scent. All the court had giggled over the story of how a very sweet-smelling bishop who called on Maria Leczynska was twitted by her on his remarkable fragrance when in fact all that he had done was to sit for a few minutes in a chair that Richelieu had occupied some hours earlier.

There was a horrified silence after Lixin had spoken, and, with the eyes of the rest of Conti's guests upon him, Richelieu rose from the table and asked for immediate satisfaction. The two men left the tent, called for their servants to bring lanterns, and then walked out of the camp and into the approach trenches. It was dark, but the unusual activity and movement of lights attracted the attention of the sentinels on the walls of Philippsburg; they opened fire as Richelieu and Lixin drew their swords and began to fight in the thin light of the lanterns. The crackle of musketry provided a background to the clatter and screech of the sword blades and the occasional grunts as one or other of the men lost his footing in the loose soil at the bottom of the trench. After a few moments, Lixin lunged forward and Richelieu was seen to have been badly wounded, but he refused to break off the engagement. White with loss of blood as well as with rage, his eyes gleaming with fury, he launched a wild, irresistible assault on Lixin and suddenly all movement stopped. Richelieu's sword was fast into Lixin's body; he was dead before the stretcher-bearers had got him back to his tent.

There was no inquiry. The insult had been public and effaceable only by a duel. The only result was that Voltaire, hearing that his protector had been seriously injured, arrived post-haste from his hiding place and narrowly missed getting himself hanged as a spy. "There are times when everything turns sour," as Madame du Châtelet wrote to another of her lovers. Philippsburg capitulated on 18 July—though the unfortunate maréchal de Berwick failed to have the pleasure of accepting the surrender, his head having been carried away by a cannon ball a week before—and the campaign ran down while France and Austria negotiated peace.

Richelieu returned to Paris and introduced his wife to her new home in the place Royale. The pair of them, under persistent prodding from Madame du Châtelet and Voltaire, kept up a constant flow of petitions and private pleadings to the *garde des sceaux*, who eventually withdrew the *lettres de cachet* and allowed Voltaire to return in the following spring. Richelieu remained faithful to his wife for several days and treated her with unfailing consideration, to which she responded with complete devotion. But it was not within his power to content himself with only one woman, and he would indeed have regarded it as deplorably shabby behaviour; he now took up with Madame de la Martellière, wife of a rich financier and the latest toast of Paris.

A great deal of her attraction for Richelieu lay in the fact that she already had not only a husband but also a lover, the duc de Durfort, and as soon as he had charmed Madame de la Martellière into surrender, he bragged about it in Durfort's presence. Durfort refused to believe him, whereupon Richelieu said that he would be very happy to provide him with proof if he would call at the *petite maison* in the rue Cadet between midnight and 2 a.m. the following night. Madame de la Martellière, quite unaware of this conversation, was startled and horrified when one of Richelieu's servants entered the bedroom in the small hours and informed his master that the duc de Durfort was outside and would like a word with him. There was worse to follow. To her utter dismay, she heard Richelieu say: "Show him in." She slid farther into the bed and pulled the sheet over her head; but as Durfort came into the room, Richelieu, whose caddishness was quite incredible at times, leaped out to greet him, dragging all the bedclothes with him and revealing Madame de la Martellière in all her perfect and familiar beauty. Durfort walked over and slapped her face and then went home.

Madame du Châtelet spent Christmas and the early part of 1735 with the new duchesse, who was expecting a child, but a miscarriage at the end of January dashed her hopes and in May, when Richelieu rejoined his regiment at Strasbourg, she went with Voltaire to spend a holiday at Lunéville. Madame du Châtelet sent Richelieu a series of letters evidently intended to kindle old flames, but there is no indication that Richelieu was tempted to accept her advances. Peace was now complete between France and Austria, and Richelieu returned to face a horde of creditors, for his standard of living when at war was even higher than when he was at home, and he was being dunned on all sides. He found some consolation in the son to whom his wife gave birth in February 1736—Louis-Antoine-Sophie, now duc de Fronsac in his turn; and early in 1737 the duchesse gave birth to a second son, but he did not long survive, having received a venereal infection from his father, it was said.

In May 1737, while his wife was away in Turin, where she accompanied her kinswoman, Elisabeth-Thérèse de Lorraine, for her wedding with Charles-Emmanuel III of Sardinia, Richelieu renewed his association with the prince de Conti and they discovered new fields for adventure. A police report of 7 June 1737 mentions that "there is a new rendezvous for love, both convenient and discreet. Several people have a key to the gallery that M. Bontemps [governor of the Tuileries] has constructed and furnished under the terrace vaults. They go in there as soon as night falls. . . . They use no lights and can see only by the light of the moon. M. le prince de Conti and M. le duc de Richelieu often go there, and the day before yesterday Madame de Vernouillet was there for an hour; two of the ladies of her company waited for her on the steps nearby, where she rejoined them."

The duchesse de Modène had re-entered his life. For many years after her marriage, Mademoiselle de Valois made frequent journeys to France, sometimes because she could not stand her unpleasant husband, sometimes because war had driven them both from their little duchy. Each time she tried to revive old yearnings in Richelieu's heart, but she had become matronly—some even said masculine—in appearance, and it was with increasing reluctance that he kept even a few of the assignations that she so persistently arranged with him. Her husband and her husband's lackeys were maintaining a close watch on her, and Richelieu wrote pleading that he had twice had narrow escapes from being detected and perhaps assaulted as he left her house and suggesting that she should not meet him again for a while. She replied that she had borrowed the keys of an accommodating abbé's house where they could meet at least twice a week, the moon and Richelieu's courage permitting. "It would be kinder to pole-axe a person at a single blow than to make her die over a slow fire, as you are doing," she complained.

§ 3

The King's marriage had failed. Maria Leczynska, devout, faithful, not very quick-witted but far from stupid by royal standards, remained submissive and possibly still in love with her husband, but infinitely wearied by his continual demands on her, for his appetite in bed was as gross as that which preceded and stimulated it at the supper table. Between August 1727, when she gave birth to twin girls, and July 1737, when her eighth daughter was born, she had ten children. "*Toujours coucher, toujours grosse, toujours accoucher,*" she summed up her existence. She began to invent pretexts for not receiving the King at night, pleading that she was ill, grumbling that she was cold and smothering him under a mountain of blankets, pretending that she was frightened of the dark and retaining one of her ladies-in-waiting to sit by the bed and read to her.

Ministers and courtiers, gathering like sharks around the sinking ship, drew closer to the King—and in particular to his *valets-de-chambre*—seeing at last an opportunity to provide a mistress and thus gain a position of power behind the throne. This was precisely the situation for which Richelieu and Madame de Tencin had been waiting, but now that it had come they fumbled the op-

portunity. They had no good candidate to put forward, and nobody was quite sure whether the time was really ripe for putting
forward anybody. Louis remained furtive and unpredictable. Some
of the women who offered themselves were too eager, others whom
their partisans thought suitable proved too hard to persuade. Eventually Mademoiselle de Charolais, herself an earlier reject, found a
candidate with exactly the right appearance, character, and talent:
Louise-Julie de Mailly, eldest daughter of the plump, pretty Madame de Nesle who fought Madame de Polignac for Richelieu's
favours in 1719. Madame de Mailly gained a great deal of sympathy at the end of her affair with Louis because of the brutal and
underhand way in which he got rid of her; but although she was
only in her early twenties when their association began, she was
no innocent (she already had one lover, the marquis de Puyzieulx), and she carried out her campaign to seduce the King with
all the skill of a practised whore. She needed the help of Mademoiselle de Charolais and Chauvelin, the *garde des sceaux*, to
persuade Bachelier, one of the *valets-de-chambre*, to introduce her
into the King's small private rooms on the floor above his state
apartments, but from then onward she was quite capable of playing her own hand.

She was tall, rather thin, not particularly pretty, but with large
eyes, well-shaped legs, and a gift for wearing clothes and walking
in an exciting, sensual way; she was also intelligent and ready to
accept advice. The palace servant who conducted her into the
King's room left her behind a screen to make her own introduction, although the King was expecting her; when she emerged
from round the side of it, she found Louis shaking with lust and
timidity, unable to look her in the face. He turned his back on her,
his hand fumbling at her dress, seeming to want to draw her into
the room; yet his actions were so hesitant that she feared the fish
would slip off the hook.

She shivered and said that she was feeling cold—a common complaint in the draughty barracks of Versailles—and asked if she
might warm herself at the fire. He nodded and watched her from
under lowered eyelids as she sat down at the chimney corner; and
she, pretending not to know that his eyes were on her, lifted her

skirts and petticoats inch by inch. There was a silence as Louis advanced slowly across the room.

"The King took hold of her leg," one of the courtly spies reported, "and her foot, which is very pretty. From there he strayed to her garter. As she had instructions not to resist so shy a man, she said: 'Oh, my God, I did not know that Your Majesty had had me come here for that. . . . I would not have come. . . .' The King flung his arms around her." Before she left, she mentioned that she was very short of money and he gave her forty louis.

In the early stages of the liaison, she shared the small house that her tutelary genius, Mademoiselle de Charolais, had taken in the grounds of the Château de Madrid in the Bois de Boulogne, within easy distance of the King's hunting lodge at La Muette. Later she was given a set of apartments at Versailles, and it was at this point that the final break came with the Queen, who pretended—or perhaps genuinely believed—that Louis had contracted a venereal disease from the association and refused to let him into her bed. He tried for four hours to persuade her. When he left the bedroom, unsatisfied, at 3 a.m., he remarked to the valet who attended him with a light: "It's the last time I shall try that." Henceforward there was no secrecy about Madame de Mailly's position as his mistress, although he was still niggardly in giving her money, and the Spanish ambassador, attending her toilet one morning, noticed that her chemise was in holes. Most disillusioned of all was the marquis de Mailly, who had set himself up with a fine carriage in anticipation of further good fortune coming the way of his wife and now had to sell it and fall back on hackney-chairs, sparingly used.

Louis had hitherto used the bedroom in which his great-grandfather had died, the middle room on the first floor of what had been Louis XIII's hunting lodge, between the *oeil de boeuf* and the *cabinet du conseil*, looking out eastwards over the *cour de marbre* to the *place d'armes* and the avenue de Paris. It was large, lofty, and draughty, and Louis used its inconvenience as a pretext for moving to the former billiard room on the north side of the *cour de marbre*. This, with the adjoining oval room and study, and the dining room, wig room, and other small rooms at the rear, formed the Private Apartments, as distinct from the State Apartments, which included the Throne Room, and the *petits appartements* on the floors above where the King gave private dinner parties, lodged his mistresses, and even kept an aviary of rare birds.

Having bravely taken the first step into adultery, he began to indulge in casual affairs with women brought to him by Bachelier. A decade of monogyny was over; during his remaining years his lust spread in a sluggish stream into stinking creeks and backwaters, draining him of all other interests. For his country he showed no care at all; nor, except that she kept him in luxury, was there much reason why he should have had any feeling for France. His mother came from Savoy, his grandmother from Bavaria, his great-grandmother from Spain, his great-great-grandmother from Italy. Like most monarchs, he was a mongrel with only a tiny fraction of pure native blood: in his case, about 3 per cent of what had flowed in the veins of the founder of the House of Bourbon, Henry of Navarre.

Richelieu was often accused of corrupting Louis, and he would have been delighted to do so; but in fact he had had no hand in this first, crucial operation: the planting of Madame de Mailly on the King. He had been on the most intimate terms with her mother, but the family had split, with bad feelings on each side. He had remained more attached to the three of her four younger sisters who were being brought up by their stepgrandmother, the duchesse de Mazarin. And Mademoiselle de Charolais, who now hated him for his neglect of her, made certain that he did not get close to her protégée.

His friendship for the duchesse de Mazarin took him into the opposing camp, for the duchesse was Madame de Mailly's sister-in-law, stepgrandmother, and bitterest enemy. Her stepdaughter by her second husband was Madame de Nesle and her younger sister was the marquise de Polignac. After Madame de Nesle's death in 1729, the duchesse had taken charge of her three younger daughters, Diane-Adélaïde, Hortense-Félicité and Marie-Anne, aged 15, 14, and 12, and had placed the 17-year-old Pauline-Félicité in the convent of Port-Royal. The eldest of the girls, Louise-Julie, was already married to the duchesse de Mazarin's brother, the marquis de Mailly, and on bad terms with her sister-in-law. The dislike between the two women increased greatly when Madame de Mailly became Louis's mistress, for the duchesse de Mazarin was Lady of the Bedchamber to the Queen and her great friend. She was also an influential woman, mother of one minister, Saint-Florentin, and mother-in-law of another, Maurepas, and her salon was always a hotbed of intrigue.

For Richelieu, the King's conversion to licentiousness brought unofficial promotion at court; he was accepted as the expert in amorous intrigue, and Louis showed a livelier interest in his witty and salacious conversation. In February Richelieu was promoted *maréchal de camp*, a rank roughly equivalent to major-general, and at the end of the year, when the governorship of Brittany fell vacant on the death of the maréchal d'Estrées, Richelieu asked Fleury to recommend him for the post. It was far beyond what he could legitimately hope for on grounds of military rank, experience, or age, but Fleury was still favourably disposed towards him and assured him that his request would be granted. But then, in the mysterious way in which such things happened at court, he found that Fleury had suddenly become inaccessible, always too sick or too busy to talk to him. Without understanding why, he began to feel the chill wind that precedes disgrace, and he sent Fleury a note saying how disturbed he was by the alarming things that were happening to him.

Fleury, always cautious about committing himself on paper, sent word by his *valet-de-chambre* that Richelieu was not to be worried and was to rest assured of the cardinal's affection. It was at Madame de Mazarin's that he eventually learned the secret of Fleury's unaccountable coolness; her daughter-in-law, Madame de Saint-Florentin, acting as the cardinal's messenger, whispered that Mademoiselle de Charolais had so frightened the comtesse de Toulouse—whose infant son had the succession to the civil governorship—with warnings that Richelieu would ride rough-shod over him, that the comtesse had implored the King not to give him the post. Instead, the cardinal was prepared to offer him one of the three lieutenant-generalcies of Languedoc, with a lieutenant-general's pay, a royal patent entitling him to special honours, and the command of the whole province, even though the other two lieutenant-generals were his seniors. It was not to be compared with the great plum that Mademoiselle de Charolais had maliciously robbed him of, but it was a notable mark of favour to a man who was only forty-two years old and had spent half of those years earning himself a reputation for irresponsibility.

The prospect of the high honours that awaited him in Languedoc stimulated his interest in protocol, and he was soon in the thick of an argument over the right of dukes and peers to kneel on *carreaux* because of their rank and not because they held certain offices. He had the advantage of having been the son of an elderly father, and, having inherited his title almost a quarter of a century before, he was fast becoming recognized as an authority on court etiquette—a subject on which in later life he was accepted as the supreme arbiter. He claimed that he had used a *carreau* in the chapel at Marly in the time of Louis XIV, that he sat in an armchair when he appeared as a suitor in *parlement*, and his advocate pleaded from behind him, that he crossed the *parquet* in front of the *premier président* when he went to and from his chair, and—a point that was currently very hot—that the *premier président* raised his cap every time he addressed him.

Madame de Richelieu was having similar preoccupations: mainly with the problem of assessing the exact degree of condescension she should display when greeting the ladies of Languedoc. Madame d'Estrées, widow of the maréchal, assured her that in Brittany she would never have dreamed of offering her hand to any of the local ladies—or, for that matter, to any foreign ladies either, though in the case of the foreigners she usually explained that this was in order not to make the Bretons envious. But when Madame de Richelieu appeared at Fontainebleau on Sunday, 16 November, to take leave of the King, she was debating an even knottier problem. She had spent the previous evening in the apartments of the duc and duchesse de Luynes agitatedly discussing whether she should take her leave first of the King and then of the Queen, or vice versa. Monsieur de Luynes was of the opinion that one must show one's respect first to the King. Madame de Richelieu, on the other hand, felt that one showed *more* respect to the

I Louis-François-Armand de Vignerot du Plessis,
maréchal duc de Richelieu (circa 1753)
by Louis Tocqué, Musée de Tours

II La place Royale, Paris

III The duchesse de Bourgogne

by Jean-Baptiste Santerre,
Musée de Versailles

IV Mademoiselle de Valois, as Hebe

by Jean-Baptiste Gobert,
Musée de Versailles

King by visiting him after the Queen when one left—though of course visiting him before the Queen when one arrived—thus, as it were, basking in the rays of the sun for as long as possible.

This she did. And it appeared that she had made a dreadful blunder, for the King failed to single her out of the crowd for any special acknowledgment. Madame d'Estrées, an insufferable busybody, assured her that *she* had had a royal bow entirely to herself each time that she had left for Britanny. Poor Madame de Richelieu explained that she had waited for the King to show some sign that he was aware of her presence and, not having seen any such sign, she had not dared approach him. The suggestion that she was in disgrace—and presumably her husband as well—was so exciting that the rest of the courtiers gathered in small groups agitatedly assessing the implications of what had happened. With his apartments humming as if invaded by hundreds of bees, Louis presently approached one of the swarms and asked what the commotion was about. On being told, he said that it was perfectly true that he had bowed to Madame d'Estrées on similar occasions in the past—but only because she had forced him into it. With which backhander both ladies had to rest content.

Richelieu transplanted his whole household, linen, silver, and servants, to Montpellier, where he installed himself in one of the great seventeenth-century mansions that struck a note of such magnificent incongruity in the red-roofed, sun-drenched southern town. He lived in vice-regal splendour, delighting in every ceremonial moment. Records were rummaged out, perused, annotated, squeezed of every drop of precedent and paradigm that might add to his honours and privileges; his every movement seemed to be attended by armed men, bowing burgesses, gunfire, or *Te Deums*. There were many who objected to his airs and pretensions, but they were either overridden or—more usually—charmed out of their resentment by some elaborate but quick-witted display of graciousness.

Only once was he known to have come off second-best: when an elderly canon, resenting his instructions to receive the military governor with a *Te Deum*, saw Richelieu before the service and asked after the King's health. Richelieu treated this as a formality, bowed but did not answer. "Monsieur le duc," the canon persisted, "I asked you how the King was." "He is very well," Richelieu replied abruptly. The canon turned to the other members of the chapter. "You hear the news of the King's health. Let us offer thanks to God with a *Te Deum*—in which the governor will no doubt be good enough to join us."

In April 1739, Madame de Richelieu returned to Paris to be with her father, who was dying. She was a lonely woman; her mother had died some years before and she had few relations who would speak to her after her *mésalliance* with Richelieu and the death of Lixin, but she was still on good terms with her eighteen-year-old brother, whom Richelieu presented at court in May.

There was misery in the countryside again this spring and early summer. The previous year's crop had been disappointing and the marquis d'Argenson, son of the fearsomely ugly *garde des sceaux* who had questioned Richelieu after the Cellamare affair, noted in his diary that the poorer people were reduced to eating grass. Louis's only contribution to the public weal was the announcement that he would not touch for the King's Evil that year. It was customary to do this after receiving the sacrament at Easter, but Louis could not take communion without declaring his sincere intention to give up his mistress. He knew that he could not bring himself to dismiss her, and in matters involving the divine wrath he was too scared to cheat. So his subjects remained scrofulous as well as hungry.

He was not, on the other hand, showing Madame de Mailly any particular favours. He was as mean as ever with money, and it had long been apparent that she had little influence with him. There was now even some doubt whether her physical charms were strong enough to hold him. When her brother-in-law wrote to ask her to obtain a place for a friend of his and added: "One word from the beautiful lips of a beautiful woman will settle the affair," she read the passage out to Louis. "A beautiful mouth!" he repeated in front of several witnesses. "You don't pride yourself on that, I imagine?"

The Richelieus did not stay long at court. Languedoc, in common with many of the provinces around the frontiers of France, had retained some remnants of self-government, including the *Etats*, the representatives of the three estates—clergy, nobility, and bourgeoisie—who met towards the end of each year, principally to vote taxes. Richelieu presided at these assemblies, and on this occasion he left Versailles in the autumn, partly to avoid the attentions of the duchesse de Modène. The poor woman, rather fatter than ever and no longer recognizable as the eager girl who had sacrificed her happiness to get his release from the Bastille, wrote to him in June: "I spend my life trying to find ways of providing you with the opportunity to see me, but to tell you the truth I am very much afraid that I am wasting my time and that the trouble is simply these *pretended* dangers that you keep discovering."

He went down to Montpellier a little ahead of his wife, for they had decided to economize, to let the Paris house and remain in Languedoc for at least two years. Madame de Richelieu found a tenant in the Neapolitan ambassador, Castro-Piagno, and the court was soon laughing over a story that before he moved in, he quartered a flock of sheep in the house, to counteract the all-pervading smell of Richelieu's scent. The duchesse, already in poor health, was not to spend the two years that they had planned in Montpellier. In March 1740 she gave birth to their third child, a girl who was christened Jeanne-Sophie-Elisabeth-Louise-Armande-Septimanie—the last because Septimanie was the ancient name for Languedoc, whose *Etats* stood as her godparents. To escape the summer heat of Montpellier, the duchesse returned to her family home in the Temple, but she was too far gone in consumption for there to be any hope for her. Richelieu followed shortly after and, for the few weeks that remained, he managed to spend more time with her and less with his mistresses.

They had been married for six years, and throughout that time she had loved him deeply. Coming into her room one day during her final illness just as her confessor, the celebrated Jesuit preacher Père Ségaud, was leaving, Richelieu asked if she were happy after receiving his ministrations. She grasped his hand and answered: "Of course, for he has not forbidden me to love you." A little before midnight on 2 August 1740 he was called from his bed; when he reached his wife's bedroom, it was evident that she was on the point of death. She summoned enough strength to speak to him, and whispered: "Oh, how vexed I am that they sent for you; I wanted to spare you the grief of seeing me die. But now that you are here—kiss me for the last time."

She died in his arms. He remained for a long time, holding her clasped to him, not wishing to admit that she was dead. Then he went to hide his sorrow on his estate at Richelieu and was faithful to her memory for about a month.

Sisters

§ 1

It was an evil summer, the year that Richelieu's second wife died. The sun would sometimes break through around midday, but the mornings and evenings were cold and overcast, and the wind stayed stubbornly in the north. Those who could afford them had roaring fires; others shivered and cursed and feared the starvation that would follow another bad harvest. Some of the bad temper and disenchantment was beginning to rub off on the King, and in late September, as he drove to Choisy, the elegant château just south of Paris that he had bought in the preceding year from the duc de Villeroy, Louis found his carriage surrounded by men and women who shouted not "Long live the King!" but "Misery! Misery! Give us bread!" He was so upset by this demonstration that as soon as he arrived at Choisy he discharged all the men working in the garden, thus proving his willingness not to waste labour on frivolities and at the same time increasing the number of starving families. Two or three days later, the inmates of Bicêtre madhouse rioted because their ration of bread had been reduced. Some escaped and roamed the streets of Paris, and forty or fifty were shot or cut down by the mounted troopers who were sent to deal with them. In the Auvergne many peasants were existing on bread made of oats and barley. "More have died of want within two years," Argenson recorded, "than were killed in all the wars of Louis XIV."

Richelieu's frequent absences in Languedoc had lost him a great deal of his standing at court. Louis, ill at ease with new faces, was prone to forget even familiar ones if he did not see them daily, and his natural furtiveness and timidity inhibited him from resuming his old relationship with them. His eyes flicked away so that the bow and sweep of the hat could be ignored; then, knowing that he had been ungracious, he would hold his victim responsible and treat him more coldly than ever. Richelieu, having seen this treatment meted out to many others, readily recognized it when it was applied to him. He knew that Mademoiselle de Charolais, through Madame de Mailly, was losing no opportunity of sniping at him in the deadly warfare of the boudoir and the bed, and it was likely that his post in Languedoc had been given him specifically to keep him as far away from court as possible.

So it was with great surprise that, returning to Versailles after his wife's death, he found himself welcomed with unexpected warmth by Madame de Mailly and her sister, the marquise de Vintimille. Pauline-Félicité de Vintimille was the second in age of the five Nesle sisters, a tall, rather plain girl—one unfriendly observer said that she was ugly, "with the ugliness that inspires fear rather than derision"—but full of bounce and vitality. She was a *pensionnaire* in the convent of Port-Royal when her sister was chosen to be the King's mistress, and, with typical self-confidence, she at once began planning to share her fate. Whether or not Madame de Mailly knew what her sister's ambition was, she brought her to court in 1738 and frequently let her stay in her own apartment. Pauline-Félicité's high spirits stirred Louis out of his torpor, and in 1739, because it would have been improper for the King to commit adultery with an unmarried woman of the aristocracy, she was found a husband, the marquis de Vintimille. Vintimille grumbled that she was cuckolding him with the marquis de Coigny and the duc d'Ayen, as well as with the King, but this was merely because he was a naturally cross-grained person. He had been rewarded with several sinecures, and it was an open secret that he had no affection at all for his wife: he said that she "stank like the devil," and he usually referred to her as "my little nanny goat."

The two sisters shared their lover in seemingly perfect harmony. Louis liked taking both women out with him in the same carriage, as when he had them called at dawn on a chilly, misty October morning in 1740 to go with him to one of his favourite entertainments: watching the stags rutting in the forest of Fontainebleau. Pauline-Félicité amused him with her sharp tongue and whetted his appetite with sudden gusts of obstinacy; Louise-Julie fussed over him, getting him new dressing gowns out of her sparse pin money and, when he had a cold, curing it with turnip soup made by her own hand. Only one small flame of jealousy flickered up: Pauline-Félicité resented the influence that the imperious Mademoiselle de Charolais had over Louise-Julie. She worked first on her sister and then on Louis, and eventually Mademoiselle de Charolais perceived that she was being invited less and less frequently to the royal suppers.

It was at this point that the two sisters suggested to Richelieu that he should propose himself for dinner with the King, as he used to do. This was a humiliating performance, involving handing in one's name and then standing at the door of the King's apartments, waiting for the list of the chosen to be read out. Richelieu, not wishing to risk a public rebuff, contented himself with giving his own supper parties in the new *petite maison* that he had rented just beyond the barrière de Vaugirard on the south side of the river, the second house that he had taken in that quarter. Here, his eyes brightly twinkling in the light of the candle that he carried, he would take his women guests on a tour of the rooms where "all is gallantry and obscenity . . . especially the walls, which have, in the middle of each panel, very immodest figures in bas-relief." Despite his reluctance, the two women assured him that they would persuade the King to give him a favourable answer, and in June 1741 he presented himself and was chosen.

The court began to stir with interest. The virtual disappearance of Mademoiselle de Charolais had created a power vacuum. Richelieu's sudden popularity with the two sisters suggested that he might be able to succeed Mademoiselle de Charolais as the *éminence grise* of the alcove, and his would-be fellow-conspirator, Madame de Tencin, at once began to pay more attention to him. The pattern of the future was obscured by an apparent lessening in the King's affection for Louise-Julie, which was expressed in sharp replies and surliness and flared into a dangerous little row when he suddenly decided to take up tapestry work—for which the necessary wool, needles, and frame were supplied by the effeminate duc de Gesvres, one of the four First Gentlemen of the Bedchamber. Louise-Julie prudently discovered a similar passion for tapestry and became so engrossed in her work one day that she failed to answer when Louis spoke to her. His bad temper got the better of him, and he picked up a knife and slashed at her tapestry, whereupon she flew into one of her rare rages. It was touch and go whether Louis would order her out of the palace, but his horror of taking any step in public saved her, and she made her peace with him over an intimate supper which she prepared and served in her own rooms.

She could be excused for being a little on edge. The King's affection for Pauline-Félicité had been proved in a way that could not long be concealed, and in September the marquise de Vintimille gave birth to a son, in whose begetting her husband protested that he had had no part, though his uncle, the new bishop of Paris, made no bones about christening the child as comte de Luc, Vintimille's secondary title. Others had so little doubt about the real father that they christened the newcomer the demi-Louis, and he grew up to bear a striking resemblance to the King. But Madame de Mailly's fears that the baby would draw the King and Pauline-Félicité too closely together were sadly unfounded, for the young mother survived the birth of her son by only a few days. Louis, greatly upset, went to Saint-Léger, a small château owned by the comtesse de Toulouse near Rambouillet, accompanied by Madame de Mailly, Richelieu, and a whole flock of Noailles, to recover from the shock—and Richelieu began to wonder whether others of the Nesle girls might not be presented as candidates for his master's favours.

Of the three that remained, one had already been Richelieu's mistress: Hortense-Félicité, a plump young woman of twenty-five, married to an officer in the Royal-Cravate regiment, the marquis de Flavacourt. Her younger sister—the youngest of all the five—Marie-Anne, marquise de la Tournelle, was a widow and currently the mistress of the duc d'Agénois, descended, like Richelieu, from the Cardinal's sister. Marie-Anne was the best looking of all the Nesle sisters and better endowed with brains than the others; it was she whom Richelieu and Madame de Tencin decided to introduce as a replacement for Madame de Vintimille—and possibly for Madame de Mailly as well—and Marie-Anne was well content to accept their help.

It turned out to be a rather long and tiresome business. Marie-Anne was very much attached to her stepgrandmother, the duchesse de Mazarin, and supported her in her quarrel with Madame de Mailly; and Madame de Mailly soon suspected Marie-Anne's intention of supplanting her and did everything that she could to keep her from court. In this she was supported by Fleury, who found Madame de Mailly docile and unambitious and did not relish the task of coping with a newcomer who might have more talent for making the most of her position. It was not until the masked ball at Versailles on Shrove Tuesday, 1742, that Richelieu was able to lead the marquise de la Tournelle up to the King and get them into conversation; within a few days he was regretting his temerity, for Madame de Mailly, with Fleury's support, persuaded the King to order him back to Languedoc to deal with some largely imaginary difficulties with the Protestants, and Louis threatened, if he argued, to give his command to the marquis de Mirepoix.

Richelieu knew that Louis would desert any of his friends if enough pressure was put on him, and he did not think the time ripe for a trial of strength with Fleury and Madame de Mailly. For that matter, he was not yet sure that Marie-Anne was prepared to give up Agénois in order to become mistress of the King, though she gave every indication of being a practical and ambitious young woman. He did as he was told: left Versailles and went down to Montpellier, where he dealt with the Protestant problems in Upper and Lower Languedoc and then went over to Bordeaux, where he was interested in the theatre and had plans for a company of actors to be formed to be supported by the cities of Bordeaux and Toulouse, playing half the year in each. From Bordeaux he made the short journey to Fronsac, where his estate, though comparatively small, brought him a useful revenue from the fords and toll bridges that he owned along the Dordogne, and from Fronsac he journeyed northward to Richelieu. He did not return to Versailles until September, and on his arrival he found the intrigues bubbling more furiously than ever.

The duchesse de Mazarin had died a few days before, and, knowing how devoted Marie-Anne was to her, he went to call on her in the apartment that had been lent to her by his old friend the duchesse de Boufflers. He did not know what progress she had made during the four months that he had been away and was disheartened to find her looking very dejected—not because of her stepgrandmother's death but because she had asked for the vacant post of *dame du palais* to the Queen and had heard no more of her request. Worse, the King had gone to Choisy, and neither she nor Madame de Flavacourt had been invited to join the party. Worst of all, the duchesse de Mazarin's son-in-law, Maurepas, had bluntly told Marie-Anne that now that his wife had inherited the Mazarin mansion, she had better take herself off to a convent— where perhaps her unhappy plight might arouse the King's sympathy. This brutal reminder of the knife-edge on which favour and fortune rested enraged her. She begged Richelieu to go to Choisy and ask Madame de Mailly to speak to the King on her behalf— adding that he might point out to Madame de Mailly that this would not only be an act of charity towards her sister but, if successful, would be proof that she still retained her influence over the King.

Richelieu drove the fifteen miles from Versailles to Choisy and arrived in time for supper, at which he managed to seat himself next to Madame de Mailly. Unfortunately, he found her, as he said, "extraordinarily indisposed towards her two sisters, and principally against Madame de la Tournelle"; but he still did not realize how far Marie-Anne's plans had progressed, or the extent to which she was deceiving him as well as the others. When he went back to Versailles with the King two days later, he called on Marie-Anne and Hortense-Félicité again to tell them that he had no encouraging news for them, and he was surprised to find Marie-Anne much less despondent than before, sitting relaxed and thoughtful in a deep armchair. Both sisters told him that they had heard nothing from the King. Richelieu, unable to offer them any comfort, was on the point of taking his leave when Marie-Anne signalled him to bend his head down; she whispered in his ear that she had been granted the place of *dame du palais*.

He was pleased but puzzled. If Louis had given her the post in face of opposition from Madame de Mailly and also from the Queen (who wanted it to go to the niece of her Grand Almoner) it must be because he was hoping for "the ultimate favour" from her. In that case, why should Marie-Anne not tell him frankly that she had ousted her sister? He called on her again next day when she was at her toilet and told her that he had not wanted to return to Paris without offering his compliments on the new position that she had obtained. Marie-Anne thanked him and agreed that, in her straitened circumstances, the perquisites of a *dame du palais* would make a vast difference. Richelieu fixed his accomplished protégée with a quizzical eye and smilingly asked her if she thought him so stupid as to come and congratulate her on a bagatelle of that kind—he was referring to Madame de Mailly's place. Marie-Anne at first pretended not to understand and then to be angry and in the middle of her display of vexation was interrupted by the arrival of the chevalier de Grille, an officer in the guards who was widely believed to be one of her more fortunate suitors. Her mood changed; she asked Richelieu not to return to Paris and, when he said that he had pressing business, she begged him to come back in the morning—a plea to which he agreed, having, as he said, "as much desire as she had, to make our understanding complete."

He did not go to Paris that day or for several days afterwards, for, on leaving Madame de la Tournelle's borrowed apartment, he learned that Louis was still at mass, and he waited to follow in the procession before taking his leave. As they walked up the *escalier des ambassadeurs* and towards the throne room where Louis would slip through a door into the narrow corridor leading to his *cabinets intérieures*, the King began to whisper to Richelieu out of the side of his mouth, looking straight before him and speaking in such a low tone that Richelieu had to crane his head sideways to catch the words. They were brief but intriguing: "Can you keep a secret?" Richelieu protested that he had given ample proof of this when he had had the honour of being His Majesty's ambassador in Vienna; but the question was not as idle as he tried to make out: Richelieu was notorious for his indiscretions, and this may have been the reason why Marie-Anne decided that it should be Louis who enlisted him in their intrigue. Richelieu, who would be only too ready to gossip about her secrets, was unlikely to risk disgrace by betraying the King's. Louis, for his part, was eager to have the support of a man of experience now that he was making his first attempt at wooing a woman for himself instead of having her delivered direct to his bedroom. Continuing to stare straight ahead as they walked through the state apartments, he muttered: "Be at my supper this evening."

Marie-Anne stayed out of Richelieu's way all that day, and he was at a high pitch of excitement when he put in his appearance at the royal supper party; as so often before, there was an anticlimax—he waited and waited, but the King did not address a word to him. He was familiar with Louis's dissembling, but this time he suspected that the King had really changed his mind, and when the fruit was brought in he decided to leave. Louis at once called him back, and he continued to stand, obedient and perplexed, until the King rose to wash his hands in the bowl that was offered to him, and at the same time nodded to Richelieu to draw near. "Wait for me," said Louis, and then went off into the Queen's apartments for a few moments' conversation with her and with those courtiers entitled to the *grandes entrées*. Since Richelieu did not enjoy this distinction, he hung around outside the King's study, but when Louis appeared shortly afterwards he walked straight past Richelieu without a sign and into the study, where he gave the evening password to the duc de Villeroy, captain of the guard. When Villeroy had left, Louis wandered out of his study again, led Richelieu as if by chance into the embrasure of the window and told him in a low voice to go and get his own supper and meet him below in the *cour de marbre* at midnight— wearing a cheap wig and a heavy *redingote*. Then, as if terrified at having taken a decision, he disappeared into the study again.

Shortly before midnight, Richelieu took up his station in the courtyard. Standing with his back to the *cour royale* and the *place d'armes* beyond it, he faced the *salon de l'oeil de boeuf* and the council chamber, flanking the old King's bedroom; on the first floor on his left were the Queen's apartments and above him on his right the clock room and the bedroom that Louis had moved into a few years earlier. The *cour de marbre* was still busy with sedan chairs and in the *cour royale* carriages were clattering over the cobbles; silhouetted against the lights from the ground-floor windows, a man in a big unfashionable black wig and a rusty coat came bustling up to him and asked: "What are you doing there?" The clothes—and the brisk manner—were so unfamiliar that Richelieu did not at first recognize the King who, snapping out "Follow me!" strode across the inner courtyard, into the *cour royale* and diagonally towards the right-hand wing where the ministers and officials were lodged. Just before reaching the corner, Louis entered one of the doorways and led the way up to the first floor; and it was at this moment that Richelieu realized they were making for the apartment of the *maître de chapelle du roi,* the bishop of Rennes—and remembered that the bishop, recently sent as ambassador to Spain, had offered to lend his apartment to Madame de la Tournelle.

It was indeed Marie-Anne whom they found inside, and a Marie-Anne for whom adventure had brought a sparkle to her usually soft, languishing eyes, a heightened flush to her much admired smooth, clear complexion. She burst into laughter at their dowdy appearance and explained to Richelieu that she had insisted on the King's bringing him with him as a protection against the tipsy coachmen and insolent porters who wandered about in the courtyard outside. They chatted a while, Richelieu marvelling at her ease of manner and wondering how often the two had met already, and then he withdrew to an ante-room, suggesting that they might have more interesting matters to discuss together. When Louis finally emerged and he conducted him back to the foot of the spiral staircase that led up to the *cabinets intérieures,* he noted with interest that the King appeared to be happy, but perhaps not satisfied.

It suited his purpose later in life to deny that he had a hand in procuring any of Louis's mistresses, and it is true that Marie-Anne did a very great deal to help herself, but there is no doubt that Richelieu prepared the way, actively encouraged the association and—but for an unhappy accident—would have achieved a position of great power because of it. After this first visit, he went as Louis' escort almost nightly and the two visitors were soon noticed and then recognized by the servants of the ground-floor tenant, the marquis de Chalmazel—who was *premier maître d'hôtel* to the Queen. Maurepas, still Marie-Anne's bitterest enemy, spread the news in the hope of nipping the affair in the bud; but Louis was too impressed by the charms of the tall, shapely Marie-Anne to be diverted from his aim of enjoying them—and she was too shrewd and strong-willed to submit to him without getting agreement to her terms in full. Madame de Mailly frequently burst into tears in public—not surprisingly, since rumour said that the King had told her: "I promised you that I would always speak frankly. I am madly in love with Madame de la Tournelle. I haven't had her yet, but I shall." Or, in a briefer and more brutal version: "You bore me—I love your sister."

On 23 October 1742, Richelieu left Versailles to join the army in Flanders, where large numbers of French and British troops were fighting each other without any declaration of war, both sides calling themselves "auxiliaries" to Prussia and Austria, who were already embarked on the war of the Austrian Succession; his duties as escort to the King were taken over by his friend the marquis de Meuse, while Madame de Tencin moved in as strategic adviser to Madame de la Tournelle—assistance which Marie-Anne neither needed nor appreciated. She was quite clear in her mind what she intended to do—which was to refuse all requests by Louis to "render his happiness complete" until he had dismissed her sister. She did not intend to share the royal favours as Louise-Julie and Pauline-Félicité had done. And in this delicate negotiation she was only distracted by the fussy intriguing of Madame de Tencin.

On 2 November, the news flashed round that Madame de Mailly had been moved from her room adjoining the King's *petits appartements* and into one occupied by Madame de Flavacourt—who had to make do with a camp bed elsewhere. Hortense-Félicité was put to this inconvenience for one night only: at 7 p.m. on 3 November, Madame de Mailly walked down to the courtyard, her plain face contorted with tears, and got into a carriage that bore her through the black night to Paris where, in the hôtel de Toulouse, the comtesse de Toulouse and many members of the Noailles family waited to offer her lodging and sympathy. She had no money and, without their help, would be forced to return to her husband, who, she feared, would beat her for her failure.

Louis, whom the regular nightly meetings had left overexcited and unassuaged, looked eagerly forward to his reward; but Marie-Anne had other demands to make: she did not intend to find herself summarily dismissed one day with neither honours nor fortune, and she was not prepared to be remunerated at the rate of forty louis a visit. Her terms for letting the King into her bed were that she should be recognized as *maîtresse déclarée*; that she should be given quarters worthy of that exalted station; that she should not be expected to slink into obscure attics to have supper with the King or to sleep with him, but that the King should entertain and sup in her rooms; that she should have authority to draw money from the treasury on her own note of hand; that at the end of the year she should be given letters patent awarding her a duchy; and that if she became pregnant, the news should be announced and the child legitimized.

Marie-Anne was a woman of coolness and determination, convinced that if she stood firm the King would give way. Others at court doubted this. Maurepas began to feel that his defeat was not really as certain as it had first appeared; Madame de Tencin sent a stream of agitated and far from brief letters to Richelieu, urging him to do something. She had managed to get her brother, the bishop of Embrun, back from Rome, where he had been virtually exiled by Fleury, and even appointed to a seat on the council, though without portfolio. With the help of the King's mistress, he could progress to the foreign secretaryship and then to the post of *premier ministre* when Fleury died—if only this stubborn girl would see sense and not pitch her demands so high.

"You did well, my dear duc," she wrote to Richelieu from Paris

on 5 November, "to send me a courier, for I was on the point of
sending you one myself and I should have had difficulty in con-
cealing his departure from the inquisitive people who are already
convinced that there is a liaison between us. . . . The cardinal is
accusing us of having organized the whole intrigue . . . and I
have shouted myself hoarse this morning trying to coach *la gimbarde* to prove to him that this is not nearly as bad as a double
adultery." Madame de Tencin made use of a *grimoire*—a code of
pseudonyms, which she varied from letter to letter, to the confusion of her correspondents and the despair of later students, since
she sometimes numbered her letters wrongly and the code names
indicated the wrong people. In this letter the "jew's harp" (*guim-
barde* or, as Madame de Tencin misspelled it, *gimbarde*) represented Marie-Anne, and the tone in which it continues sufficiently
explains how this officious and conceited woman so often succeeded in antagonizing the intelligent and stubborn younger one.

"I shall begin again tomorrow, trying to stuff into this *gimbarde's* head what I want her to say on Wednesday. . . . M. de
Maurepas . . . believes that la M[ailly] will make it up with the
King and ruin you. They are also planning to give him a young
girl and have la M—— return with all the honours and appearance
of favour. I know for a fact that they have been searching for such
a girl. . . ." They had even called in the assistance of a well-
known procuress. And there was another, quite unexpected, cause
for alarm. "A woman's mind is a strange weathercock, and they are
saying that the one in question [Marie-Anne] has fallen passion-
ately in love with the princesse de Conti. This," Madame de
Tencin commented with great restraint, "is a further inconvenience."

From Marie-Anne, Richelieu received letters of quite a different
tone: confident and calm. She told him that Louis was denying
that Richelieu had had any hand in the change of mistresses, "and
in fact that pleases me better. I do not wish to seem to have
sought that advantage, nor to have had my friends do it for
me. . . ." She was intoxicated by her triumph over her sister:
"Meuse is sure to have told you of the trouble I had in sending
Madame de Mailly packing; but I have succeeded in having her

ordered not to return unless she is sent for." The annoying thing was that Louis kept snuffling around her, or sending her notes, asking to be allowed to let Louise-Julie come back to Versailles on condition that he promised never to see her. "I have received one just this moment in which he tells me that if I refuse him this, I shall soon be rid of both him and her; apparently meaning that they will die of grief, the pair of them. Since it would not suit me at all to have her here, I intend to stand firm. . . . He shall decide between her and me. . . ."

Even the enmity of the quiet, all-powerful Fleury did not alarm her. "So long as the cardinal is alive I shall not be able to do everything I wish. This has prompted me to get the old rascal on my side by making approaches to him—the appearance of trusting him will perhaps win him over. . . ." She greatly enjoyed all the excitement she had created: "You can well imagine that everybody is up in the air and all eyes are on the King and me. . . . As for the Queen" (who had trusted her and been her benefactor) "she gives me black looks, but that's all in the game." She joked that she acted on the Queen "like a dose of opium," for whenever she was on duty for the week as *dame du palais* and consequently had the privilege of supping with the Queen, the enraged and embarrassed Maria Leczynska pretended to doze off after the meal and remained with her eyes closed until Marie-Anne left to visit the King at midnight. Unlike her sister, who used to entertain the King with imitations of the Queen, Madame de la Tournelle restricted herself to singing the latest of the street ballads that were inspired by their affair.

Many people had jumped to the conclusion that the King's latest love affair had now been consummated; but they were mistaken. "He must have told you that the affair was completed between us," Marie-Anne wrote to Richelieu, "for in his letter to me this morning he tells me to disabuse you, since he does not want you to think that there is any more to it than there really is. It is true that when he wrote to you he counted on it being this evening; but I raised objections to the performance, and do not regret having done so."

On Monday, 12 November, Louis took her to Choisy, hoping

that he might obtain there what had been denied him at Versailles; but she remained adamant. She saw that he had not yet got her sister out of his mind, for the Blue Room, where Louise-Julie had always slept, was left vacant and Marie-Anne had to be satisfied with the one that was usually allotted to Richelieu. Louis came and tapped at her door that night; there was no answer, and he returned, prancing with rage and frustration, to his own room.

Madame de Tencin had written to Richelieu on the previous day, giving him "a good piece of information that I hope you will make use of. M. de Maurepas went to Issy yesterday to suggest to the cardinal that he should bring Madame de Mailly back to Versailles. My brother will tell us everything that he knows about it. *La gimbarde* wants to see you. Yesterday evening she came to tell me that if you come to Paris during the next stay at Versailles you must let him [the King] know. . . . That is to say, he wants you to come here. . . . It is important that you should link up with M. de Soubise, the Rohans hate Maurepas almost as much as we do. . . ."

Richelieu realized that the crisis point had been reached. Madame de Tencin's anxious appeals had made little impression on him, but the news that both Marie-Anne and the King were wanting to see him convinced him that he could now step in, lead the intrigue to a conclusion that was satisfactory to both parties, and establish himself as their closest friend. Playing the pander in this way did not worry him at all. As he wrote to one of his women friends: "I would have no great scruples about being useful to my master in his love affairs; one makes a present of a pretty picture, a handsome vase, a jewel, and I see no reason for blushes in putting a monarch in the position of enjoying the most delightful thing in the world—a woman. . . . One owes services of every kind to the master who reigns over us, and one may offer him a woman just as well as anything else."

He reached Versailles on Friday, shortly before the King, who returned very sulkily from his fruitless nights of supplication at Choisy. Everybody remarked on how well Richelieu looked—the intrigue had indeed had a rejuvenating effect on him—and kept a sharper eye than ever on his movements, noting that he supped that evening with Madame de la Tournelle and spent much time in conversation with her before and after the meal, and that on Saturday he ate with the King in private—the *petit souper*—accompanied by two of his cronies: Meuse and the prince de Tingry. Next week, the King's party set out for Choisy once more, to stay there from Wednesday until Saturday.

The subject of Richelieu's discussion with Marie-Anne was just how far she could go in taming the King without depriving him of his titbit for so long that he lost interest. Although he craved women, he had not, in this as in any other sphere of activity, any real application or persistence in the face of difficulties. He must be made to suffer a little in winning his new mistress, in order to condition him against running after another and to squeeze from him as many benefits as possible; but the lesson must not be so painful or prolonged that he quit the classroom in disgust. Fortunately for the two conspirators, Richelieu, during the sessions when he advised Louis on how to achieve felicity, was able to assess exactly how near the royal impatience was to the point where it might topple over into indifference.

Louis's lingering devotion to Louise-Julie was a matter of great concern to Marie-Anne, and she insisted that it should be broken down. When they arrived at Choisy on 21 November, Louis made a significant surrender: Hortense-Félicité was given the room that Marie-Anne had occupied the week before; Richelieu was given a room near the library; and Marie-Anne was at last installed in the Blue Room that had always been her sister's. She was triumphant and looked more enchanting, gayer, more desirable than ever. That night Louis, bright-eyed with expectation, scratched at her door—and there was no response.

Once more he returned to Versailles, overheated and sulky. As far as anybody could tell—and the eyes of the whole court were permanently trained on him—it was nearly a month since he had had a woman: an intolerable disruption of his routine and a dangerous strain on his nervous system. Like a circus animal trained by the most humane methods, he was broken, bewildered, and ready to be whipped through the final hoop. He had given orders for the furniture to be left undisturbed in Louise-Julie's former apartment, assuring Marie-Anne that he would never let her sister approach him closely again but that he felt she should be allowed to retain just one room at Versailles. Now Marie-Anne gave him the last order: he would cancel his instructions about the furniture and give up all hope of ever recalling Louise-Julie.

By the first week of December, the furniture had been moved out and a stout bar placed across the door that used to communicate with Louis's apartments. And on Sunday, 9 December, the royal party set out for Choisy once more. During the journey, the King drew a snuffbox from his pocket, and his companions in the carriage remarked on its unusual design in moss-agate and enamel. The guests were allotted the same bedrooms as on the previous occasion, and the following morning Meuse called on Marie-Anne in the Blue Room before she had got out of bed. She put her hand under the bolster and, with a smile, produced the royal snuffbox. Victorious on all fronts, she had at last surrendered to her defeated lover.

Richelieu was more than content; the King was snared, his mistress was a clever woman, and Richelieu was her closest friend. By a happy coincidence, a magnificent new toy had just arrived in time for his celebration. He was off to Languedoc for the annual opening of the *Etats*, and the other members of the house party gathered on the curved flight of stone stairs at the front of the château at 9 p.m. on Thursday, 13 December, to watch him descend by the flickering light of the torches carried by the servants, clad only in his nightshirt and dressing gown. Awaiting him on the semicircular drive was his new carriage, with a box at the back containing several days' supply of food and in front a compartment stacked with baking dishes and joints of meat, which one of the lackeys could take on ahead and have placed in the oven of the next hostelry; so that, travelling or at rest, he need never be kept waiting a moment for his meal.

But the greatest surprise for the onlookers was when the servants opened the door of the carriage and revealed a bed, then turned back the sheet and blanket and removed the warming pans. (The idea, though nobody remarked on it at the time, may have come to Richelieu from his illustrious namesake, for the Cardinal, when travel became a burden to him, used to favour a barge. He would lie in bed as the vessel glided smoothly along the rivers and, on arrival at a town, would be transferred to a litter on which, any obstructive walls or too-narrow windows having been demolished, he would be carried directly into the ground-floor room which was to serve him as a bedroom.)

Richelieu, basking in the envious stares and shouts of admiration, removed his dressing gown and stepped into bed. Pulling the sheets around him, he motioned the postilion to close the carriage door. "You may wake me at Lyon," he said, as the horses were whipped up and the *dormeuse* clattered slowly over the cobbles.

§ 2

For Madame de Tencin, Marie-Anne's campaign to enslave the King had been only the first step in her own plan to promote her brother's career; but she soon found to her disappointment that Marie-Anne was tired of her tutelage and not anxious for her friendship. "Madame de la Tournelle paid her New Year's Day calls with Mesdames de Boufiler and Luxembourg," she wrote indignantly to Richelieu on 3 January 1743. "In passing my brother's door, they suggested to her that she should write her name in his book. Madame de la Tournelle refused. They insisted but could not persuade her. She said that she did not know him; now you will remember that she dined with him during a visit that he made to Paris before he was cardinal. If you had been here, things would have gone off differently. . . ." She was, as usual, full of warnings and forebodings: "My brother, who arrived this morning, told me that I must caution you that they are doing all they can to estrange us from Madame de la Tournelle, and that they never cease telling her that you turned the King against her sister and will do the same for her if you remain in close friendship with the master. It is beginning to be clear that the lady is as lofty as the mountains. She intends to have power and she will not be controlled. You know all this better than I and you can see how necessary is your presence here."

Nor was this all. Having previously perplexed him by putting the wrong number on a letter, thus leading him to misinterpret all the pseudonyms, she now announced that she would be forced to give up the use of her *grimoire* altogether. She had found out that some of her letters had been intercepted, and the officials of the King's *cabinet-noir*, having also been confused by the pseudonyms, had "managed to give them a meaning which could be a thousand times more dangerous than the true one." Despite so many years of practice, it appeared that Madame de Tencin had neither the gifts nor the temperament for conspiracy of the highest order. Richelieu remained unperturbed, even when Fleury's death, at the end of January, produced a violent struggle for office among the politicians, all of whom—and the Tencins in particular —were plunged into despondency when Louis announced that henceforward he would be his own *premier ministre*. When Richelieu returned from Montpellier in February, he found everybody convinced that Louis would not persist long in his intention to be the active head of the council. Maurepas was once more trying to strengthen his position by sniping at his rivals, among whom Richelieu, Marie-Anne, and the Tencins figured prominently. There was a larger crop of scurrilous *chansons* than usual, and Louis remarked to Richelieu one day that Maurepas had got off lightly. "Not very surprising, Sire," Richelieu replied, "since it was he who wrote them." It was true. Maurepas, a witty, shortsighted, impotent man, had a genuine gift for light verse. He had been a minister for twenty years and still had a few more to run before his malicious pen wrote him out of office.

As the year developed, Marie-Anne became dissatisfied and worried. She could not blame herself for having trusted Louis's word, but Richelieu should have known better and advised her to get something more substantial than promises. She had not received her separate establishment; there had been no more word about the duchy that was to be given her. When Richelieu rejoined the army in the spring, her letters were cautious and anxious. She told her "cher oncle" (the name that she gave him to mark his relationship to her lover, Agénois) that she was no longer certain of Louis's affection and that he seemed to resent her hold over him. Now that she had surrendered to him she was having to fight hard to retain her influence.

"The King has said that affairs of state must be of no interest to me, since I never speak of them. But you understand that I do not wish to show any desire to know, so as to make him more eager to instruct me. He has told me too often that my sisters interfered in things, for me to wish to imitate them. One must bide one's time and not do anything unless one is sure not to be reproached for it. He is often bored with work and the less I speak to him about what is going on the more I believe he will want to talk about it with me; and that will be the most propitious time to act. I shall always be ready to follow your advice and I shall do nothing without consulting you."

That Louis was taking seriously his position as his own *premier ministre*, and that he knew that Richelieu would be behind Marie-Anne in any attempts that she made to interfere, was made clear by a hint in a letter that he wrote to Richelieu on 13 June. Writing in his own hand but sometimes referring to himself in the third person, as he often did, he addressed Richelieu as "Your Excellency" in memory of his ambassadorial days and spoke of Marie-Anne as "the princess"; "The King has spent two very peaceful days with the princess, and perceives every day that she is more and more deserving of his confidence. She does not have that desire to know things which I did not like in her sisters and which often vexed me. . . ." He felt it his duty to strike a gallant tone with Richelieu, who was now serving under the maréchal de Noailles on the other side of the Rhine. He told him that he was missed by many of his women friends: "There is one who, they insist, in order to find the strength to support [your absence] is consoling herself with somebody who is on the spot. I do not know how Your Excellency will take that. . . . It is not only the women of your acquaintance who are consoling themselves for those who are absent; it is an infectious complaint; and since it pleases two persons and displeases only one I see nothing very much against it, particularly since it also amuses a great many others."

Britain and France had still not declared war on each other, but on 27 June 1743 George II, at the head of a combined British and Hanoverian army, marched into a trap set for him by Noailles at Dettingen—and then had the good fortune to blunder out of it,

thanks to the stupidity of Noailles's nephew, the duc de Grammont. The French suffered heavy casualties in the battle and had
to retreat; while George, in his hurry to extricate himself, left his
wounded on the field to fend for themselves. Richelieu sustained
no injury, although he had his horse shot under him, but among
the French dead was the duc de Rochechouart, one of the four
First Gentlemen of the Bedchamber. Richelieu, with considerable
effrontery—for the post was above anything he could expect on
the grounds of birth—wrote to Marie-Anne and asked her to try to
persuade the King to give him the vacant appointment.

Marie-Anne replied at once, congratulating him on having come
out of the battle unscathed but saying nothing about the prospect
of his getting the vacancy. The King scribbled a few words of
greeting across the top of the letter, but he, too, made no mention of Richelieu's petition. In his next letter to Marie-Anne, Richelieu complained of the way the King was treating them both,
and she replied, chiding him for his *"humeur de chien"* but admitting that her own affairs had not improved since she last wrote
to him. The King had given orders for her to be found an estate
with an income of twenty thousand livres, but the *contrôleur*
seemed unaccountably unable to find one. However, she was certain that the delay would not be long, and she invited Richelieu to
suggest a name for her new duchy. "Let me know what you think
about this, for when you are not in a bad temper, I consider you a
sound adviser and have confidence in you."

The only scraps that were flung to Richelieu that summer as a
reward for his loyal pandering were promotion to Lieutenant-General and a letter from the King telling him that he had replaced
the *intendant* of Languedoc, whose harsh treatment of the Protestants Richelieu considered both unwise and unnecessary. The
replacement, Le Nain, was not the man that Richelieu had suggested, and Marie-Anne wrote almost timidly at the foot of Louis's
letter: "The King commands me to send you a little good night
and I obey with the greatest pleasure. I did not receive the letter
in which you spoke of your intendant until after the matter was
concluded. I think I have heard you speak well of M. le Nain; and
I flatter myself that you will not be vexed. . . ."

But in October all was changed. Marie-Anne, bubbling over with joy, wrote that "The King has had the kindness to give me the duchy of Châteauroux, in the most gracious possible way; I am overwhelmed with gratitude, as you can well believe. . . . It will not be announced until Monday, because I wanted you to be the first to know. . . . I am delighted that those cursed English have had enough and that we shall have the pleasure of seeing you again at any moment. . . ." The estate from which she derived her new title had been a royal domain, and its rents were farmed out for 85,000 livres, more than four times as much as she had expected. This was a great gesture indeed, both as a financial reward and as proof of her power over the King; and now Richelieu was to share in the harvest.

He returned from Germany at the end of October, and on 21 November he was granted the privilege of the *premières entrées*; but the climax of his good fortune was not reached until after he had left for Languedoc and the usual winter session of the *Etats*. On 22 December, the four-year-old duc de Rochechouart who, despite Richelieu's pleas, had succeeded his father as First Gentleman of the Bedchamber, suddenly died of water on the brain; the dead child's relations, and those of other First Gentlemen, past and present, pressed their claims; but on 26 December, it was announced that the appointment had been given to Richelieu.

"At last," sneered one of his enemies, "the King has made Richelieu a gentleman." But the insult was easy to swallow, for in the hierarchy of Versailles the First Gentlemen followed immediately on the princes of the blood. The King, when he retired at night, gave instructions as to the hour at which he was to be called in the morning and at that time, which, even if it happened to be mid-afternoon, was officially "daybreak" for Versailles, the King's relations were entitled to enter his bedroom, then whichever First Gentleman was on duty that year. These were admitted to the alcove, the area behind the gold balustrade which partitioned the bed from the rest of the room, and remained there while the King got up and put on his slippers and dressing gown. He then walked out through the little gate in the balustrade and sat in a chair to be fed and dressed while the *premières entrées—*

officials, higher clergy, and those holding special *brevets d'entrée*—
were admitted. Having eaten his light breakfast, the King changed
from nightshirt into shirt and breeches, behind his dressing gown
held by two valets; and when he was fully clothed, he passed into
his study and two more sets of inferior *entrées* were admitted.
The whole process was gone through in reverse order when he
went to bed at night, and minor variations of it occurred whenever he changed his clothes during the day. It was attendance at
these ceremonies, and particularly participation in them, the holding of a candle, the handing of a shirt, that conferred glory and
substance on a courtier, and for those who had not been born
royal the next best thing was to be at the heart of it all—as a First
Gentleman of the Bedchamber.

Within a few days, Marie-Anne's former admirer, the chevalier
de Grille, was given command of the King's Company of horse
grenadiers; and when she appeared in a new pearl necklace that
Louis had given her and that the courtiers valued at 100,000 livres,
there could be no longer any doubt about the extent of her influence. She determined to use it in an attempt to make Louis into a
king; and her first step was to persuade him to take the field with
his armies, as his ancestors had done, and as George of Britain and
Frederick of Prussia still did.

She was an unprincipled woman, grasping and ruthless, yet she
might, had she been luckier, have stood behind the weakling King
and forced him to acts of courage and wiser, wider decisions which
could have altered the whole history of France and Europe and the
world. For the greatest error of eighteenth-century France, France
of the *ancien régime*, was that during the forties and fifties,
through the selfishness and laxness and even cowardice of the
King and the small governing class, she dissipated her energies on
inconsequential campaigns in Europe, while overseas she threw
away her empire and ensured that the colonization of the world
should be continued in the English tongue and not the French.
Nothing that France did after the reign of Louis XV could alter
this. The map of the world had hardened, the channels of history
were set, the adventures of Bonaparte were irrelevancies. The
basis of strength and glory had been destroyed.

There is no reason to suppose that the duchesse de Château-roux was inspired by any high ideals in urging Louis to take command of his troops. Both she and Richelieu knew that the *auréole* of martial fame has never failed to win the devotion and support of the French. Misery and misgovernment would be forgotten once the King had been present on the field where his soldiers won him a brilliant victory; the taste of glory might even lead him to a taste for power and some activity more honest—though possibly more dangerous—than his present obsession with hunting and fornication. So it was in an ecstasy of optimism that Marie-Anne wrote to Richelieu at the beginning of February 1744: "I hasten to tell you, dear uncle, that the King has decided to go on the next campaign. He has just given me his promise, and I can assure you that nothing in the world could please me more. . . . Maréchal de Noailles will retain the command; there will be two armies, one under his orders and the other under the comte de Saxe, of whom there are high hopes. . . ."

Now that she had got the royal courage to the sticking point, she let her hopes stray to the future. She continued: "The cardinal always reigned for him until now: it is time for him to show that he can reign on his own account. I am not deceiving myself when I credit him with the qualities to govern well; all that I fear is his excessive trust in his ministers. He judges and sees more clearly than they do, I am certain, but he often good-naturedly defers to their opinions which are less valuable than his own. It is to be hoped that he will have a will of his own. . . ." She concluded by telling Richelieu that the King had agreed to take him as one of his aides-de-camp.

Richelieu returned on Saint Valentine's Day to celebrate the success of his and Marie-Anne's plans and to take the oath as First Gentleman of the Bedchamber, although he would not be exercising his office that year. He attended the King at his *coucher* and *lever* and was in the party that Louis took to La Muette, where fortune continued to smile on Richelieu, and he won a good deal at cards. The guests included three of the Nesle sisters: the new duchesse de Châteauroux, the marquise de Flavacourt, and the middle sister of the five, Diane-Adélaïde, who had become the second wife of the duc de Lauraguais, son of one of Richelieu's former mistresses, the duchesse de Brancas. Diane-Adélaïde was a short, plump girl, noted for her equable disposition and extremely coarse language; the King, who had nicknamed her *la rue des mauvaises paroles*, after a street in Paris, had been ogling her for some time.

It was not only at the French court that the growing influence of Richelieu and Madame de Châteauroux had been noticed. Frederick of Prussia, who had made a separate peace with Austria and deserted his French "auxiliaries" in 1742, now decided to go to war again and saw more chance of enlisting Louis's help if he negotiated with him through his mistress instead of through the Minister of Foreign Affairs. In March, Richelieu received a note from the comte de Rothenburg, a former friend who had married a daughter of Madame de Parabère, and, after losing 180,000 livres at the gaming tables, had renounced his French citizenship and entered the service of the King of Prussia. Rothenburg asked Richelieu to arrange a meeting at some place where he could arrive and leave without being recognized: a request that presented no problems to Richelieu, who had recently rented in the rue de Clichy the *petite maison* which was to last him for the rest of his life. Its *petite* quality was strictly relative, for the house was guarded by a porter's lodge, and there was room for a gardener's cottage in the acre and a quarter of grounds, but for secrecy it was peculiarly well suited: the wall that flanked the rue Blanche, at the rear, had no less than four separate exits.

Rothenburg told Richelieu that Frederick was willing to guard France's eastern frontiers if she would declare war against Britain and keep the British and Hanoverian troops occupied in Flanders. Rothenburg's instructions were to deal only with the King and to reveal his mission only to Richelieu and the duchesse de Châteauroux. Would Richelieu be good enough to arrange an interview for him with the duchesse? Richelieu set off at once for Choisy and on arrival was told that Madame de Châteauroux was entertaining the King alone in her room. Ignoring the startled looks of those around him, and with an impertinence that even his urbanity could not entirely gloss over, he half-opened the door and heard Louis ask him sharply what brought him there. He replied that it was an occurrence that would surprise the King as much as it had himself and that he had felt he must not lose a moment in telling him; he then slid into the room, closed the door behind him and repeated his conversation with Rothenburg.

Marie-Anne, seeing immediately that an alliance with Prussia would increase Louis's chances of winning a victory in Flanders, asked him eagerly what he thought of the proposal; but he was still ruffled by the interruption and as unwilling as ever to take a decision or express an opinion. "It could be very good, but we must think about it," he replied; and Richelieu, somewhat crestfallen, bowed and retired. But at supper Marie-Anne whispered to him that Louis had agreed to see Rothenburg, and, as soon as they returned to Versailles, Richelieu took the Prussian emissary for an interview with the King in Marie-Anne's apartment. Frederick's proposal was accepted; France declared war on Britain; and on 4 May, Louis set off to join his armies in Flanders, accompanied by Richelieu.

Marie-Anne went off with Diane-Adélaïde to stay with the army contractor, Pâris-Duverney, at his estate at Plaisance, a little beyond Vincennes. She was glad to get away from Versailles, where she feared snubs from the Queen—and perhaps worse; for the docile and pious Maria Leczynska was so annoyed with the new mistress that she appeared to be actively supporting her sister, Hortense-Félicité, in her attempts to supplant her. Of Diane-Adélaïde, Marie-Anne appeared to have no fear at all. She had heard the rumours that, in the days of Louise-Julie's supremacy, Diane-Adélaïde had sometimes shared the royal bed with her, during the same night, and that Louis had found refreshment in turning from the lean vigour of the one to the generous opulence of the other's "firm, white abundant breasts and great buxom buttocks." But Marie-Anne considered her too lacking in either malice or social graces to be a serious rival and had made no protests about Louis's recent renewed interest in her. But of *La Poule*, as Hortense-Félicité was nicknamed, Marie-Anne was not at all so sure; two years older than herself and one year younger than Diane-Adélaïde, she was clever and attractive enough to be a formidable adversary, even without the Queen's backing.

Madame de Tencin, certainly, had no doubt about the seriousness of the situation, and by 24 May she was again sending urgent warnings to Richelieu. "The Queen has told her that [before he left for Flanders] the King quizzed her at supper; she added that she had no better friend than her and that she wished to be her confidant. La Flavacourt replied that she would tell her everything; that, if the thing happened, she would submit only from fear, since she had no liking for the King; but that she did not want to be hunted from the court, or to find herself forced to live with her husband. . . . But here is something more important: La Flavacourt writes to the King almost every day; her letters are sent from Versailles or Paris; they are addressed to little Le Bel [*premier valet-de-chambre*]. . . . Madame de Châteauroux must be on tenterhooks, both because of the Queen's conversation and because of the letters."

She was indeed. Marie-Anne was convinced that the man behind the mounting intrigue against her was her arch-enemy, Maurepas, whose wife had not recovered from the mortification of seeing the penniless little Marie-Anne take her *tabouret* at court while she herself continued to stand. Marie-Anne implored Richelieu to provide her with evidence of some kind that might help her to procure Maurepas's disgrace and then reverted to the threat from Hortense-Félicité. "I have not whispered a word to the King, for I think that would be useless by letter; when I arrive I want to bombard him with everything I know, so as to make him confess if there is any foundation to it." Before Louis left, it had been agreed that she should not accompany him to the front, since the expense of providing for her and her establishment under such conditions would shock people and throw doubts on his seriousness as a military leader. But he was incapable of remaining continent for long and readily agreed when Marie-Anne suggested that she should join him.

There was a great difference between the confident woman who had so coolly captured Louis and the worried mistress who thought she saw him slipping from her. "Does the King still seem to think about me? does he often mention me? is he sad at not seeing me? . . . It would be impossible to write to me more punctually or with more civility and friendliness. Yet . . . the moment when they deceive you is often the one when they try all the harder to hide their intentions." Too tormented to wait for Richelieu's reply, she was already bumping northwards in her carriage, accompanied by Diane-Adélaïde.

The King showed discreet astonishment when they arrived at Lille on 10 June, but when he received them in private there was no doubt about his delight. The maréchal de Noailles, on the other hand, did nothing to hide his disapproval; and he was right, for the strait-laced Flamands were well acquainted with court gossip and, knowing all about Louis's previous simultaneous affair with the two elder Nesle girls, were outraged to see another two arrive together and share the same apartments.

While the civilians murmured, the soldiers set new words to old indecent songs and sang them under the sisters' windows. But Marie-Anne had come only to protect her own interests, not to distract the King from his war; she begged him not to sacrifice to Venus the energy that he should reserve for Mars, and within a few days had packed him off to the trenches outside Ypres. In just over a week the town surrendered: a very considerable success, though not perhaps quite what Marie-Anne described it in a jubilant letter on 26 June: greater than anything Louis XIV ever achieved.

Her jubilation was premature; soon after Louis had gone to the coast to inspect the defences at Dunkirk, Calais, and Boulogne, a succession of couriers began to arrive from the east bringing the alarming news that Maria Theresa's brother-in-law, Prince Charles of Lorraine, at the head of eighty thousand Austrian troops, had eluded the French army on the Upper Rhine, crossed into Alsace, and was marching towards Paris. Louis at once set off to intercept him between Metz and the frontier, offering his soldiers double pay if they would march at double speed, while the sisters followed at one day's delay, catching up with the King each time that he halted for more than one night. On such occasions, the sisters and Louis would sup and sometimes sleep at lodgings which Richelieu discreetly commandeered in his own name; but Louis's face was easily recognizable and, under the influence of wartime emotions and the lowering of standards of good behaviour which attends the presence of large bodies of soldiers, his subjects sometimes greeted him with more ribaldry than reverence. At Laon, for instance, he was seen when leaving Richelieu's quarters after dining with Marie-Anne and Diane-Adélaïde. Amid sardonic shouts of *"Vive le Roi!"* he pulled up the skirts of his long coat, took to his heels, and ran desperately down the road until he found a walled garden in which he took refuge.

On the morning after this inelegant display, Richelieu left for Paris, planning to rejoin the army at Metz; he had appointments with some of his women friends; he hoped to see Rameau and smooth out the difficulties of his collaboration with Voltaire. There were probably private conversations to be held in connection with his political aspirations, for the marquis d'Argenson was convinced that Richelieu counted on becoming *premier ministre* very shortly and admitted that when he spoke to him during this flying visit Richelieu's views on affairs of state were both confident and sound. It was a pity that Richelieu was not with Marie-Anne when she arrived at Rheims, for she was greeted with the news that her lover, Agénois, had been wounded in Italy, and she was so distressed by this that she had to take to her bed. When Louis visited her, she was still so little able to control her grief that he very nearly guessed the true reason for it, but his natural talent for looking on the dark side led him to conclude that she had contracted a dangerous malady and would die. He was so terrified of death that the approach of it in others always drove him to extremes of callousness or morbidity; and when he left, he could talk of nothing but the arrangements he would make for her funeral and the designs that he would prepare for a really magnificent tomb. Despite these attentions, Marie-Anne was well enough to continue her journey the following day.

§ 3

The town of Metz—though it had not known until 22 July that the King intended to honour it with his presence—was determined to welcome him in a manner worthy not only of a sovereign but also of the man who had taken Menin, Courtrai, and Ypres and was about to drive the insolent Austrians back across the frontier

v Madame de Mailly, as *La Madeleine au désert*
by Jean-Marc Nattier, Musée du Louvre

VI Madame de Tencin

by Jacques Aved, Musée des
Beaux Arts, Valenciennes

VII The duchesse de Châteauroux, as Dawn
by Jean-Marc Nattier, Musée de Marseille

(a task which Louis already knew would not be too difficult, since Frederick had sent word that he would relieve the pressure by invading Bohemia). The most presentable of the burgesses were formed into four battalions, the officers in scarlet coats edged with gold braid, white vests and gaiters, and gold-braided hats with white cockades. The young men of good family, four hundred in all, their ages ranging from nine to thirty, made up two separate corps, their uniform resembling that of the burgesses except that their buttons were silver and their cockades blue and white. They were preceded by an ensign carrying a standard of white taffeta on which was depicted an eagle soaring near a golden sun, and by a band of hautboys, bassoons, and tambours, with blue and white aiguillettes and blue flounces faced with red. The whole parade was under the command of Monsieur Perrin, the town syndic, easily distinguishable from his troops by the gold braid, three fingers in width, which edged his blue coat, double-edged his sleeves and pockets, and rimmed his silver-moiré waistcoat.

While these rich uniforms were being hurriedly stitched in every tailor's shop in town, the troops were instructed in manoeuvres and the manual of arms until they could march in step and present their muskets, swords, and lances with all the grace and precision imaginable; and the streets were filled with the noise and bustle of scores of carpenters, painters, and plumbers. On the place du Pont des Morts, two grottoes, carpeted with turf and garlanded with ivy, concealed twin fountains ready to gush wine; twenty-foot-high fountains of water spouted from sanded, grass-edged basins thirty yards farther along the road; and at an interval of another thirty yards there rose the centrepiece of the whole display, a triumphal arch forty-five feet high, forty feet wide, and twenty feet deep, constructed of timber and canvas and painted in exquisite taste by men drawn from as far afield as Nancy and Lunéville.

It was at 11:30 on the morning of 4 August that the sound of gunfire from the village of Moulins, followed by the booming of the signal-guns from the beflagged look-out vessel on the Moselle, announced the approach of the King. To the accompaniment of handclapping and the shouting of loyal sentiments, he rode across the bridge with the maréchal de Noailles on one side and the duc de Villeroy, captain of the guard, on the other, and halted to inspect the companies of burgesses and the corps of noble cadets; then, sullenly handsome and sitting his horse well, he acknowledged the applause of the ladies in the semicircular tiers on either side of the *arc de triomphe* and rode on under it towards the cathedral, where he dismounted and went inside. The bishop sprinkled him with holy water, offered him a portion of the Holy Cross to kiss, and, after a motet and the *Domine salvum fac regem,* conducted him to the forecourt where he mounted his horse and rode under more triumphal arches to the Hôtel du Gouvernement, at whose gates two decapitated lions' heads gaped in stony astonishment while wine spurted desultorily from their mouths. Louis was conducted to his apartments on the first floor, and the rest of the building was soon bulging with officers of the royal household.

Marie-Anne and Diane-Adélaïde made their entry later in the day, as privately as could be managed, and were taken to the apartments of the *premier président* of the provincial *parlement* in the abbey of Saint-Arnould, just across the road from the Hôtel du Gouvernement. This road, wide enough for two carriages to pass, was much frequented by the citizens of Metz. When they discovered that the thoroughfare was blocked by a close-boarded wooden gallery that had been built to link the duchesses' lodgings with the King's, they were scandalized as much by its interference with the traffic as by its immoral implications; and, the town authorities having set up fire-pots and torches everywhere, it was easy to observe through the cracks in the boards that there was a constant coming and going between the apartments on either side of the street.

The day after his arrival, which was also the day on which Richelieu rejoined him, Louis attended mass, dined in public, and inspected the fortifications; the next day he stood at his window in the Hôtel du Gouvernement and watched a loyal parade of Jews in the courtyard below and then went to inspect more fortifications; and on the 7th he inspected the barracks, an iron foundry and still more fortifications before giving a dinner in honour of Marshal Smettau, who had brought the welcome news that Frederick was at that moment marching into Bohemia. On Saturday, 8 August, he was to attend a *Te Deum* in the cathedral before moving off with the army next day, but he awoke with a bad headache and the ceremony had to proceed without him. Some attributed his indisposition to the fact that he had spent much of the previous day in the hot sun and had perhaps over-eaten at the banquet; others suspected that he had again indulged in his habit of sharing his bed with both sisters at the same time and had overextended himself. He had been showing signs of increasing fatigue ever since they joined him at Lille.

Richelieu at once took charge of the royal patient, despite the fact that he was not the First Gentleman *en exercice* that year, brushing the duc de Fleury aside with the firmness of a close friend dismissing an awkward servant. He had kept up the interest in medicine and black magic that had involved him in the scandal at Vienna, and he now felt Louis's pulse, nodded his head very knowledgeably, and confidently informed La Peyronie, the first surgeon, that there was nothing seriously wrong with the King. Chicoyneau, the first physician, seeing that the favourite and the King's mistresses were determined to make light of the affair, readily handed the conduct of the case over to La Peyronie, anxious not to do anything that might offend them and thus lose him a post which brought him in 40,000 livres a year, with another 15,-000 livres or so from the grant of patents for secret remedies and mineral waters.

Because of the King's headache, the gunfire and the ringing of bells, which had been going on without respite since he entered the town, were suspended during the evening of 8 August; but by the following morning, his headache was worse than ever and his temperature had risen. Richelieu refused to allow anybody other than the doctors and the two sisters to enter Louis's bedchamber and throughout the day an agitated crowd of court officials cooled their heels in the ante-room, concerned about the King's health and still more about the cavalier fashion in which they had been deprived of their privileges; the only times that they or the princes of the blood were allowed into the bed-

room were for the morning mass and to receive their formal
instructions in the evening, and they were briskly ushered out
afterwards. As soon as Louis had complained of sickness, Richelieu
had seen that Marie-Anne's position, and consequently his own,
was in grave danger; for if the King believed that his illness was
serious, his fear of death and hell would set him clamouring for
his confessor, and the priest would certainly refuse his ministrations unless Louis agreed to get rid of his mistress. Richelieu
tried to forestall this by warning the doctors, and anybody else
who would listen to him, that the King was of such a nervous
nature and would read such dire implications into any suggestion
that he should make his confession, that the shock of such a proposal might well kill him.

The courtiers whom Richelieu was keeping at bay in the ante-
room were divided into several groups, among which only a very
small one—that of his fellow aides-de-camp and some of the
younger men—had any liking for him. Of the others, the church-
men, led by the cantankerous and fearless bishop of Soissons,
hoped to regain their hold over the King; the princes of the blood
and the high officers of the household, led by the duc de Bouillon,
were eagerly awaiting an opportunity to humble the upstart
favourite. The politicians, led by Maurepas, were ready to fight
with professional viciousness against the threat of interference by
Richelieu and Marie-Anne and the dreadful prospect of losing their
jobs.

On Tuesday, 11 August, the game suddenly swung their way.
La Peyronie unexpectedly announced that he was no longer prepared to take the risk of letting the King die without the ministrations of the Church, and he formally notified the bishop of
Soissons that he considered the King's life might be in danger.
Whether or not he was bribed by Maurepas to say this—as Richelieu always maintained—is not possible to prove; but the suspicion
seems to be borne out by the fact that La Peyronie told the duc de
Luynes some days later that he thought the King had nothing
worse than a slight attack of sunstroke. On Wednesday morning,
before mass, the bishop spoke seriously to the King, recommending that he send for his confessor, Père Pérusseau. Louis, fleeing

as always from a decision, plaintively replied that he was not feeling well enough and must think about it. His thoughts brought
him no comfort; and later in the day, in the act of kissing Marie-
Anne, he suddenly thrust her away from him, saying: "Oh,
princess, I think I am doing evil." She tried to embrace him again,
but he resisted, adding: "I think perhaps we ought to separate."

Richelieu appreciated that his enemies would now play continually on the King's fears, and his only hope of preventing them
was to keep Louis entirely shut off from the rest of the court.
Accordingly, when the senior officers of the household came for
their instructions and passwords that evening, Richelieu told them
that the King no longer wished to give these in person and had
asked Richelieu to pass them on for him. There was an immediate
uproar. Bouillon, shaking with rage, swore that he would never
take orders from a Vignerot. The comte de Clermont thrust his
foot in the door and shouted: "What! A lackey like you refusing
admission to his master's closest relations?" Clermont, followed by
the duc de Chartres, shouldered his way into the room and strode
across to the King's bed, protesting at being kept out. Louis made
no reply, and, with the protests thus tacitly accepted, Richelieu
realized that his blockade was broken.

He entered the royal bedchamber at seven the next morning
to find Marie-Anne sitting beside the bed. They talked in a
desultory way while Richelieu went through his morning ritual of
feeling the King's pulse, after which he assured him that, although
his headache might not have gone, there was no increase in his
fever. Louis did not reply, but a few moments later indicated that
he was indisposed; when Marie-Anne modestly left the room, he
sat up in bed and began to roar in a surprisingly strong voice:
"Have them enter for mass! Have them enter for mass!" Then he
turned to Richelieu and said: "Take her back to her apartments."

Louis's shouts were heard in the ante-room, where Maurepas's
supporters at once took them up, yelling for the attendants to
open the doors and to fetch the priests. Richelieu, on his own
confession, completely lost his temper, and for a few moments he
and Louis were raging at each other. Then he calmed down and
went to Marie-Anne in the adjoining room, where he found her

much less astonished by the trick than he had expected; she told
him that the King had been talking since dawn about the sacraments.

Richelieu walked with her through the wooden gallery to the
abbey, and they had scarcely arrived in her rooms when a messenger appeared with instructions from the King that she should leave
Metz at once and find some other place to stay, at least four or
five leagues away. The news of her disgrace had spread rapidly and
there was already a crowd collecting in the street when Richelieu
hurried off to consult the duc de Belle-Isle, governor of Metz,
whose room was directly above the King's bedchamber. He found
Belle-Isle ready to do everything he could to help—the two most
pressing problems were to find a house for Marie-Anne to live in
and a carriage in which she could get there, since her own was too
well known in the town—and, after warning him that Madame de
Châteauroux's enemies would do their best to create disturbances
in the streets, Richelieu went back to the abbey to reassure her.
As he was returning to the Hôtel du Gouvernement once more,
a second messenger stopped him and told him that the bishop of
Soissons had refused to administer the sacraments to the King
until Madame de Châteauroux had left Metz and that the messenger had orders to remain at the abbey until he could report that
she had gone.

Richelieu snapped at him that he had just left the duchesse;
that she was packing and expecting a carriage to be sent by Belle-
Isle; that even if she went on foot she could not get away any
quicker; and that unless somebody did something to disperse the
hostile mob that was collecting in the street it would very soon
be impossible for anybody to get in or out of the abbey. He then
went off in search of the bishop, whom he described as "devout,
hot-headed, but of good faith and capable of listening to reason."
He found Soissons in the King's ante-chamber and explained the
impossibility of getting Madame de Châteauroux to leave immediately; to which the bishop replied that he understood this
perfectly well but still did not intend that the sacraments should
be administered until he was sure that she had gone.

The bishop's position was impregnable, for the King had gone completely to pieces. He had been yelling almost uninterruptedly for his confessor, and, as Richelieu and Soissons were talking in the outside room, he had a mild fainting fit. The duc de Bouillon came running out for a bottle of smelling salts, shouting: "It's happened!" Half of those in the ante-chamber took this to mean that the King was dead, and Louis himself appeared to be of the same opinion when Richelieu swaggered into the bedroom, took a spoonful of the soup that stood in a bowl on a side table and pushed it firmly between the King's lips with one hand while, with the other, he clasped the royal wrist and confidently assured Louis that his pulse was quite steady. But it was no good; his spell was broken.

He returned to the abbey for the third time, thrusting his way through the crowds that were clustered outside the door and up and down the street. He found Marie-Anne white-faced but full of spirit and advised her not to remain in the neighbourhood but to make direct for Paris and to stay there until the trouble had blown over. Then he took her down to a side door where carriages bearing Belle-Isle's arms and with their blinds drawn were waiting; he bustled her in, with Diane-Adélaïde and three other companions, and they were driven rapidly away. At the front of the abbey, the crowd was cheering and jeering while workmen, on the bishop's instructions, tore down the wooden gallery.

Once more Richelieu walked back to the Hôtel du Gouvernement, and on the way he felt a note being slipped into his hand by a stranger whose face he could not see and who disappeared into the crowd; he stopped beside a sentry in the courtyard and unfolded the piece of paper; the message was anonymous, warning him that there was a hue and cry against him and that it would be safer for him to leave Metz. He went on into the building and, as he mounted the stairs to the first floor, another note was handed to him—almost identical with the first. He found the ante-chamber and the King's bedroom seething with people, "more tightly packed than the opera pit on a first night." The comte d'Argenson, Minister of War and younger brother of the diarist, pushed his way towards him and then, as he hurried past, whispered: "I am going to Le Bel's room; I will wait for you there; do not fail me."

Richelieu entered the *valet-de-chambre*'s room by one door as Argenson came in by another. "They are blaming you for having dragged him into all this evil living," Argenson said. "If you take my advice, you won't show yourself in there—or at least keep well away from the bed so that the King does not see you." It was clear that Argenson had decided that Richelieu had lost and had already gone over to the enemy; Richelieu wondered who had sent him to warn him away from Louis, and whether it was he who had sent the two notes. He knew that the building was teeming with his enemies: the priests, the officers of the crown, the princes of the blood, the Maurepas clique, the disapproving notables of Metz who had been summoned to see that the King made his submission; but Richelieu had never quit a battlefield or a gaming table. Ignoring Argenson's warning, he returned to the ante-chamber; his back very straight, his face expressionless, a small, neat, almost dainty figure moving in a heavy cloud of scent, he made his way through the throng, into the bedchamber, up to and beyond the wooden barrier in front of the bed, and took up his position facing both the King and the bishop.

Soissons was determined to make the most of this moment, and Louis had played into his hands by saying that he was too weak to speak, for the bishop had answered that he would speak for him. In a strong voice that carried to the door of the room and beyond, he announced that the King desired to ask pardon of God and his people for the scandal he had caused. He recognized that he was unworthy to bear the titles of Very Christian King and Eldest Son of the Church. He promised to accept all the conditions that the bishop laid upon him, including the banishment of the duchesse de Châteauroux. Louis, frightened that even a bishop might omit some of the magic formula that would rescue him from eternal fire, at this point unexpectedly squeaked: "And her sister, too!"

Richelieu stood erect and dapper as all his plans collapsed around him, his eyes flicking from the King to the triumphant bishop. "After the anathemas against Mesdames de Châteauroux and Lauraguais," he said later, "I had no doubt that it would be my turn; and I was ready with my answer, which I would have given him at the top of my voice. But he did not say a word, and I never knew what prevented him."

§ 4

Marie-Anne, meanwhile, was jolting along the roads to the west of Metz, suffering all the hazards and inconveniences of a hasty departure: the house that Belle-Isle had found her turned out to have no beds, indeed no furniture of any kind, and there were no horses at the relay station. She sent back notes asking if Richelieu could drive out and see her the next morning; if he would inquire whether she had any saddle horses at Metz that could be sent to her; if he would make sure that her servant called on Bachelier or Le Bel and asked for news of the King: "I must have news several times a day, otherwise my head will begin to spin and I certainly do not need that, for I must have it clear to cope with everything that is happening to me. Please tell Mmes. de Boufflers and Luxembourg that I thank them for their kind attentions but that I have not the strength to write to them." She darted first south and then north, unable to make up her mind where to take refuge and trying, for pride's sake, to avoid meeting the Queen, whom she knew to be coming to Metz and bringing the detested Hortense-Félicité with her in response to a panic message that Bouillon had sent to Versailles.

No sooner had she left Metz than Richelieu reflected that his advice that she should go to Paris had been overhasty; if the King died, the news would be there before her and the mob might give her a very rough handling. He sent her a message suggesting that she should go to Montjeu, where he had been married, and which had been inherited by his wife and now passed on to his daughter. But by this time she had regained some of her confidence, and, after discussing it with Diane-Adélaïde and her three other companions, she wrote to him that they all thought it would be a mistake: "Since they have left me at liberty to go to Paris, I ought to go there, and I will see that I arrive at night so they will not be able to insult me; if we have the misfortune to lose the King, I need to be in Paris; and if he recovers I should be better there, too. . . . To tell you the truth, dear uncle, I have not lost all hope.

. . . Please believe that my decision is the best one, you know how much I love you; everything that is happening is very peculiar, but what does it matter if the King recovers. . . ."

Instead of heading southward, they now made for Bar-le-Duc and the Paris road; and at Bar-le-Duc she received the first news that there was an improvement in Louis's condition. Her natural optimism and self-reliance returned, and she wrote to Richelieu at ten o'clock in the morning: "I do not know, dear uncle, why you do not want me to be hopeful, since the improvement is considerable. . . . I can well believe that as long as the King's head is weak, he will be deeply devout, but as soon as he has recovered a little I wager I shall come trotting smartly back into his thoughts and in the end he will not be able to resist talking about me and will ask Le Bel or Bachelier what has become of me."

She had decided, after all, not to go to Paris. The other three women would continue, but she and Diane-Adélaïde would go only as far as Sainte-Menehoulde and wait there for further news. If the King recovered, she wished to be closer to him, "not for him to see me, for I do not count on that happening quickly, but for him to send me word; if he dies, I shall go to Paris and wait there to talk with you. . . ." But she did not believe in her heart that he would die and she was already dreaming of revenge. "If he recovers, dear uncle, how marvellous it will be! Mark my words: I am convinced that this is a blessing from heaven to open his eyes and to bring down the wicked. If we come clear out of this, you will have to admit that our lucky star will take us far and that nothing is impossible for us. And I have high hopes."

Before she arrived at Sainte-Menehoulde, her mood had changed entirely; and she wrote to Richelieu telling him to ignore her decision to stay there: "My letter had scarcely left me when I reflected that it would be ridiculous—we shall leave here tomorrow morning without fail." She commiserated with Richelieu on the persecutions and humiliations that she was sure lay in store for him and told him that, whatever happened, she no longer had any wish to return to court. The reason for this sudden depression was clear from the last paragraph: as her carriage left Bar-le-Duc, it passed a convoy of vehicles being driven furiously from the other direction. Despite all her dodging about, she had failed after all to avoid the Queen's retinue, and at one of the carriage windows, she saw the smug face of *La Poule*, her hated sister, Hortense-Félicité, riding on towards Metz and all the opportunities that awaited whichever woman could catch the King's eye as soon as he was on his feet again. "Oh, my God, what is all this? I give you my word it is all finished as far as I am concerned. One would have to be a madwoman indeed to think of beginning all that all over again. . . . Try to calm your mind and do not fall ill."

The Queen arrived at Metz just before midnight on 17 August, and when she appeared at Louis's bedside, he embraced her and asked her forgiveness for all the grief he had caused her in the past; he was showing signs of recovery, but the fears of hell-fire were still strong in him; one of his first actions was to deprive Richelieu of his mission to the court of Spain to bring back the Dauphin's bride. Fearing that this was the prelude to even blacker disgrace, perhaps banishment from the court, as with Marie-Anne, Richelieu took himself off to the army, which had continued its march towards the Rhine under the maréchal de Noailles. Marie-Anne wrote to him from Paris, saying that she was "overjoyed at the King's good health. His fear of the devil is like that of M. le comte de Clermont, who ran seven leagues without stopping with his sword in his hand. When he returns to his senses, I shall have no more worries; he will miss me madly and will be full of repentance for everything that he has said and done. . . . And I can tell you now that we shall return more brilliant than ever." She regretted that he had had to leave the King, but added: "You did well to forestall the order [to leave the court] for they say that it would not have been long in coming. All this is incredible, and one would think one was dreaming—but it will be our turn soon, dear uncle."

By 3 September, the King's health was sufficiently restored to justify a *Te Deum* in the cathedral and the rekindling of the illuminations. The whole of France had been breathless over the King's illness (although, as so often in its history, its concern was born not so much from respect for him and his government as from fear of what might succeed them), and among the many congratulatory songs composed in celebration of his recovery was one that referred to him as *"le Bien-Aimé"*—a nickname that stuck to him for the rest of his life, becoming more and more laden with bitterness and sarcasm as the years went by. On 8 September he showed himself at the first-floor windows for the first time, and on the 14th he went for a drive.

All this time the unhappy Maria Leczynska had kept a close watch on him. It had been six years since revulsion and exhaustion had prompted her to forbid him her bed, but she now felt it her duty to do everything in her power to encourage his return to a Christian decency of conduct and regular marital habits. She dressed her attendant ladies in coloured ribbons and herself in soft shades of pink; and she had the good sense to make sure that Hortense-Félicité did not get anywhere near the convalescent. There was muted gaiety and breathless anticipation in her household, a secret, smiling, wistful and triumphant, hymeneal hum in the air. And one morning, when all agreed that the King's vital forces must at last be entirely restored, the ladies—for the first time for so many years—set two pillows on the bolster of the Queen's bed in her bedroom on the ground floor of the Hôtel du Gouvernement. Alas! There had already been too many jokes about the ladies' pretty dresses and their too obvious hopes; the King was embarrassed, was already missing Marie-Anne, and was growing increasingly resentful of the way in which he had been humiliated by those who wished to reform him. The Queen's slumbers remained undisturbed; she accompanied Louis to Lunéville, to see her father and mother, but when she asked if she might go with him as far as Strasbourg, on his way to join the army, he answered sharply: "It is not worth while."

All this had been closely watched by Richelieu and Marie-Anne, for, although they were far away, they had many observers working for them at court. Madame de Tencin's brother, the cardinal, wrote to Richelieu in September, telling him that the maréchal de Noailles did not seem to be in favour; that Argenson had some letters from Richelieu in a portfolio that he put in front of the King, but Louis had pretended not to see them; that nobody was yet in a position to read the King's mind. A more certain augury

that the tide was turning in their favour was that Argenson, the
nimble trimmer, began writing to Richelieu again, offering his
assistance. All this information was sent on by Richelieu to
Marie-Anne, who showed remarkable skill in reading Louis's mind
and predicting his actions. While Louis was deciding whether or
not to go to Strasbourg, she wrote to Richelieu: "I believe that
if he goes alone it will be so that he can more easily get rid of the
Queen and return to his usual way of life; I am even convinced
that that is the way he is thinking and that he is at present pon-
dering over all these possibilities. I think the first time he sees his
aides-de-camp he will be a little embarrassed, but you must try to
put him as much at his ease as possible."

She enclosed a long memoir accusing Maurepas of having fo-
mented all the trouble at Metz and asked Richelieu to give this
to the King when he thought the moment was propitious. "There
is plenty of good fortune coming our way, dear uncle. We have
had some rough moments in the past, but they are over. Have a
little more confidence than usual in what I tell you; these are
not dreams; you will see for yourself that they will all come true.
All this is based on the knowledge I have of the man we are dealing with, and I assure you that I know every twist and turn of his
soul."

The embarrassment that Marie-Anne had foreseen when Louis
met Richelieu among his other aides-de-camp was avoided by
Noailles's sending Richelieu back to Louis's headquarters at Saverne, between Lunéville and Strasbourg, early in October, carrying news of the progress of the siege of Freiburg. The atmosphere
when he entered the headquarters building was tense, but Louis
acted as if nothing out of the ordinary were happening, talked
freely with him and kept him for dinner. The King was alone in
his study when Richelieu went to take leave of him, but he made
no mention of the events at Metz, and Richelieu, knowing that
any attempt to confront him with a difficult subject would merely
annoy him, remained silent. But after he had left the study and
was walking through the ante-chamber, Le Bel sidled up and
handed him a note asking for the return of all of Madame de
Châteauroux's letters.

Louis had ordered Le Bel to hand these letters to Richelieu for safekeeping at the beginning of his illness, and they were at the moment in his baggage at Freiburg; he went back to the study to explain this to Louis, but when the King saw him he leaped to his feet as if he had an urgent mission elsewhere and, without waiting for Richelieu to open his mouth, said, "Just as you wish; as you wish," and disappeared. But the next day he sent Richelieu a long, confidential letter discussing the complaints of the Prussians and Russians that Noailles was not pressing the war hard enough, and then adding as if it were an afterthought: "Were you given something during my illness, and what have you done with it?" Richelieu found the letter waiting for him at Freiburg and returned to Saverne to hand over Marie-Anne's letters to the King, and with them her long memorandum of grievances against Maurepas. Events began to move swiftly: Freiburg fell on 6 November; Louis returned to Paris on the 13th and was greeted by a jubilant population, celebrating his victory, as well as his return to health; the streets were illuminated but, as so often happened with Louis's jubilees, a strong wind blew all the lights out within an hour and flattened the triumphal arch that had been erected at Versailles. On the 15th, ears were pricked when the King mentioned Richelieu in favourable terms; on the 19th, he confirmed all the knowing winks by appointing the duchesse de Brancas, Richelieu's former mistress and Diane-Adélaïde's mother-in-law, lady-in-waiting to the not-yet-arrived Dauphine.

The hour of vengeance that Marie-Anne had dreamed about was at hand. Louis had no sooner arrived at Versailles than he was imploring her to return to him; but she would agree only on her own terms. These included the instant disgrace of the Grand Chamberlain, the Grand Master of the Wardrobe, the First Gentleman of the Bedchamber, the bishop of Soissons—Bouillon, La Rochefoucauld, Fleury, Fitz-James—those who had witnessed or plotted her discomfiture. Only one victim was withheld from her: the one whom she most wanted sacrificed, Maurepas. His witty, dirty talk enlivened council meetings so much that Louis could not bring himself to dismiss him, but Maurepas had to grovel and, like the perfect politician that he was, he eagerly embraced the opportunity to do so.

On Wednesday, 26 November, he was summoned to the wig room, and Louis talked to him in private; he then left for Paris and at six in the evening called at the house that Marie-Anne had recently taken in the rue du Bac. He asked to see Madame de Châteauroux, and, on her instructions, the servant who answered the door told him that she was not at home. Maurepas sent in his name again and received the same answer. It was not until he said that he came with a message from the King that he was admitted and taken up to the bedroom where Marie-Anne, who had been indisposed, was chatting with Noailles's son, the duc d'Ayen.

Ayen took his leave, and Maurepas, stumbling over his words, announced that he was the bearer of a communication from the King, which His Majesty had himself dictated to him and had ordered him to read to her. Marie-Anne, who was quite familiar with the contents of the letter and had herself dictated a great deal of it to Louis, nodded coldly, and Maurepas began to read: The King was extremely annoyed by all that had occurred at Metz and by the improper way in which Madame de Châteauroux had been treated, and he begged her to forget it. "I am well aware that the King had no part in what happened," said Marie-Anne. The King hoped that as a mark of her forgiveness she and her sister would return to their apartments at Versailles; he would take every opportunity to give them proof of his protection, esteem, and friendship; he would reinstate them in all their appointments.

Maurepas then handed her a personal letter from Louis and began to stammer protestations that anything she might have heard against him was untrue and that he was extremely embarrassed. "I can well believe that," interjected Marie-Anne, savouring the moment and remembering the time when he had told her she had better get to a convent, after the duchesse de Mazarin had died. He asked permission to kiss her hand before he left. "That doesn't cost much," she snapped as she held it out to him.

Word of Marie-Anne's great triumph and Maurepas's humiliating defeat reached Richelieu in Montpellier, where he had gone direct from Freiburg for the opening of the *Etats*, at the end of November. His dreams were now rosy indeed; all his former plans were possibilities again, well-nigh certainties; with this brilliant and courageous woman as his friend and instrument, there was nothing that he might not hope for: the highest offices in the royal household, the council, the army: he could have any and perhaps all of them. His feet were on a path that would lead to power and glory comparable with that of the Great Cardinal. . . . And ten days later his dreams were shattered, the path had crumbled beneath his feet.

Marie-Anne, excited by Maurepas's visit, developed a fever the following day and kept to her bed. And the day after that she remained in bed, with the fever persisting. The doctors were unable to make anything of it; the inevitable rumours of poisoning began to circulate; she drifted into delirium, screaming with pain and at unknown horrors. After many hours of agony, she died on 8 December, at the age of 27 and without ever having made her victorious return to Versailles.

Louis, terrified of death, had not dared visit her, and on the night that she died, he drove from Versailles to La Muette, where he shut himself up with Ayen and others who had seen her during her illness, refusing to talk to anybody else or to deal with business of state. Richelieu returned from Montpellier and reached Versailles late on Christmas Eve, a few hours after Louis's return; he was met by the marquis de Meuse, who told him that the King wished to see him privately that night. Louis attended midnight mass in the chapel and then took Richelieu up to the *petits appartements* under the rafters, where he had so often entertained the rejected Louise-Julie, as well as Pauline-Félicité, who had also died suddenly and very young—and now Marie-Anne. . . . He produced the letters that Richelieu had returned at Saverne and began reading them and weeping. The two men faced each other in the quiet room, and Louis went on reading and weeping until five o'clock in the morning.

Feats of Arms

§ 1

Madame,

    M. le duc de Richelieu a reçu ordre du Roi de vous avertir de sa part qu'il y aura bal à Versailles mercredi 24 Février 1745, à cinq heures du soir.

    S.M. compte que vous voudrez bien vous y trouver.

    Les dames qui dansent seront coiffées en grandes boucles.

It was his inaugural year *en exercice* as First Gentleman of the Bedchamber; the invitation was to the ball in celebration of the wedding of the Dauphin and the Infanta Maria Teresa Rafaela; and the fact that it was sent out in his name represented an initial victory in the arena of petty punctilio which he now entered with as much gusto as he had brought to his campaigns against the Austrians or his sadly ended efforts to establish Marie-Anne as the royal mistress. A battle had been raging for three weeks, ever since he and the duc d'Ayen had come into open conflict at the King's *débotter* over whose privilege it was to send out the tickets for the ball that was to be held in the *manège*, the former riding school. Ayen, who was doing his quarterly tour of duty as Captain of the Guard, claimed that, since the Captain of the Guard unquestionably sent out the tickets for the ballet, he was also entitled to send them out for the ball. Richelieu, combing the records and the memories of the oldest courtiers, discovered that at the wedding of the King's grandmother, the princess of Bavaria, the proceedings had become so disorderly that the Gentlemen Ushers had had to call in the bodyguard, thus proving that

135

the ball had been originally policed by the Gentlemen Ushers, who were themselves at the orders of the First Gentlemen. Ayen protested that the ball had then been held in the *salon d'Hercule*, and what happened in the *salon d'Hercule* was no precedent for what should happen in the *manège*, but Richelieu dismissed this as irrelevant, stuck to his guns and not only vetted the list of guests but personally signed each ticket.

Although his disgrace in the previous autumn had lost him the honour of going to Madrid to fetch the future Dauphine, he was sent to meet her at Orléans as the representative of the King, the Queen and the Dauphin, taking with him the boxes upon boxes of presents that had been cluttering his rooms at Versailles for days; some were presents from the King to his new daughter-in-law, but most of them were gifts for her to offer to other people, including thirty-six fans, twelve gold watches, eight gold scent-bottles and four of rock-crystal, thirty snuffboxes, a dozen tooth-pick cases, scissors, penknives, and scores of other small objects. Richelieu also carried with him the King's permission—amounting to an instruction—for her to wear rouge, without which her very fair complexion would have appeared almost corpse-like at a court where women's faces were completely masked with make-up.

The Dauphine was eighteen, almost three years older than her husband, who had never seen her and knew from advance descriptions only that she was "neither tall nor short, well built and with a noble air, very white-skinned and extremely blond, even to her eyebrows and eyelashes." Her least attractive feature was her nose, "which is large and not very agreeable, and appears to be joined to her forehead without any bridge." It was comforting to learn that "all who know her say that she is intelligent and very anxious to please." Her affability was put to its first test on the afternoon of 23 February when *La Princesse de Navarre*, the musical *divertissement* over which Voltaire and Rameau had squabbled for the best part of a year, was performed in the covered *manège*. It was generally considered to be long, tedious, and not saved even by the mechanical marvels of its final transformation scene, in which the Pyrénées split and retreated into the wings to reveal a pink-garlanded Temple of Love. Richelieu, however, was entirely satisfied; though it was well known that the covered *manège* was the province of the Master of the Horse, it was the First Gentleman, once more, who had issued the tickets. And at the ball the following day, when the lieutenant of the bodyguard marched his men up to the *manège* and informed the Gentlemen Ushers that he had orders from the duc d'Ayen to station them inside the barrier, Richelieu appeared as if from nowhere and sharply told him to get outside and stay outside: by order of the King. The lieutenant did as he was told. If there had been no precedent before, Richelieu had made sure that one was established now.

The minutiae of protocol fascinated him; he was everywhere in the fight for privileges, defending them, usurping them, framing them, above all, codifying them:

Entrées chez M. le Dauphin

The ladies of Mme. la Dauphine will have the same *entrées* in the Dauphin's apartments as the Queen's ladies have in those of the King.

When Mme. la Dauphine passes through the Dauphin's cabinet to go to mass or elsewhere, nobody shall follow her through the said cabinet except her *dame d'honneur*, her *dame d'atour* and her *chevalier d'honneur*.

Mme. la Dauphine's *dame d'honneur* will have the *grandes entrées* in the King's apartments at all times.

The *dame d'atour* will enjoy these only when she is in attendance on Mme. la Dauphine.

If the *dames du palais* of Mme. la Dauphine attend her when she goes to the King's apartments in the morning and he is still in bed, they will remain in that room of the apartments in which the King's *premières entrées* wait, and only the *dame d'honneur* and the *dame d'atour* will enter with Mme. la Dauphine.

If this is during the *débotter*, they will remain in the *chambre à balustre* until the King is dressed and has passed into the *chambre des perruques*; they will then be shown into the *cabinet du conseil*, which they may also enter when in attendance on Mme. la Dauphine at other times, if the usher is present.

The *chevalier d'honneur* of Mme. la Dauphine will accompany her into the *cabinet du conseil* at all times that the King is not in bed.

It was with this kind of thing that he occupied most of his time and that of scores of clerks, or with backstairs commerce of patronage by which, at the end of March 1745, he obtained a pension of 2,000 livres for Voltaire, together with the promise of a post of Gentleman in Ordinary and the title of His Majesty's Historiographer; though there were some who said that the poet had received greater help from another of his friends: Madame le Normant d'Etioles, who was shortly to embark on her nineteen-year reign as Madame de Pompadour. Richelieu's later denial that he had anything to do with establishing Madame d'Etioles as Louis's *maîtresse déclarée* is as casuistical as his similar statement that he knew nothing of Madame du Barry's succession to her in that office. He is sure to have met her in the worlds of literature, politics, and finance where they had many common acquaintances: Voltaire, Madame de Tencin, and Le Riche de la Pouplinière, the farmer-general who became the most celebrated of Richelieu's cuckolds; but it may be true that he did not at first think of her as a mistress for the King, since she lacked the necessary qualifications of birth: women of the middle and lower classes were acceptable for *passades* (passing affairs), but the aristocracy jealously guarded the ancient privilege of offering their own wives as the King's regular harlots.

There was no question about the humbleness of Madame d'Etioles's birth; as Jeanne Poisson she was the granddaughter of a butcher on her mother's side and a weaver on her father's; her mother was a woman of loose reputation, while her father, a senior clerk to an army contractor, had fled the country to avoid prosecution for swindling. Mademoiselle Poisson's beauty had won her a tiny but very rich husband, son of the chief treasurer of the mint and nephew of her mother's lover; his fortune provided her with almost everything she could desire, including a private theatre on his estate at Etioles. But there remained one dream unfulfilled: since her earliest girlhood her ambition had been to become the King's mistress. As there was no way in which she could approach Louis closely enough to catch his eye in Versailles, she determined to impress herself upon him outside. As he hunted through the forests that surrounded the royal residences and that he denuded of game with bored but dedicated ferocity, he would catch tantalizing glimpses in a clearing or a neighbouring ride of a woman dressed in flouncy pink, driving a pale blue carriage (or sometimes the frills were blue and the carriage was pink), a fragile, sugary-fondant beauty. She was slender and graceful, a little above average height; her oval face was set in a mass of curls, light brown with red highlights; her dimpled smile revealed perfect teeth; and the play of light in her eyes could turn them from deepest black to brightest blue. To her physical attractions she added a wealth of accomplishments: she was a skilled and graceful horsewoman; Crébillon had taught her how to declaim lines; she sang and accompanied herself on the clavecin far better than the usual amateur.

Although she managed to attract Louis's attention and was among the many women followers of the hunt to whom he sent carcasses of the thousands of deer that he so tirelessly slaughtered, there is no indication that he met her even informally while hunting; the first occasion on which they spoke together inside any of the royal palaces was almost certainly the public masked ball held in the *galerie des glaces* on 25 February 1745. Unlike the ball in the *manège* the previous evening, this had the minimum of formality and no tickets were issued, one man in each party being required to unmask, give his name and accept responsibility for his companions. As more and more carriages from Paris clattered into the forecourt, bright with the lights that outlined the whole front of the château, and as their passengers got out and streamed up the *escalier de marbre* and the *escalier des ambassadeurs*, it became increasingly difficult to identify these *bourgeois* visitants from another world, and an appearance of respectability was all that was needed to obtain admission. Soon the throng became so great and the pressure so insistent that the oaken barriers were shattered and the dancers flooded uncontrolled through the surrounding rooms with their subsidiary orchestras and sideboards laden with refreshment.

A certain number of pockets were picked, but the guests' behaviour was tolerable on the whole, though ignorance of the identity of their betters occasionally resulted in distressing incidents. There was a lack of chairs and the dowager princesse de Conti, as much to manifest her rank as to rest her limbs, asked one of the masked men to give her the one on which he was sitting. She met with a refusal and, realizing that her voice had not been recognized, she took off her mask—only to be met with the same blank look and firm refusal. "We must be in very bad company here," she exclaimed as she billowed away.

The Queen entered the *galerie des glaces* followed by the Dauphin and his bride, dressed as a gardener and a flower girl, for the odious pretence that the rustic poor were to be envied for their idyllic existence was current at the court long before Rousseau published or Marie-Antoinette was born. Shortly afterwards, eight men disguised as yew trees came in from the private apartments. Word that one of them was Louis brought all the pretty Parisiennes flocking round, flirting their richly embroidered skirts and plucking off their masks in the hope that eager glances and propitious smiles might arouse the interest of the King, who had now been more than nine weeks without a known mistress. Unfortunately, it was difficult to decide which of the identical yew trees concealed the person of the King, and the wife of one of the presidents of the Paris *parlement* submitted to being carried off to an attic bedroom and irrevocably committed to the twiggy embraces of one of them before discovering that she had made the supreme sacrifice to a mere gentleman-in-waiting.

Madame d'Etioles had no such problems, for she was led up to the King either by Richelieu or by Binet, one of her distant relations who was *valet-de-chambre* to the Dauphin. The King was enchanted by her beauty, her gaiety, and her cool confidence. A day or two later he met her again at the masked ball given at the Hôtel de Ville by the merchants of Paris and saw her home in a hired carriage to the hôtel de Gesvres, in the rue Croix-des-Petits-Champs, which had been rented for her by Charles le Normant de Tournehem, her husband's uncle and her mother's lover. On 29 March, she was present at a ballet in the *manège*, and on

1 April, she saw the Comédie-Italienne perform in the small *salle de spectacle*, occupying a box at the side of the stage where the King could feast his eyes on her. At some time within the next three weeks, the decision was taken that Louis's appetite had been sufficiently aroused, and Binet introduced her to the smelly intimacies of the royal bedchamber. On Thursday, 22 April, Louis gave a supper in his *petits appartements* to present her formally to his cronies, Richelieu, Ayen, Boufflers, and Meuse.

Her hold over Louis was complete from the outset and so firmly exercised that Richelieu was in no doubt that she was a more dangerous opponent than any he had yet met at court. She was as intelligent, unscrupulous, and emotionally uncommitted as himself; beneath the frothy lace and rosy frills was a cold and calculating whore whose head guided every action, a delicate Sèvres figurine with a heart as obdurate as the glaze on her pink and white cheeks. She knew at once that Louis was easy prey, his lust making him the captive of any pretty woman who set her mind to it; and in Richelieu she recognized a man whose ambition, though more fitful, was as fierce as hers. She would never trust him as an ally, and he was too proud to be her lieutenant; he must therefore be an enemy.

It was not long before he felt the pressure of her antagonism. After the evening service on Sunday, 2 May, the King worked in his study with the bishop of Mirepoix, who had charge of the portfolio of benefices. The abbess of the rich and fashionable Abbaye-aux-Bois had recently died, and Louis asked the bishop if Richelieu had spoken to him about a successor. The bishop replied that both Richelieu and Madame de Brancas had urged him to give the appointment to the youngest of Richelieu's sisters, who was then abbess of the Cistercian Abbaye-du-Trésor, near Les Andelys; but, Mirepoix added, he understood that Mademoiselle Vernem, sister of the late abbess and herself abbess of Caen, was a very deserving case.

"She shall have it then," said the King, and signed the order giving her the benefice. Mirepoix remarked contentedly that Richelieu would be very angry. "He should expect it," Louis replied. "He was recommending his sister to me a moment before you came in, under the pretence of speaking of something else. I told him that he was too forward, that he shall not have the abbey." Within a few hours, this rebuff was public knowledge and Feydeau de Marville, the Lieutenant-General of police, reported to Maurepas that in café gossip "M. le duc de Richelieu's shares have dropped considerably." But it was no more than a tiff, a momentary exasperation on the part of the King, his annoyance cleverly fanned by Madame d'Etioles.

§ 2

Four days later, Louis set off for Flanders and the army, this time taking the Dauphin with him. The year before, the young man had been kept at Versailles, but now that he was a married man he was to have a chance to win his spurs. The thought of both the King and his only direct heir facing the danger of enemy fire aroused great excitement in the château; very early in the morning, the Queen waited at the end of the passage leading to her room and, when the Dauphin appeared, smothered him with farewell kisses; then, with Mesdames her daughters, she followed him to the King's bedroom for the *lever*, which the Dauphine was too upset to attend. The royal warriors left soon after 7 a.m., Richelieu and Ayen having the honour of riding with them, and by Friday evening they were at Douai, where news was awaiting them that the Duke of Cumberland, who had landed at Ostend, was marching at the head of 30,000 Dutchmen, 25,000 Britons, 8,000 Hanoverians, and some Austrian infantry and cavalry units, to relieve Tournai, which had been besieged by Maurice de Saxe since the end of April.

Louis was on the road again at five the next morning and arrived that day at the castle of Pont-de-Chin, close to Saxe's headquarters; on Sunday he inspected the troops and confirmed Saxe in command of the army and then listened to the reports of the reconnaissances of the previous week. Cumberland, having marched eastward from Ostend to Brussels and then southward from Brussels towards Mons, had assembled and reviewed his troops at Soignies and was now in a position to advance westwards on Tournai by any of three roads but could not use all of them with-

out the risk of having one of his columns cut off. Saxe had set out
a thin arc of troops on the right bank of the Scheldt, facing the
general direction of Cumberland's advance, and supported them
with most of his cavalry, which were of no value during the siege.

From the waterlogged meadows along the bank of the Scheldt,
the open ground rose gently to the village of Vezons in the distance. On the left, the slope was steeper, rising to broken ground,
cut by ravines and often thickly wooded, across which the road
from Tournai to Mons ran through Notre-Dame-aux-Bois and on
to Barry wood before reaching Vezons. On the right, where the
village of Anthoin stood on a slight eminence among the water-
meadows, a ditch, deepening to a ravine, ran forward to the village
of Fontenoy and then swung at right angles across the plain,
ending midway to Barry wood. It was along the Mons-Tournai
road that Saxe expected Cumberland to advance, and in the plain
bounded by Anthoin, Fontenoy, Barry wood, Notre-Dame-aux-
Bois and the river that he hoped to defeat him.

At Fontenoy he cut down the trees and burned the houses on
the far side of the ravine to deprive the enemy of cover as they
advanced; on the outskirts of the village and at Anthoin, he threw
up redoubts. Another two were set up at the near corner of
Barry wood, at the side of the Mons road, each large enough to
shelter an infantry battalion, as well as artillery. On Sunday, an
overcast, squally day, Cumberland's advance guard came in sight,
moving about on the heights around Vezons and behind Barry
wood. Saxe sent two battalions of the Grassin regiment forward
to keep them under observation and withdrew to his tent, where
he was tapped for the dropsy.

Maurice de Saxe, born in the same year as Richelieu, a man of
iron courage but with few other virtues, was the illegitimate child
of Augustus the Strong, Elector of Saxony, a distinction which
he was said to share with three hundred and fifty-three other
bastards. He was boastful, uncouth, and overbearing; he was a
foreigner and a Protestant. For all these things he was detested
by the French generals who served under him. They criticized his
plans and claimed that a commander who was suffering so acutely
from the aftereffects of dropsical tapping that he could not sit a

horse and had to be transported around the field in a light wicker-work basket was not fit to perform his duties. Saxe brushed their objections aside. "His courage, his severity with himself—and his love of command," as Richelieu said with excusable malice, pre-vented him from handing over his command to a more nimble general. There was also the consideration that none of his rivals had half his military talent, though he did not perhaps show it to its best advantage in this battle.

On Monday, Louis was up at dawn, inspecting the positions that Saxe had chosen; the rain and wind of the previous day had waned a little. As the King rode from Anthoin towards Fontenoy, a shout went up that the enemy was on the move: three columns could be seen advancing down the slope. But while they were still out of range, they halted for the rest of the day, their pioneers preparing tracks for artillery and munition wagons through the woods on the left and their cavalry making skirmishes across the stream that ran from Vezons to the Scheldt. Saxe brought up the remainder of his troops and by nightfall had placed in position 100 cannon, 59 battalions of infantry, and 106 squadrons of cavalry.

On Tuesday, 11 April, Louis returned to the battlefield at dawn from the château de Calonne, where he had spent the night. He was accompanied by the Dauphin, maréchal de Noailles, Argenson, the Secretary for War, Richelieu, as general officer-in-waiting, and an escort of 200 infantrymen, gendarmes, light horse and musketeers. The dawn was grey with a mist hanging heavily over the fields as Louis halted at the gibbet on the hill at Notre-Dame-aux-Bois. As he looked forward along the Mons road, which dipped down to the corner of Barry wood, skirted it, and rose to Vezons, he had on his left the 13 squadrons of the *maison du roi* and 4 squadrons of gendarmerie; and in front of them another 8 squadrons of cavalry; and in front of them, facing the rear of Barry wood, the Normandy brigade, the marines and the Irish brigade, the latter linking the two redoubts at the side of the Mons road. Forward to his right, covering the plain from the redoubts to Fontenoy, were 6 battalions of the *gardes françaises*, 4 of the Aubeterre brigade, and 4 of the King's regiment. From Fontenoy, held by the Dauphin brigade, the line turned sharply back at right angles, following the deep ditch to the river, guarded at each end by Crillon's regiment and the Swiss and in the middle by 3 regiments of dragoons. In the centre, supporting the *gardes françaises*, Aubeterre, and King's regiment, were another 8 battalions of infantry and behind them 2 lines of cavalry of 24 and 32 squadrons each.

The enemy had begun moving into position at dawn, and at 6 a.m. four clouds of smoke puffed out and were followed by the reports of the cannon fire that had given the signal for the advance. Two columns of Dutch infantry, supported by cavalry, advanced on the French right between Anthoin and Fontenoy, came under heavy fire from the batteries in the two villages and, deciding that the task was beyond them, halted out of range and remained there for the rest of the battle. In the right centre, British and Hanoverian troops began a frontal attack on the village of Fontenoy, but without cover and with the ravine preventing them from getting to grips with the defenders, they were mown down by artillery and musketry fire; finally their attacks wilted and ceased. It was during these two assaults on the right of his line that Saxe made his first and almost fatal error: he ordered his second line of infantry from the centre to the right flank. For, as they marched off to their right, the bulk of the British infantry, supported by skirmishers who had penetrated Barry wood, moved diagonally across the French front and, in three columns, came through the gap between Barry wood and the end of the ravine, heading directly for the left of the French line and dragging their artillery with them.

The guns that Saxe had placed in front of his infantry were now booming incessantly, and under this murderous fire the British troops began a series of magnificent, cumbersome manoeuvres. Marching to the slow, deliberate pace of the guards who headed the column, they wheeled left as soon as they had cleared the end of the ravine and marched along its near side until they had filled the whole of their front; then, with a right turn into line, they advanced a few paces and halted, leaving room for the next column to march into the arena behind them. Thus, halting and advancing, they continued to move forward, closing ranks as men dropped under the fire from the French guns, and halting once more as they came within range of the first redoubt at the side of the Mons road, at the point of Barry wood. Once more, with the impressive, appalling artistry of the barrack square, the great mass of men began the huge wheeling movement of a half-left form. They were now marching into a pocket, with the batteries of Fontenoy and Barry wood on their left and right and the French infantry in front of them.

The British halted. On both sides, the guns had been withdrawn, and now only the lines of infantrymen faced each other, in four ranks, company by company, stretched across the plain. Lord Charles Hay stepped forward, doffed his hat, and invited the French to fire first. The comte d'Auteroche, lieutenant in the grenadiers, declined the honour, since, at that range, muskets were so erratic that whoever fired first would be at a disadvantage, unable to reload before the enemy charged and, with bullet or bayonet, made deadly certain. The French advanced in their turn; except for the clatter of their equipment, there was complete silence as they tramped across the fields still tacky from rain; "I believe there has never been a spectacle so beautiful and at the same time so terrible," one of them wrote later. The British were at a distance of thirty yards when the French saw the first two ranks of the enemy kneel and take aim; and as the French did the same, they saw officers walking along the British lines, calmly tapping the muzzles of their men's muskets with their canes, keeping the fire deadly and low. The volleys crackled out. The French began to reload and then, to their astonishment and dismay, saw the men who had fired at them double round to the rear, while four more ranks, their muskets already loaded, took their places. The French line wavered, and a new line of British troops, their bayonets fixed, came charging at them, shouting their weird "Huzza! Huzza!"

The French infantry crumpled and ran. From the rear, their cavalry came galloping through and over them; but these too drew back as the British infantrymen dropped to their knees and, like automatons, delivered their withering rapid fire. The French cavalry in their retreat overran their infantry once more, and between the British and the river there seemed to be nothing but masses of struggling, bewildered, leaderless men. While the French tried to re-form, the British recommenced their steady forward march, and at the far end of the battlefield their reinforcements still filed into position to the beat of the drum.

Something was missing, however, from this model demonstration: the cavalry should have followed up the breakthrough, slashing the demoralized enemy into segments, turning the flanks, riding down the redoubts from the rear, chasing the tattered remnants from the field—and the cavalry could not get through on either side of the British infantry because of the fire from the redoubts at Fontenoy and Barry wood. Saxe, hoping to close the pocket and seal the British infantry in a bag, ordered his troops on both flanks to attack, but the French army, unlike the British, had not yet adopted the brutal Prussian discipline that made a man more frightened of his officer's displeasure than of his enemy's hate. Combining overenthusiasm with lack of practice and co-ordination, the troops on the right flank attacked long before those on the left were ready, so that each was driven back in turn.

For the moment it was stalemate. The British had failed to outflank the batteries in Fontenoy and at Barry wood, and, until they silenced them, they could not bring their cavalry into action. The French had also failed to cut off the head of the British advance and had been beaten back by superior firepower. The attackers were as tightly wedged and apparently immobile as a square peg in a square hole, but they had shown superior discipline, and, although they were being fired on from three sides, their morale was higher. Saxe had lost control of the battle, and it seemed only a matter of time before the British continued their ponderous march and split the French forces or drove them into the Scheldt.

Around the gibbet of Notre-Dame-aux-Bois there was great hubbub and confusion. The night before, with habitual foreboding, Louis had commented that this was the first occasion that the King and the Dauphin had been together on a battlefield since the dreadful *débacle* of Poitiers. And now, as disorganized packets of men rode or stumbled about behind the French lines in the plain below him, the shadow of an equally disastrous defeat loomed closer. Behind them, out of sight beyond the wood, sappers were already piling straw and faggots under the arches of the bridge that led to Tournai, so that it could be burned to prevent pursuit as soon as the King and the Dauphin had got across. To Richelieu, sitting his horse at a few paces from the King and listening with increasing contempt, this talk of retreat was madness. Pride and his natural audacity prompted him to reject all thoughts of failure; he edged his way over to the King and asked permission to ride to the left flank, which was partially hidden from them by a rise in the ground, and find out what was happening there.

He arrived at a moment when the marines, thrown back in an earlier attack, had re-formed and were once more about to advance. Eager for action instead of the defeatist talk that he had been listening to up on the hill, he charged with them and saw for himself how pitiably they were broken by the unwavering British fire. Pressing his way through more groups of scattered and discouraged troops, he galloped back to the gibbet, where he found the generals, apparently even more demoralized than their men, shouting among themselves and assuring the King that the battle was lost and that he must retire across the Scheldt while he still could.

Richelieu joined in the shouting, but with a very different theme: that they were far from defeated and that to attempt to retreat across the Scheldt by the single bridge that was available would mean the total annihilation of the army (he did not yet know that the bridge was to be burned after the King's escape and the army left to its fate). "Sire!" he pleaded, "only Your Majesty's presence can restore our position and bring us victory." He paused, but there was no supporting voice. He urged that the British were still unable to bring their cavalry into action; that cannon firing small-shot would create dreadful havoc in their tightly packed ranks; and that a concerted charge from all sides could break them and drive them from the field.

"And where would you get your cannon?" somebody asked, for

the French artillery was now either sealed off in the redoubts or overrun by the British infantry.

"Close at hand," Richelieu replied. "I saw four guns as I rode back just now." His confidence, tinged with more than a little scorn, provoked the usual military response. "The maréchal de Saxe has forbidden that battery to be moved," he was told.

"Monsieur le maréchal could not foresee what has happened," said Richelieu. "And the King has only to command."

Louis's face was flushed with embarrassment and anger: anger because he felt that the shouting and confusion around him detracted from his dignity; embarrassment because he was about to be confronted with a decision which only he could take. "Your Majesty!" said Richelieu. "Do you command me to march with those guns?" The crimson on Louis's cheeks deepened as he hesitated. Then, loudly and firmly, he answered: "Yes, that is my order!"

Richelieu sent an officer to get the guns limbered up and drawn round to face the centre of the British line, and other messengers to both flanks to order the commanders to make a concerted attack as soon as the guns were fired. While the guns were being wheeled into position, he assembled a motley collection of troops from the household cavalry, the gendarmerie, the carabineers, infantrymen, orderlies, and grooms—any with a horse to ride or weapon to wield. Louis had spoken mournfully of Poitiers; it was Richelieu who was to revive the great traditions of French chivalry, the magnificent wild onrush of horses and men that had broken on the English steel and arrows at Crécy and Agincourt, but on this day was to charge to triumph.

The line of French infantry facing the British centre parted and unmasked the cannon that had been placed into position behind them. The gunners touched their lighted matches, and the small-shot tore through the British infantrymen, tumbling them over like toys. Before they could re-form, as the boom of the guns still echoed, Richelieu came racing from the French lines with his rag-bag of supporters yelling and screaming behind him, while from the flanks the infantry advanced: the marines, the Irish brigade, and, trying to retrieve their honour, the French and Swiss guards, who had so disgraced themselves by breaking and running earlier in the day.

Richelieu leaned forward, reins loose, half-standing in his stirrups, a small, ferocious man, glowing with Gallic fury and intoxication; and as he flung himself at the centre of the British line, there was nothing but death that could have halted him and the men behind him. The unyielding, impenetrable wall of redcoats trembled and then cracked. Suddenly the British were in full retreat, leaving behind them their artillery and three or four thousand dead and wounded. It was 1:30 in the afternoon.

The messenger whom Richelieu sent to carry the news to the King found him, on the recommendation of Noailles, far beyond the crest of the hill and about to cross the bridge over the Scheldt. Louis turned back immediately and rode up and down the battlefield, receiving the congratulatory cheers of his victorious soldiers. When Richelieu galloped up to him, Louis placed his hand on his shoulder and said: "I will never forget the service you have just done me."

Saxe, on the other hand, managed to forget not only what Richelieu had done but almost everything else that had happened. "The enemy," he said in one report, "attacked us in a position where I was able to take all the advantage that years of experience have given me. One might say that our dispositions made victory certain for us, because, having retained considerable reserves, I was able to bring up constant reinforcements of fresh troops."

In bragging, however, Saxe was faced with a formidable opponent, for Richelieu had Voltaire write a poem in celebration of the battle of Fontenoy. Voltaire, who had smartly hitched his wagon to Pompadour's star, was glad of an opportunity to flatter her by celebrating her royal lover's triumph and gave the first reading of his epic at her country house at Etioles. The poem went into five editions in a fortnight, not so much because of its literary worth—although it had an enormous sale of ten thousand copies in ten days—but because the author withdrew each new edition in order to correct the more flagrant errors that had been pointed out to him or to insert the names of still more members of the aristocracy to whom he wished to toady. But no matter which edition, Richelieu remained the hero of the final charge.

Yet even victory gave rise to weighty problems. As soon as the Queen received the news, she gave instructions to the master of the chapel music that a *Te Deum* should be sung at mass the next morning; no sooner had the superintendent of the chamber music heard of this than he protested that it was *his* duty to arrange a *Te Deum* on such occasions. Maria Leczynska, brought up by a father who frankly disliked ceremonial, never entirely appreciated the sanctity with which privileges were surrounded at Versailles, and thought that she was being merely reasonable when she sent word to the superintendent that she considered it would be best to stand by the arrangements she had already made. The superintendent, far from convinced, followed the master of the chapel music round the chapel next morning, collecting up his sheet music and substituting his own, until the Queen arrived and he had to withdraw, defeated.

News of this shocking affair reached Richelieu at Tournai, where the interrupted siege had been resumed. He sent a very stiff letter to the master of the chapel music and almost as severe a one to the duchesse de Luynes, the Queen's lady-in-waiting.

"I have been compelled, Madame, to acquaint the King with the fact that, despite his decisions in favour of the superintendent of chamber music, the abbé Blanchard [master of the chapel music] has been able to find protection in the Queen's entourage for his having conducted the *Te Deum* for the battle of Fontenoy, which H.M. has greatly disapproved; I will not conceal from you, Madame, that but for the favour with which I know you honour the abbé Blanchard I would have suggested to the King that he should be punished for his boldness in having dared to revive a dispute which was lost and decided long ago. Consequently, Madame, if a similar argument should arise over the *Te Deum* for the capture of Tournai, I beg you, Madame, to be good enough to inform the Queen of the King's commands. . . ."

This was too much for the long-suffering Maria Leczynska, who tore the letter up and told her lady-in-waiting to reply that she dared not show it to the Queen; but Madame de Luynes pointed out that this would make matters worse, since part of the letter purported to be written on the King's behalf. Instead she sent Richelieu a curt but not impolite acknowledgment, saying that the Queen had already forestalled the King's commands by asking for a second *Te Deum* to be performed. The news of the fall of Tournai arrived very shortly after Richelieu's letter, and the Queen somewhat wilfully instructed the abbé Blanchard to sing a *Te Deum* at the mass she was on the point of attending but covered herself by making it clear that this was not an official *Te Deum* but merely a substitute for the psalm; and at the same time she complied with Louis's orders by telling the superintendent of the chamber music to arrange for the ceremonial *Te Deum* to be sung three days later.

Alas! The unfortunate woman did not know that what made a *Te Deum* official or unofficial was not mere words from her, nor even the fact of its being supervised by the master of the chapel or the superintendent of the chamber music. It depended entirely on whether or not a royal chaplain, either hers or the King's, was present at the time, and whether or not he was wearing his stole. And by unhappy chance her chaplain *was* there and *was* wearing his stole. It was a blessing that she had Maurepas with her, to draw up a memorandum explaining exactly what had happened, and what had been her intentions, so that the King should not be vexed and no precedents created. Richelieu remained suspicious and touchy; three weeks later, when the Queen cautiously had Madame de Luynes write to ask for the King's approval to her having Madame de Belzunce dine at her table, Richelieu sent back a very short and disrespectful answer, saying that he had read the letter to the King, whose reply was that he was too busy campaigning to be bothered with such matters.

This was quite untrue; Louis was not at all busy. The momentum of the campaign was slackening, though the French advance continued almost unopposed now that Cumberland had withdrawn with most of the British troops to deal with the Jacobite rising; and the King was beginning to fidget for his mistress. He had enjoyed a taste of the simple life at the Château de Chin, basking in the double glory of Fontenoy and Tournai and showing great favours to Richelieu, who lodged on the lower floor, next to the

Dauphin. When they moved on to Ghent, Louis fell into the habit of rising early and wandering into Richelieu's room for a chat before Richelieu got up; in the evening he would often walk into Richelieu's quarters after his own dinner and talk to the company at table there, sometimes staying on to play dice. It was evident from all these very gracious attentions that Louis had been as impressed by Richelieu's recent display of courage at Fontenoy as he had long been by his ready wit and courtly manners and success with women. The marquis d'Argenson, envying and disapproving at the same time, recorded in his diary this portrait of Richelieu at fifty.

"The duc de Richelieu is the King's favourite whenever he takes the trouble; but he is not content with the most flattering familiarity with his master unless he can improve his fortune thereby, above all by obtaining a ministry; he is possessed with the desire to enter the council. . . . At the moment he restricts his ambition to gaining command of the army; but he hopes and prepares for it more by presumption than by work. The soldiers fear his eventual promotion; none of them wants to serve under him; he is accused of being frivolous, hasty and careless. . . . He possesses all the experience and wisdom necessary to manage men, but he tries to influence them more through their weaknesses than their good qualities; he studies the former but rejects the latter as irrelevant. He despises our ministers but takes great care not to offend them; yet his satiric temper shows through his politeness and smooth talk; he is feared and detested. The most useful quality that he has for the ministry is what is called *style*: I doubt if even his great-uncle, the famous Cardinal de Richelieu, had a more vehement and positive way of talking than he has. . . . But if the misfortunes of this realm ever gave us a second Richelieu, could one be sure that good fortune would still come to the aid of imprudence? . . . He has been very popular with women. The rivalries and jealousies of coquettes have brought him many triumphs; never any true passion, much debauchery, sensual satisfaction without pleasure; he deceived the members of a feeble sex and mistook the senses for the heart. He is not fortunate enough to possess a single friend; he is frank through want of care,

distrustful through contempt for men, disagreeable through in-
sensibility and misanthropy."

§ 3

On Tuesday, 7 September 1745 Richelieu drove into Paris in the
train of carriages that brought Louis and the Dauphin back from
the wars, through streets crowded with cheering people and
draped with tapestries and bunting all the way from the porte
Saint-Martin to the Tuileries. On Wednesday he accompanied the
King to a *Te Deum* at Notre Dame and in the evening to a grand
ball at the Hôtel de Ville, where the Queen, the Dauphin, and
the Dauphine were in the King's party dancing downstairs, while
Madame d'Etioles, who had not yet been presented at court, had
to content herself with supper served in a private room—and with
the letters patent that she had in her pocket, granting her the
marquisate of Pompadour.

On the following Tuesday, Richelieu was at Versailles, still in
attendance on the King and waiting, in common with hundreds
of others, for the presentation of the new marquise by the
princesse de Conti, the same dowager who had been so upset at
the company that she found herself in at the Dauphin's ball. She
had been reconciled to her present task by the promise that the
King would pay off her debts. Long before the appointed time—
six in the evening—the *galerie des glaces*, the *oeil de boeuf*, and
the *chambre de parade* were crowded with courtiers, all hoping
that the new, lowborn mistress would make some ludicrous mistake in the unfamiliar and infinitely complicated court procedure
and language. The throng grew so dense that when the princesse
de Conti arrived, she had to thrust her way through by sheer force
of elbows. She was followed by her own lady-in-waiting and by
Madame de Chau-Montauban, Madame d'Estrades, and the new
Madame de Pompadour, all of them in full court dress and agleam
with diamonds. The princesse de Conti struggled through the
outer rooms and into the *cabinet du conseil*, where the King, in
accordance with custom, was seated in an armchair with his back
to the fireplace.

The princess made the presentation, and the marquise de

Pompadour advanced, making three curtsies as she did so. She looked nervous, and the King was more shifty-eyed than usual. After only a few words of conversation, she withdrew; the small flotilla re-formed and, with a rustle of silks and glitter of jewels, walked back through the banks of outthrust faces and hard, intent eyes to the Queen's apartments, where Maria Leczynska greeted her so graciously that the new mistress was quite over-come and, as she knelt to kiss the hem of the Queen's gown, pulled off her glove so clumsily that she broke her bracelet. Not even the barely civil greeting that she received from the Dauphin, whom some onlookers claimed to have seen sticking his tongue out at her, could spoil her pleasure. It is to Pompadour's credit, whatever her motives may have been, that she always treated the mild-mannered, unhappy Queen with the utmost respect.

There was now so much goodwill in the royal ménage that when Pompadour and Louis went to stay at Choisy later in the month, the Queen did them both the honour of going there to dinner. Richelieu and Pompadour were guests at her table, and Louis came over after the meal to talk and show her the recent alterations in the house which the King's mistresses knew so well and the Queen scarcely at all. Afterwards she went to the parish church for a two-hour service and returned contentedly to Ver-sailles late that evening.

In October, Louis moved on to Fontainebleau, where the court usually spent six weeks each autumn, and Pompadour was given the ground-floor rooms formerly occupied by Marie-Anne. Ma-dame de Lauraguais and Richelieu had adjoining apartments over-looking the *jardin de Diane* on one side and the *cour des fontaines* on the other, a sign of favour since they had once been those of the duc d'Orléans and the duc de Chartres. The gossips, noticing that the King's dinner guests were being changed more frequently and that Richelieu was less often in his company, took this to indi-cate that Richelieu was falling from grace and being replaced by the duc d'Ayen, who was assiduous in his attentions to Pompa-dour. A more likely explanation is that Richelieu was too occupied with his plans for the invasion of Britain, a feat that would crown his exploit at Fontenoy and, he hoped, win him a marshal's baton.

Louis had long been impressed by the argument that the Stuarts were the only kings of England who had consistently shown friendship to France and already—early in 1744—he had given permission for an expedition to be mounted under the command of Saxe to invade the south-east of England. The vessels were dispersed by a storm, and the project was abandoned. The young Charles Edward Stuart waited disconsolately in Paris for a year, living on promises, until in July 1745 he secretly left for Scotland, where he raised the Stuart banner at the head of Loch Shiel on 19 August and on 17 September in Edinburgh was proclaimed Prince Regent on behalf of his father, James VIII. While he marched on into England with the victory of Prestonpans and the surrender of Carlisle behind him, the French began fitting out a new expedition to support him. It was undertaken with the customary lack of secrecy; by November, it was being widely discussed, and by December, anybody who wished could discover the details of its composition: eighteen battalions of infantry, nine squadrons of dragoons (including the Septimanie regiment that Richelieu had raised in Languedoc), an artillery train, and a great quantity of weapons, ammunition, and stores to be distributed to the rebellious Britons whom it was hoped to find on landing.

Richelieu asked Saxe to make diversions in Flanders, hoping to persuade the British that this was where the expedition was headed and trick them into leaving some of their troops there, but by now Whitehall knew as much about his plans as he did. After conferring with Saxe in Ghent in the last week of December, Richelieu moved to the Channel coast to organize the embarkations at Calais, Boulogne, and Dunkirk. A small convoy with 400 men of the Royal-Ecossais and 200 of the Irish brigade had successfully made land between Montrose and Peterhead after eleven days at sea; but the remaining ships were still in harbour awaiting troops and stores.

A body of marines arrived, but the naval officer in command at Calais produced regulations which forbade marines to be put aboard privateers and insisted that they must wait for regular men-o'-war. Richelieu protested to his old enemy, Maurepas, who was still Minister of Marine, and soon there were great drifts of correspondence shifting backwards and forwards between Versailles and the coast, between Richelieu and Maurepas and the marquis d'Argenson, who had been made Foreign Secretary the year before, and his younger brother, who was Minister of War, each shielding himself and blaming another. And to all these were added the plaints of the comte de Tressan, appointed to the command of the advance guard and thirsting for the opportunity to land at Dover and storm the castle, and alternatively begging Richelieu for a week's leave so that he could visit his mistress.

On 8 January, the younger Argenson sent Richelieu a letter that was evidently intended less for its recipient than for the record. He acknowledged two letters from Richelieu, "by which I see that not only is your situation still the same, but that you seem to discover each day new obstacles to the execution of your enterprise. You alone, Monsieur, since you are on the spot, can judge properly whether these obstacles are more or less difficult to overcome, and your zeal in the service of the King does not give H.M. any reason to doubt that you will make use of every means and resource in this enterprise whose importance you appreciate better than anybody else.

"H.M. is convinced, therefore, that you will not miss the first moment that seems favourable for you to embark and reach England, where, if the news is to be believed, Prince Edward is beginning to slow down in the progress that he has made, and would thus seem to have more need of the diversion. . . ." Prince Charles, or Prince Edward, as the French called him, was at that moment back in Stirling, pursued by Hanoverian troops.

While sending assurances of the King's confidence, Argenson made it clear that in his own opinion Richelieu was dragging his feet. "Until I received your last letter I thought that the spring tides began on the 6th or 7th of this month, and your letter of the 2nd appeared to confirm this opinion, since it informed me that you would profit by them to leave within four or five days. What is disturbing about this is that the longer your operation is delayed the more public it becomes, and allows the enemy even more time to counter your plans."

The enemy had known all about the operation at least three months earlier, thanks to the loose talk of everybody, including Argenson, but it was true that continued delay could only harm the prospects of success, and Richelieu took steps to ensure that all the blame was not laid at his door. Three weeks later, Argenson wrote, complaining that Richelieu's friends had been spreading a story that he had been ready to leave, but Argenson had held him up. Argenson protested that he had issued movement orders much earlier than usual and that the artillery had been either at Dunkirk or loaded on to canal barges at Ypres and Saint-Ouen before the end of November. If there had been any hitches caused by faulty naval cooperation, that was Maurepas's affair.

Saxe joined Richelieu in complaining about Argenson, alleging that the minister was more of a hindrance than a help; while Richelieu told his friends that it was all a plot by Argenson and Maurepas to discredit him. At the beginning of February, 700 men of Clare's regiment and Berwick's were ready to embark with medical stores and arms and munitions for the dissidents that they hoped to find awaiting them: two thousand pistols and sabres, forty cases of lead and twenty-six 200-pound barrels of cartridges. But the delays continued, aggravated by the reluctance of the naval officers to hazard their ships.

By the middle of the month, Richelieu had despaired of ever getting the main body afloat; he returned to Paris on the pretext of illness and wrote to Saxe saying that the obstacles were insurmountable, and he was restoring his troops to Saxe's command with the exception of the Irish regiments, whom it was still thought possible to embark. They left for Scotland at the beginning of March, but their cause was already lost. On 16 April, the Duke of Cumberland won the only victory of his inglorious career on the grey heath of Culloden.

Richelieu was disappointed of his marshal's baton; the court sniggered over the malicious verses written about the fiasco; there were some cynical songs in the streets—and that was all. The expedition, never really begun, had therefore never really failed; it was just one of the many unhappy projects that went amiss in this unhappy reign. From May until June, Richelieu was in attendance on the King in Flanders, where Saxe overran Brabant and captured Antwerp and, after giving Richelieu command of one operation, criticized him for losing men through recklessness. It was not a cheerful campaign and, for those at the royal headquarters, made rather more mournful by the Dauphin's preoccupation with the approaching birth of his first child.

The Dauphine had never properly settled down at Versailles; her native haughtiness and her natural repugnance for the morals of the people around her kept her estranged from many of the members of her own household; she was lonely and frightened at the thought of the experience that awaited her. The Dauphin, who cared for her in an oafish, well-intentioned way, tried to comfort her by canvassing all the men he met, asking them if they had been present at their wives' *accouchements*, if the women had screamed and suffered much, if the birth had been preceded or followed by much pain. He derived a morbid satisfaction out of these interrogations, and, since everybody he questioned knew the reason for his asking, each assured him that nothing untoward had happened, so that in the end he had formed a truly remarkable picture of childbirth. "Cheer up," he would say to his wife. "Madame ——— had the most jolly lying-in imaginable; her husband has just been giving me the details."

In his eagerness for information, he was sometimes careless about the people to whom he put his questions: an army chaplain, for instance, who blushed in an interesting way; the duc de Gesvres, the butt of so many court jokes, who had been divorced for impotence more than thirty years before, after a long and painfully frank inquiry. And in the end his confidence and his assurances to his wife proved to be ill-founded. The Dauphine gave birth to a daughter on 19 July and died three days afterwards, without having known much happiness in less than twenty years of living. The Dauphin was heart-broken. Whenever her name was mentioned or some object reminded him of her, he burst into tears and assured those around him that he could never forget her.

While the palace was in mourning for the dead Dauphine, Richelieu was progressing with a love affair whose ingenuity and audacity made a great impression on his contemporaries and which a later age commemorated in a play: the cuckolding of La Pouplinière. Alexandre-Jean-Joseph le Riche de la Pouplinière was one of the forty farmers-general who bought from the state the right to collect various indirect taxes and shared the profits among themselves; he was a man of great wealth, a patron of the arts, and some dozen years before had taken as his mistress a young actress named Thérèse Deshayes, whose mother, Mimi Dancourt, was a friend of Madame de Tencin. Madame de Tencin, never able to resist meddling in other people's affairs, decided to make an honest woman of her friend's daughter, and, when the contracts of the farmers-general came up for renewal, she threatened La Pouplinière that she would use her influence to have him dropped from the list unless he promised to marry Thérèse. It was no great hardship. He was forty-five and she twenty-four at the time of their wedding in 1737; she was as intelligent as she was beautiful and presided with grace and wit over the town house opposite the Royal Library in the rue de Richelieu and over the country estate at Passy where her husband built a theatre in which he produced his own and his friends' plays.

Among their frequent guests were the painters La Tour and Vanloo; Vanloo's wife, who created the vogue for Italian songs and singers; the incompatible twins, Rameau and Voltaire; the ambitious Madame d'Etioles, whose passion for amateur theatricals equalled their own; the maréchal de Saxe and the duc de Richelieu. La Pouplinière offered a particularly warm welcome to Richelieu, for the First Gentleman was in charge of the King's companies of actors, as well as of court entertainments, and might use his influence to get one of the farmer-general's plays produced in public. Richelieu's amatory reputation did not worry him, for he knew that Thérèse was frigid by nature, refusing his own infrequent demands now that she was no longer impelled by cupidity to accept them. Enfeebled by earlier excesses, he was willing to accept his wife's refusals so long as he could enjoy the envy in other men's eyes; and he watched contentedly as she turned down one distinguished suitor after another, among them Saxe's and Richelieu's close friend, Meuse.

Had La Pouplinière understood Richelieu's character better he would have realized that this was precisely the sort of challenge that he could never resist accepting. There were still very few women who could withstand him when he really set his mind to it, and sometime in 1744 he successfully seduced Thérèse in an armchair which he had given her and which she thenceforth kept as a love-totem in her boudoir. This cold, unkindled, desirable woman suddenly discovered that she had fallen in love, desperately, deeply, without restraint. She wrote Richelieu passionate letters, visited him at his *petite maison*. Inevitably, La Pouplinière was told one day that his wife was in the habit of receiving Richelieu in private and for long periods. He forbade Thérèse to see Richelieu, and she assented so meekly that his suspicions increased and he had her watched. On 22 April 1746, just before Richelieu left for Flanders, La Pouplinière's spies told him that Thérèse had spent the afternoon in the *petite maison* at Clichy.

There were guests for supper that evening in the mansion in the rue de Richelieu, and nobody noticed anything unusual in La Pouplinière's sulky behaviour; he had often been bad-tempered recently. But when all the company except one of Thérèse's women friends had left, he flew into a fury, accusing his wife of disobeying and betraying him; as she got up from the table, he boxed her ears with such force that she fell to the floor. Her friend began to protest but was given such a thundering cuff in her turn that she ran out of the house and went in search of Richelieu; La Pouplinière returned to his wife, who was still lying on the floor, and kicked her repeatedly in the face and chest until his rage was exhausted, hurting her so badly that her doctors had to bleed her three times the next day and twice more within the following twenty-four hours.

Richelieu was in a quandary. He could not go to plead for Thérèse or offer her his protection, because La Pouplinière was a common man behaving in a common way; it was even possible that he might so far forget himself as to strike Richelieu, who could scarcely demean himself by demanding satisfaction in a duel. He could, indeed, draw very unfavourable comparisons between La Pouplinière's vulgar outburst and his own conduct when he caught his first wife misbehaving.

A nobleman, in his less formal moments, might punch his wife in the head or kick her in the ribs, but he would do it strictly privately and without fuss, and seldom for such a frivolous reason as suspecting her of adultery. He would take it for granted that his wife would have a lover, and perhaps several. (The elderly Monsieur de Barcançon was showing his contemporary, the duchesse de la Vallière, round his garden one day, when he suddenly halted his gouty promenade and told her that as a handsome young man he had been madly in love with her. "Oh, my God," said the duchesse, "why didn't you speak up? You could have had me just as all the others did.")

Since Richelieu deemed it unwise to call on La Pouplinière himself, he persuaded his old friend the duchesse de Boufflers to represent him. But La Pouplinière was not to be appeased or persuaded. He was still in a tearing rage, and, when Madame de Boufflers reproached him for having treated his wife so brutally, he answered that in a few weeks' time, when she was recovered from that dose, he would give her the same treatment again. It was with matters in this unsatisfactory state that Richelieu had been forced to leave Paris and attend the King at the wars, but as soon as he returned, and was firmly refused admission to La Pouplinière's by the *concierge*, he began to plan the continued cuckoldry of the impertinent farmer-general.

By a stroke of good fortune, the house next door to La Pouplinière's became vacant, and Richelieu rented it under an assumed name, putting in a caretaker who did not know his identity and entering it only in disguise. The whole affair had a rejuvenating effect on him, and he resorted not only to disguises but to a stratagem which he had first used thirty years before—and in this same rue de Richelieu—when he found a way of entering Mademoiselle de Valois's bedroom by way of her jam cupboard. He ensured communications with Thérèse by the seduction of her maid, Mademoiselle Dufour (although, to conserve his energies, he entrusted this task to his Italian valet, Stefano); and he prepared to make an entry into Thérèse's boudoir from an adjoining room on the second floor of his own house.

This time there was no convenient jam cupboard to cover a gap in the wall, and the furniture could not be disturbed, for fear of arousing the suspicions of her jealous husband. But Richelieu had brisk powers of invention in these matters, and one evening two masons, who had been collected in a hired carriage and driven to Richelieu's house with their eyes blindfolded, were taken up to the second-floor room, where they removed the back of the fireplace on his side and on Thérèse's and replaced hers with a similar sheet of iron mounted on hinges and bolted on Richelieu's side. The work was completed in a single night when La Pouplinière was away from home, and from that time forward Richelieu would tap on his side of the iron backplate, wait for Thérèse's answering tap to signal that the coast was clear, and then slide back the bolt; when he emerged from the chimney to join Thérèse in one house, Mademoiselle Dufour made the reverse journey to Stefano in the other.

§ 4

The Dauphine was no sooner dead than the King, his ministers, and most of the court were busy with projects for the remarriage of the Dauphin, to ensure the succession and to cater to the lumpish Bourbon lust for women. The Dauphin, a simple fellow prepared in principle to show affection to any woman put into bed with him, was for the moment too upset to take part in the discussions, but the choice was easy to make, although it was kept secret for some months. Augustus of Saxony, who had evicted Maria Leczynska's father from the throne of Poland for the second time, had recently signed peace terms with Frederick of Prussia and, in return for a three-year subsidy of three million livres and Louis's promise to address him as "Majesty," was willing to revoke his alliance with Austria. Louis accepted the proposal and suggested that the new friendship should be cemented by marrying the Dauphin to Augustus's 15-year-old daughter, Marie-Josèphe. As compensation to Richelieu for having been deprived of the honour of fetching the Spanish infanta after his disgrace at Metz, and also because he was endowed with the graces that most became a royal emissary, the King appointed him his special ambassador to go to Dresden and bring the Saxon princess home. Richelieu was also to have secret talks with her father on the possibility of his negotiating peace between France and Austria.

The news struck terror into the heart of Augustus, who was

almost bankrupt and well aware of Richelieu's taste for luxury. Entertaining him on a suitable scale, Augustus complained, would take a large bite out of the first year's subsidy that Louis was giving him. His prime minister, von Brühl, sent anxious dispatches to the Saxon ambassador in Paris, von Loos, imploring him to do his best to have Richelieu's appointment cancelled. But it was too late; the King's decision had been made known; and on 8 December 1746, Richelieu left for Dresden with an entourage that included twelve gentlemen of noble birth, eighty-four pages, half-a-dozen running footmen, fifty ordinary footmen, and a dozen of his favourite *heyduques* in their romantic Hungarian costumes. Everywhere on the journey he was greeted with royal honours, which he received with better grace than his master would have shown, and a great deal of relish. As von Loos had written to von Brühl: "The courtesies shown to the duc de Richelieu will make a great impression on his mind; he is vain and by flattering and applauding his magnificence he can easily be won over, since he prides himself on being one of the grandest seigneurs of the realm."

He arrived in Dresden on the evening of Christmas Day, and on 27 December reported to the elder Argenson (who was replaced a few days later at the Ministry of Foreign Affairs) on the secret part of his mission and also on the future Dauphine: "I think that her face will be found pleasing in France, and particularly her grace. . . . She speaks French very badly." To the maréchal de Saxe, who was the princess's uncle on the wrong side of the blanket, he was more explicit: "I found her charming; she is not in any way a beauty, but she has every imaginable grace; a large nose, full, fresh lips, the most lively and witty eyes in the world, and indeed I assure you that if there were any like her at the Opéra there would be a scramble to bid for them."

His letters were shown to Louis who, far from taking offence at Richelieu's comparison of his future daughter-in-law with a dancer at the Opéra, wrote to him from Versailles on 4 January: "I am most eager to see her, and my son to hold her; for he says that it is high time that his bachelor state ended and the final days are always the most difficult to bear. If she had been put up to auction, would you once upon a time have been among those who cast covetous eyes on her? Certainly her bosom must be well developed to have roused your interest. My son has set his heart on her and I gather that he would prefer her to be sweet-smelling: he has urged Madame de Brancas" [the bride's *dame d'honneur*, who was to meet her at Strasbourg] "to see that she has a bath before he meets her, which confirms my suspicion that the poor late-lamented did not do this often enough."

The distasteful style that Louis favoured in his letters to Richelieu sprang from his admiration for him as a *dompteur de femmes*. The King was still timid and quite restricted in the scope of his lechery; at thirty-six he had had fewer mistresses than most of the men at his court; he contemplated Richelieu's score with the awe of a small boy, and tried to adopt a man-of-the-world blend of wit and cynicism which he hoped would impress his friend the duc. When, for instance, Richelieu reported that the duc d'Ayen had taken a new mistress, Louis wrote back: "*S'il éjacule autant qu'il sue, j'estime la pauvre fille au moins hydropique.*" It was usually rather clumsy, adolescent stuff, but he got pleasure from it and Richelieu was only too ready to pretend to be vastly amused by it, although he sometimes received an uncomfortable sideswipe: such as the suggestion that he would *once upon a time* have coveted the young princess. Richelieu was not pleased at being patronized in matters of sex by a man only fourteen years his junior.

On 7 January, Richelieu made his official entry into Dresden to offer the Dauphin's proposal of marriage. It was the pomp and splendour of Vienna all over again: the ornate procession, the resplendent costumes, the uniformed attendants casting handfuls of money into the gaping crowds. In the evening he entertained the royal family in the palace that they had lent him. Outside, fountains spouted red wine and white; inside, a choir sang the cantata *Amor Insuperabile*. After the guests had retired to the salons, the citizens of Dresden were admitted to inspect the superbly decorated banqueting hall, where some fingered and then filched the figures carved in icing sugar that adorned the tables. When his servants came to warn him of what was going on, Richelieu ordered that no action should be taken; shortly afterwards, he was told that one or two of the smaller but valuable objects— he had brought a large quantity of silver forks and spoons and dishes from his stocks in Paris and Montpellier—had begun to disappear. With a truly seignorial wave of his hand, he ordered that there should be no interference with the pleasures of the good people of Dresden; within a few minutes, they had stripped the dining room of every piece of silver in it.

The next two days were taken up with more secret talks and with the presentation of the procuration authorizing the bride's brother to wed her on behalf of the Dauphin, the signing of the marriage contract, and the exchange of presents. The wedding took place on the 10th, at five o'clock in the afternoon in one of the state apartments, since the Catholic chapel in the palace of this preponderantly Lutheran state (the bride's grandfather had changed his religion to qualify for the throne of Poland) was too small to accommodate all the guests. Richelieu and his retinue toured the palace until eight o'clock, presenting their compliments to the numerous members of the royal family (the House of Saxony's excellent record for fertility had been checked by the French foreign ministry before the marriage was mooted). Then they all sat down to a gargantuan wedding feast. The meal, punctuated by the boom of jubilant gunfire, included 143 different dishes, among them such delicacies as pigs' ears and cows' udders in orange sauce, and was followed by a ceremonial torch dance in the ballroom where, to the accompaniment of drum and trumpet, gunfire without and belches within, the royal party marched round two by two in order of precedence, carrying flaming and stinking torches, which dripped wax on to clothes, now and then set fire to wigs, and brought still brighter hues to sweaty cheeks already crimson with too much food and drink. It was not a setting in which the French envoy-extraordinary could feel himself entirely at home.

In the morning of 14 January, after a round of farewell visits, the young Dauphine descended the palace steps with Richelieu on one side and the commander-in-chief of her father's Polish army on the other. Her mother, her sister, the princess Maria-Anna, and her brothers, the princes Xavier and Karl, burst into tears; and her father wore a look of deep satisfaction, as Richelieu's imposing cavalcade, escorted by a squadron of Saxon cavalry, set off on the long winding route to Strasbourg, where he presented to the Dauphine her new household, among whom the preponderance of his old mistresses and rake-helly friends—Madame de Brancas, Madame de Lauraguais, the maréchal de la Fare—gave proof of his continuing favour with the King. Madame de Brancas, after one look at the girl's pale, lightly freckled, somewhat blotchy skin, suggested that it would benefit greatly in French eyes from a lavish application of rouge (and later, no doubt, broached the subject of a bath).

Their progress through France was accompanied by receptions and rustic rejoicings, the Dauphine dining in public attended by Richelieu and La Fare. At Troyes, soon after she had sat down to her state meal in the bishop's palace, Madame de Brancas handed her a letter that had just arrived by courier. The Dauphine broke the seal, unfolded the paper, read it, and then, to the surprise and interest of the onlookers, burst into tears and hurried from the room. It was all an unhappy misunderstanding: Madame de Brancas, recognizing the Dauphin's handwriting and seal, had assumed that the letter was for his wife, but it was in fact for herself. In it, the Dauphin thanked the duchesse for her eulogies of the princess, but—his sentimental nature having been touched by the thought of marrying twice in two years—he added that whatever charms she might prove to have she would never succeed in making him forget his beloved Maria Theresa.

It was on this sad note that she met Louis and the Dauphin, who rode out from Choisy to greet her: the King kindly and attentive but the Dauphin stony-faced and miserable despite the girl's clumsy attempts to flirt with him. At Choisy, she was presented to the Queen and Madame de Pompadour, and the whole party moved on to Versailles, where the château was more brightly lit than ever, for in the previous month the old lanterns with their yellow candles had been replaced by new lamps burning colza-oil. Next morning her tiring-women spent three hours getting her into a wedding dress so heavily embroidered and so thickly encrusted with jewels that the skirt alone weighed thirty pounds more than a cavalryman's cuirass. The wedding was soon after midday, and, when they had received congratulations and taken dinner with the King's daughters, the newly married couple went to the ball in the *manège de la grande écurie*. To the surprise of the other guests, the Dauphin opened the ball with his sister, Madame Henriette; it had been a long, cold journey from Dresden and the bride was suffering from chilblains.

The dancing ended at nine, when the King rose and led the way in to supper; after supper Madame de Brancas accompanied the Dauphine to her room for the ceremony of putting the bride to bed, the *femme-de-chambre* handing the nightgown to the duchesse de Chartres, the duchesse de Chartres to the Queen, and the Queen to the Dauphine. The Dauphin, his premature obesity emphasized by the nightshirt in which he also had been formally arrayed, was then brought in; the young couple disappeared from view behind the bed curtains; the doors were opened to admit all who had the right of *entrée*; and the curtains were drawn apart again. For minutes on end the courtiers stared at the fat young prince and his foreign bride; and while Marie-Josèphe stared composedly back, the Dauphin put his head under the bedclothes.

When the onlookers had been shepherded out and the ladies-in-waiting had drawn the curtains round the bed once more, the Dauphin's head emerged from the blankets, and Marie-Josèphe saw that he had been crying. "Let your tears flow," she said to him in her halting French, remembering the letter that she had read by mistake at Tours. "Do not fear that I shall be offended; on the contrary, they show me what I may hope to merit myself, if I have the good fortune to win your esteem." The Dauphin dried his tears and, like a good Bourbon, settled down to enjoy what Providence had sent him; but, as Saxe reported to the Elector next day, "nothing happened during the night, despite the enterprise of M. le Dauphin, and all ended with much disturbance and no sleep." The Dauphin seemed gloomier and more gawky than ever at their first public dinner and the subsequent ball which went on till dawn, but the next evening, when Saxe was working with Richelieu and von Loos on the Austrian negotiations, Louis summoned the marshal to his study. "The job's done," the King told him. "She's Madame la Dauphine. It happened this afternoon."

Richelieu played an increasingly large part in foreign affairs during the months that followed: the marquis de Puyzieulx, who had succeeded the elder Argenson as Foreign Secretary, caught smallpox and Richelieu continued to work on the Austrian project with the senior under-secretary, without informing Maurepas, who replaced Puyzieulx during his absence. Richelieu, dreaming of military preferment, had hoped to be given a marshal's baton on his return from Dresden, but his hints were ignored; when he accompanied Louis to Flanders on yet another campaign in May 1747, it was still as an aide-de-camp. It was only when the maréchal de Boufflers died in Genoa of smallpox, and the maréchal de Noailles urged Richelieu's claims as his successor, that he was at last given command of an army, rather grudgingly, since Louis had a higher opinion of him as a witty companion than as a general.

Richelieu passed through Paris towards the end of August and sailed from Monaco early in September; after a hazardous voyage in which he was almost captured by a British man-o'-war and his ship nearly sunk in a storm, he arrived at Genoa to find the situation far from rosy. During the previous year, the combined French and Spanish armies in Italy had been heavily defeated by the Austrians at Piacenza and chased back over the Var. The Austrians marched on deep into Provence, and Toulon and Marseille were saved only by a successful uprising in Genoa, which threatened the Austrian bases. From February 1747 onwards, the French had been slipping scratch battalions past the British naval patrols in the Mediterranean, but these were unable to prevent the Austrians from surrounding Genoa. Renewed French attacks in the west relieved some of the pressure, but when Richelieu took over command of the garrison of 14,000 men—7,000 French, 4,000 Spanish and 3,000 Genoese—the town was still threatened by several concentrations of Austrian troops in surrounding fortresses.

After a lavish reception in the Doge's palace, Richelieu inspected the town fortifications and gave orders for new work to be put in hand. But a defensive war was completely alien to his nature, and he at once began to plan turning the tables on the Austrians by besieging their principal base at Campo-Freddo. He organized four columns, whose duties were to lay the siege, to cover the besiegers, and to provide diversions, while the villagers along the route were ordered to mend the roads sufficiently for guns to be brought along them. Richelieu, at the head of one of the siege parties, led his men by night to Marcharolo and learned on arrival that all his columns had reached their set positions, only one having had to fight an engagement on the way.

The investment was complete; all that remained was to dig the approach trenches, set up the guns, and batter and charge a way into the town. But first he must bring up the guns, and it now appeared that, despite Richelieu's orders, the independent-minded peasantry of the Genoese Republic had failed to mend the roads and refused to be coerced into doing so. While he sat impotently outside the walls of Campo-Freddo, Genoa was open to attack; after a conference with his corps commanders, he returned dejectedly to his base.

He was preoccupied with the next Austrian attack, which he was sure would come as soon as they had brought up reinforcements and might be launched from any direction, for the Genoese Republic, a thin strip of land crushed against the Mediterranean by the weight of Piedmont and Parma, was surrounded by enemies on all sides, even by the British at sea. His own feeling was that the attack would come from the east, and he spent much time on detailed inspection of the frontier defences, though he was also at Genoa sufficiently frequently to enjoy the favours of one of the dancers at the Opéra.

Whenever couriers could slip through the British blockade, he received passionate letters from Thérèse de la Pouplinière, whose love for him had grown even greater in his absence. In January she complained that he wrote coldly to her. He protested that this was not true, and next month she replied: "My dearest heart, you love me more than anyone you have ever loved. But is that true? I always fear that it is only the kindness of your heart that prompts you to say such things to comfort me and lend me patience. . . . I long for you with such impatience, and it grows so from day to day, that I scarcely know how to last out until nightfall, and from night to morning, and then to the end of the week, the end of the month. Oh, my love, what torture!"

She was worried about her health and feared that she had cancer as a result of the beatings her husband had given her. "The maréchal [de Saxe] was urging me yesterday to have a cautery. I did not answer him. In the end he said, 'If the trouble comes from a blow, do nothing; but if it is in the blood then a cautery is very necessary.' To get rid of him, I said into his ear, 'Monsieur, I shall do nothing of the kind.' That silenced him. . . . In any case, I do not want it; its usefulness is less apparent than its unpleasantness."

A new surgeon had come to examine her and had gone away shaking his head. "I am much tempted to give up everything and await my fate. . . . Sweetheart, if this should be my last letter, as I always fear it will be, do not worry about me and be convinced of my love—it grows with every moment and will endure as long as I live. As you shall see when you return."

To avoid her husband's watchful eyes, the correspondence with Richelieu was handled by Thérèse's maid, Dufour, and Richelieu's valet, Stefano, who had remained in Paris; it was carried to and from Genoa in Richelieu's personal mail or in that of Guymond, the French Minister. But Thérèse was nervous and fidgety, worried about her health and yearning for her lover; she began to suspect that Guymond was talking too much; then she warned Richelieu that Stefano had another sweetheart and that Dufour was complaining that he did not pay her enough attention. She caught Dufour searching her clothes and discharged her: "The slut was reading and keeping all my letters, taking them out of my pockets when I went riding," she wrote to Richelieu. "What risks I have been running!" In April, she sent him another agitated note: the pain in her breast was worse and she was suspicious of Stefano; she begged Richelieu not to employ him as a messenger any more.

In Genoa there were other problems. Richelieu now had sixteen

French battalions and eight Spanish under his command and had formed another from Austrian deserters. Still gravely outnumbered, he persuaded the Piedmontese to agree to the immediate exchange of prisoners and then embarked on a series of raids, one of which, a land and water-borne attack on Viareggio, netted him the whole garrison of 409 Piedmontese, whom he at once exchanged for more than half a battalion of his own men. The Austrians attacked from the west and were repulsed with losses of four to one; then in June they advanced from the east in great strength, but once again he held them off. This time was the last, for the Austrians agreed to an armistice which came into force in the middle of the month.

Richelieu, with his usual impatience, asked to return to Versailles instead of remaining on in Genoa to supervise the armistice terms and guard against Austrian bad faith. Maréchal de Belle-Isle, writing to him "as I would to my brother," urged him not to do anything impetuous. "You must not spoil all the good you have done. You have won a great deal of honour and reputation; you have shown that you are capable of handling the most difficult affairs, both military and political. Your rivals are furious. . . ."

But Richelieu was in no mood to be sensible. He suspected that there were rewards for his success in Genoa that he might have begged from the King at Versailles but which he would not obtain from a distance. He changed his mind and decided to ask for permission to go to Rome and call on the Old Pretender, whose son he had tried to serve in 1746 and whose mother he had known at Saint-Germain. Belle-Isle wrote back in even greater agitation: "M. de Puyzieulx [the Foreign Secretary] is making mountains out of it because of the present situation; he claims that, commanding an army which has attracted so much attention, particularly in Italy, everybody is keeping an eye on your movements and that, if they see you paying a visit to King James, the English in London will take offence; they won't believe it is a private matter and it will have very bad consequences. M. d'Argenson has written me a personal letter in his own hand on the same lines; and adds that, not wishing to displease or contradict you, he will not say anything to you. . . ."

Forbidden to return to Versailles or even make the journey to Rome, Richelieu had to be content with receiving the title of Nobleman from the Genoese and having his name inscribed in the Republic's Book of Gold, while waiting for the completion of the statue that they had ordered and proposed to put up in the main square. He continued to bombard Belle-Isle, the Tencins, Argenson, Puyzieulx, anybody and everybody with complaints of the treatment that he was receiving, protesting that his services merited a better reward. And in October he received it: permission to return home and a letter from the King promising him a marshal's baton. He arrived in France just in time to open the *Etats* of Languedoc on 24 November. In Paris, Thérèse eagerly awaited him.

Thérèse, her whole life transformed now that she could count on seeing her lover early in the new year, gaily accepted Saxe's invitation to be his guest at a review on 28 November of the Uhlan regiment which he had raised and which was quartered at Saint-Denis. The day was eventful from every point of view. To give the Uhlans more space for their manoeuvres, the review took place not on the usual Plaine des Sablons but in some fields southwest of the Etoile, to the detriment of the vines and late autumn crops that had been growing there. A vast square of land was cordoned off by the French and Swiss guards who, resentful at having to line the arena for foreign troops, dealt so firmly with any spectators who tried to push past them that several people were badly bruised with musket butts, and one fashionable gentleman was carried away dead from a bayonet wound. The jumble of carriages became so impenetrable that later arrivals had to climb down into the cold, sticky mud in order to get a glimpse of the proceedings and were relieved when, at 2:30 p.m. Louis arrived from La Muette with Saxe, who was dressed in the uniform of colonel of the Uhlans: green, with Hungarian boots, a pinchbeck helmet with a horsehair plume and a turban of Russian leather: a sight that stirred many feminine hearts. His troops carried pistols and ten-foot lances, the colonel's company being composed entirely of Negroes on white horses; from 2:30 until they were lost to view in the autumn dusk, they wheeled, trotted, and executed mock engagements with the aid of their artillery drawn in light carts. Despite the mud and damp, the spectators cheered up a little and agreed that it was a very pretty display.

La Pouplinière had refused to accept Saxe's invitation to the review, on a plea of urgent business; but in fact he was employing the afternoon in an examination of Thérèse's boudoir. After the treacherous Dufour had been dismissed, she had blackmailed Thérèse into paying her a pension on condition that she did not inform La Pouplinière of Thérèse's correspondence with Richelieu, but as soon as she heard of Richelieu's return, Thérèse ceased payment and told Dufour she would get no more—rather belatedly, since Dufour seems to have been receiving a retainer from La Pouplinière from the earliest days to spy on Thérèse. Knowing that the secret of the chimney was almost impossible to discover from La Pouplinière's side of the wall—all the bolts and visible parts of the hinges having been fixed on Richelieu's side—Dufour planned to frighten Thérèse, while thriftily reserving some information for later, by telling La Pouplinière to "ask Madame the secret of her boudoir." La Pouplinière, scarcely on speaking terms with his wife, decided to inspect the boudoir himself, taking with him his lawyer, Ballot, and the celebrated mechanical engineer, Vaucanson, who had often helped him with his theatrical presentations.

It was Ballot who noticed that, although the boudoir floor had been carpeted and the room was evidently intended to be put to winter use, there was neither fuel nor kindling in the grate. He struck the back of the fireplace with his stick and remarked on the hollow sound. At this point one of the servants hurried out of the house to find Thérèse to tell her what was going on.

By the time the catastrophic news reached her, the light was failing and the rain was beginning to drench the Uhlans, the resentful French and Swiss guardsmen, and the thinning ranks of spectators. She sat in damp misery until the end of the parade, not daring to return home alone. She told Saxe what had happened, and he gallantly offered to escort her, but, when they arrived at the house in the rue de Richelieu and Saxe knocked at the door, he was told by the *concierge* that the servants had been given instructions that Madame de la Pouplinière was not to be admitted. "You know me, man!" Saxe bellowed. "And you know there is no door that can be closed against me!" He pushed the door open and bowed to Thérèse: "Come, Madame, enter your home."

It was soon clear that it was not to be her home much longer. Her husband came rushing towards them, wild-eyed and stuttering with fury; and, although Saxe tried to calm him, pointing out that a public scandal would do nobody any good, La Pouplinière was beyond reason. After the servant had left to warn Thérèse, Vaucanson had examined the grate and discovered the secret of the hinged backplate, kneeling with his head thrust into the chimney piece, transfixed with admiration at the workmanship, while his host strode up and down in a frenzy of jealousy and rage. La Pouplinière told Saxe that he was prepared to pay Thérèse an allowance of 8,000 livres a year and give her 4,000 livres to buy some furniture, but he would not allow her to remain in his house or to take anything from it.

The boudoir that she had prepared for the reception of her lover, the *bergère* in which she had dreamed of being once more enfolded in his arms—she would see them no more. She went to stay with her mother in the Chaussée d'Antin for a while, and then found an apartment in the rue Ventadour, where Richelieu, still in Languedoc, sent her money to tide her over until she could manage to get a larger allowance from her husband. Soon Paris was ringing with songs about Richelieu's latest exploit and the toy-sellers were offering tiny models of chimneys with revolving backplates, some of them made of gold or decorated with precious stones and much admired as novel Christmas presents. "Nothing was ever better invented," Louis wrote to him in admiration, "and it was easy to identify the inventor. I regret not having seen it myself, for I could not have resisted trying it. But you must console yourself that you will henceforward be able to get your little comforts more easily and without spoiling your clothes with soot."

§ 5

Richelieu returned to Versailles at the end of the year ready for his second tour of duty as First Gentleman and for a decisive battle with Madame de Pompadour. The atmosphere at court was electric, for the new mistress had already shown that she intended to rule in every department of state as well as in the King's life, to dictate to ministers as well as to courtiers, while it was common knowledge that Richelieu believed the moment propitious for him to make a bid for power and, though the prospect of his succeeding pleased nobody, many of the politicians were agreed on supporting him as a means of getting rid of Pompadour. As the elder Argenson wrote in his diary: "He arrives covered with glory and with a reputation for prudence won in the defence of Genoa; he has found reward and renown in the baton of a Marshal of France and in the statues that have been raised to him at Genoa. Here is something to make Madame de Pompadour tremble! All her supporters fear his coming and he is considered capable of striking a strong blow for the glory and security of the realm, of sweeping away the lowborn, tyrannical mistress and putting another in her place."

When the King kept him talking in private until 2 a.m. on the day that he arrived, it was clear that Richelieu had retained all his old ascendancy despite fifteen months of absence. His ante-rooms were crowded with suitors soliciting the honour of attending at his own *lever* and, as he made his way to the King's apartments, his path was hedged with obsequiously bowed heads. But the reputation for prudence that had so impressed and surprised Argenson did not last long. As so often in his life, Richelieu found it impossible to ignore a challenge, although the dispute was of no importance; and he now got himself involved in a quarrel with Pompadour which had no connection with the very real grievances against her and in which he was almost certain to be de-feated.

Although Pompadour had first attracted Louis by her beauty, it was by her ingenuity in providing him with distractions that she continued to hold him. She realized that the changes of scene that his moody nature craved, satisfied with the incessant journeying from one royal abode to another, needed to be supplemented by a change of interest. This she supplied by staging plays, ballet, and opera, performed by amateurs for the King's intimate circle; in these she had an opportunity to entrance him still further with her near-professional talent. Amateur theatricals were no new thing at court; they had been presented at Marly and in the comtesse de la Marck's apartments at Versailles. But almost always they had been for the amusement of the players rather than the audience; Pompadour brought to them a new brilliance, lavishness, and expertise.

At first she had these entertainments performed in a small gallery leading off the *cabinet des médailles* (which served as a dressing room) but during the court's *voyage* to Fontainebleau in 1748, she had a larger and more convenient theatre constructed, which could be put up in twenty-four hours and dismantled in seventeen, on the magnificent but infrequently used *escalier des ambassadeurs*. She appointed one of her favourites, the duc de la Vallière, as director of the theatre: a flagrant breach of the privileges of the Gentlemen of the Bedchamber, who controlled all official entertainments given in the royal palaces and were also responsible for the *escalier des ambassadeurs* since it formed part of the King's apartments and was used every New Year's Day for the solemn procession of the chevaliers du Saint-Esprit in their rich velvet cloaks embroidered with gold and silver flames, as they marched to the annual service in the chapel.

News of Pompadour's action reached Richelieu before he left Genoa and, although he was not *en exercice* that year, he wrote a "very respectful but very firm" letter to Louis, protesting against the infringement; and as soon as he got to Versailles he threw himself into the fray. On 4 January 1749 he transferred the Queen's concert to the Dauphine's apartments from Pompadour's theatre on the staircase; at the same time, he warned the musicians of the royal chamber that they were not allowed to play elsewhere without specific permission from himself. Meeting La Vallière in public one day, Richelieu acidly asked him if he had been appointed Fifth Gentleman of the Bedchamber, and how much he had paid for the position. "For my own part," he added, "I have never received a franc and would not accept a million in return for one inch of my territory."

Argenson recorded gleefully that "he makes no bones about clashing with the little Pompadour and treating her like a wench from the Opéra, having had great experience with that sort of woman—as with every sort of woman. Though she is mistress of the King and dominates at court, he will torment her, he will wear her down, and already there is a change to be seen in the snubbing of her minion La Vallière." Argenson noted, too, that Richelieu was making outspoken attacks on two of Pompadour's protégés: Puyzieulx and Saint-Séverin, both of them ministers. He blamed them for the unfavourable terms of the Treaty of Aix-la-Chapelle, claiming that he could have got much better ones if he had been allowed to continue with the negotiations he began in Dresden two years before—which everybody knew to have been broken off because Pompadour wanted Louis to go to war. And, having blamed Pompadour for the treaty, he laid upon her shoulders the burden of shame for the way in which France had behaved towards the Young Pretender.

One of the conditions of the treaty had been that France should expel the Stuarts from her territory, and it was because of this that Richelieu had hoped to be allowed to go to Rome to offer his personal apologies to the Old Pretender. But Prince Charles Edward, who was still in Paris, refused to believe that he could be treated so shabbily and in December had still failed to leave. As he got out of his carriage at the Opéra one evening, he found himself pounced on by four guardsmen, who dragged him into the Palais Royal and there searched him, disarmed him and bound him hand and foot before bundling him into a coach and taking him under armed escort to Vincennes. White with rage, as the ropes were tied round his wrists he said: "You may do anything you wish; for you do not dishonour me, you dishonour yourselves." And in this the whole of France concurred, learning that he had subsequently been thrust across the border into Savoy, and feeling a sense of national humiliation at having been forced into this mean action by British pressure.

The Jacobites, many of whom were now linked by marriage with influential families, rallied to Richelieu, knowing that they would get no help from Louis as long as Pompadour reigned. The tide was flowing for him, and his confidence and arrogance grew daily. There was misery and discontent throughout the country. The taxes, inefficiently collected, were irresponsibly squandered; thousands of livres poured out of the national purse as the monstrous royal household straggled from one residence to another, stayed a few days, and then roamed on again. The vast sums that the King paid for the châteaux that he gave his mistress at Montretout, at La Celle, at Bellevue, at Crécy in Normandy, and the "Hermitages" that she built at Versailles, Fontainebleau, and Compiègne, and the mansions that she bought in Versailles and in the Champs-Elysées, were only a tiny proportion of what she expended on their decoration. There was no minister who would venture a criticism, for they owed their positions to her or knew that she was strong enough to have them dismissed; but the people in the street knew and, for the first time, the King was being continually attacked in rhymes and caricatures.

Richelieu continued to pay court to Pompadour, offering her elegant witticisms and polished compliments as if nothing had happened between them. But when Louis was setting off for a two-day visit to the "petit château" at La Celle, she begged that Richelieu should not be included in the party. Louis smiled and refused. "You don't know Monsieur de Richelieu," he said. "If you chase him out of the door, he comes back through the chimney."

During these two days at La Celle, the King spent a great deal of his time with Richelieu and observers contentedly watched Pompadour's vexation. Louis, who from his earliest days had shown destructive and sadistic tendencies, delighting as a boy in ripping the lace off his courtiers' sleeves, stamping on their gouty toes, firing a pistol close to the head of his pet deer, undoubtedly found pleasure in his mistress's distress; but he was her slave in the end. A few days later, when Richelieu was attending the débotter, Louis asked him casually: "How many times have you been sent to the Bastille? "Three times, Your Majesty," Richelieu replied. "And for what reasons?" Louis asked.

Richelieu took the hint. He had been preparing for a reversal and now spread the word that he had never opposed the use of Madame de Pompadour's theatre; that he considered the entertainments given there to be the personal and private amusements of Pompadour and therefore no concern of the First Gentlemen of the Bedchamber; that he had raised the matter only because it was his duty to ensure that the First Gentlemen did not lose any of their privileges; and that Pompadour and La Vallière had shown themselves so much in sympathy with his views that everything had been easily arranged: in future Madame de Pompadour would inform the First Gentleman of anything that she required, and he would pass the instructions on to the *intendant des menus plaisirs*. It was a piece of face-saving that deceived nobody. On the other hand, Richelieu had not entirely retired from the fight. He repeated his instructions that no orders from Pompadour or La Vallière were to be carried out without his permission. And late in January, during a visit to La Muette, when Pompadour retired to bed early with a sick headache, he relieved his feelings by jumping up and down on the floor of the room above hers.

Celebrations in honour of the Treaty of Aix-la-Chapelle were continued well into the new year, in the hope of convincing the populace that the peace had brought some profit to France, but many of them were as ill-fortuned as the peace itself. At the firework display on the quai Pelletier, there was a panic during which some of the spectators were crushed to death and others forced over the parapets and drowned, while the soldiers who had been sent to keep order took advantage of the confusion to carry off and rape several incautious young women. Richelieu, deputed to deliver a congratulatory address to the King, commissioned Voltaire to write it for him. The poet, unwilling to lose the credit, showed the speech to Madame de Boufflers, who took a copy of it and, either carelessly or through natural malice, showed it to some other academicians. When Richelieu began to deliver the address, he became conscious of whispering near at hand and was startled and annoyed to realize that an old enemy, the abbé d'Olivet, was reading the same speech, *sotto voce*, but with the difference that Olivet was one word ahead. Richelieu hesitated for a moment, then put down his script and continued with the speech impromptu.

As Easter approached, he was involved in an argument about the peers taking part in the ceremonies of the Last Supper and the Adoration of the Cross, on which the King had promised him satisfaction two years before and which the princes of the blood were opposing. Pompadour, who had her own quarrels with the princes, came out in favour of Richelieu, and this temporary alliance gave rise to rumours that she believed her influence to be waning. The names of possible successors were bandied about: the comtesse de Forcalquier, a very pretty woman who had been proposed as a rival to Madame de Mailly eight years before, and Pompadour's cousin by marriage, the marquise d'Entrades. Another group thought that Richelieu was planning to turn on Pompadour the trick that had been used against him at Metz: to direct Louis's thoughts towards religion and persuade him to exile his mistress and complete his Easter duties.

A common hatred for Pompadour had brought two of Richelieu's bitterest enemies—Argenson and Maurepas—much closer to him. Maurepas in particular was offended by Pompadour's highhanded treatment and took great exception to her ordering him "in the King's name" to cancel a *lettre de cachet*. He avenged himself by producing a punning quatrain which suggested that she was suffering from an unpleasant sexual disorder, but it had no sooner begun to circulate than the court witnessed a startling repercussion which left no doubt in anybody's mind about Pompadour's continuing authority. At his *lever* on 23 April, Louis went out of his way to be affable to Maurepas, a danger signal which the minister was too overconfident to notice. The King then left with Richelieu for a visit to La Celle and from there, at one o'clock in the morning, he sent a messenger to Argenson with a letter that he was ordered to hand to Maurepas personally. It was his dismissal; after more than a quarter of a century as a minister, he was sent into exile on his estate at Bourges.

Richelieu's position was unaffected by Maurepas's disgrace; indeed, since they had been bitter enemies so long, it could be read as a point in his favour. The King's friendship was warmer than

ever, and Richelieu excited envy and won himself a few more enemies by constantly parading in the Bellevue uniform of purple
and gold that was reserved for the King's intimate companions, or
the green and gold that was worn at Choisy, Crécy, La Muette
and La Celle. When Louis returned to La Muette from Compiègne (the farthest that his voyages ever took him), Richelieu
entertained him at dinner in the *petite maison* in the rue de
Clichy. Pompadour came with him, and again a fortnight later
when they took supper at the house that Richelieu had built himself at Gennevilliers since being appointed lieutenant of the royal
hunt.

In September he was out hunting with Louis at Rambouillet,
and many gossips were convinced that he was about to be named
First Minister. There was further proof of his influence when he
persuaded Machault, the *contrôleur-général*, to send for La Pouplinière and threaten to remove him from the list of farmers-
general if he did not increase Thérèse's allowance to 20,000 livres
a year. And when Saint-Séverin fell ill at the end of the year, Richelieu hopefully deferred the meeting of the *Etats* in Languedoc until January, in the belief that before that time he would be given
Saint-Séverin's seat in the council.

He was disappointed. Louis admired him, envied him—and did
not trust him. In any case, his dream of becoming First Minister
would never have been fulfilled as long as Pompadour remained
the King's mistress, for she already exercised all the powers of
that office. Disgruntled, Richelieu went off to Montpellier, where
he had to deal with a mutiny from the *Etats*.

§ 6

The *contrôleur-général*, Machault, who had been appointed by
Pompadour in 1745, was faced with the problem of trying to liqui-
date the greatly increased national debt, which was all that France
had to show for Saxe's victories and her own expense of blood. It
was useless to attempt to economize on the amount that the
King spent; Pompadour, who lived at the rate of two million livres
a year, would discharge any minister who suggested it. It was fool-
ish to think of abolishing the system of farming taxes; not only was

VIII Louis XV

by Carle Vanloo, Musée de Versailles

IX Madame de Pompadour

by Maurice Quentin de la
Tour, Musée du Louvre

x The *bal masqué* in the Galerie des Glaces, Versailles, February 25, 1745
by Charles-Nicolas Cochin, Musée du Louvre

it easy to work but it was also bolstered by bribes to everybody of consequence, including ministers and members of the royal family. Of all the taxes, whether farmed or not, it was estimated that between 30 and 50 per cent never reached the royal treasury; and of those that were levied, almost none fell on the people most able to pay.

Machault's plan was to accept the fact that the clergy and nobility would continue to evade the two principal traditional taxes, the *taille* and the *capitation*, and to revive a temporary tax that Louis XIV had first introduced in 1710. This, a 10 per cent income tax, had in the past been levied only in time of war; Machault now reduced it to 5 per cent, made it permanent, and set up boards of assessors to ensure that it was collected fairly. This *vingtième* was greeted with howls of protest from the *parlements*, and encountered the greatest opposition of all in the *pays d'états*, those provinces where the *Etats* retained the right of assessing their own taxation. At the meeting of the *Etats* of Languedoc in January 1750, the attack was led by the clergy, since the church would be the greatest loser if taxation were equitably applied. Richelieu, whose private views were in accord with those of the *Etats*, was anxious to arrive at a compromise, but his plea for moderation was brushed aside by the archbishop of Albi. The *Etats* refused to vote any taxes at all, unless they were given a share in the assessment of the *vingtième*. Richelieu, on orders from Versailles, dissolved the assembly; but on his own initiative he continued negotiations with the leading members and eventually persuaded them to agree to the assessment of the *vingtième* at half the last levied *dixième*. They had thus made their point of being their own assessors, but the right of future assessment and collection passed to the crown.

Richelieu returned to court at the end of April to find the temperature chilly in every respect. Machault thought he had not been firm enough; there was a biting north wind; the rebellious spirit in the provinces was reflected in Paris, where a rumour that the police had been ordered to collect stray children to be sent to Louisiana was followed by another—that the children were being slaughtered and their blood used to cure lepers—and by a brief, violent, terrifying flare-up that revealed the hatred below the surface and then as suddenly died away. Richelieu danced attendance on Louis, who still addressed him as *"mon cher Richelieu,"* through a July so swelteringly hot that at one guard-mounting fifteen soldiers died of heat-stroke after standing in the midday sun. The weather soon turned stormy, and he pottered about on small intrigues, getting a pension for a colonel who had once served under him, writing to warn Voltaire of Louis's displeasure at his having thrown up the post of historiographer-royal to enter the service of Frederick of Prussia. He brought his children to be presented at court: the ten-year-old Septimanie, a pretty girl who was being brought up by her aunt, the abbesse du Trésor, and the duc de Fronsac, who, at fourteen, was smaller than his sister. Louis visited him more frequently at Gennevilliers, now that he had taken to shooting rather than chasing his quarry on horseback. The King was an expert marksman, accustomed to killing two or three hundred animals every time he went out, and he still wandered restlessly from one estate to another, slaughtering as he went. During 1750, he spent only fifty days at Versailles.

Pompadour's apartments were now the acknowledged centre of court intrigue and power; she received ambassadors, appointed ministers; in her reception room, there was only one chair—her own—and her visitors, however illustrious, remained standing in her presence. Richelieu, remaining on terms of polite hostility with her, shared her box at the opera at Fontainebleau one evening and entered into conversation with an Italian visitor who had a seat below them. The foreigner, who amused them by making, in his imperfect French, two inadvertently indecent puns, was a man whose reputation in one sphere was to eclipse even that of Richelieu: a certain signor Casanova de Seingalt.

Blocked in his ambition to play a part in politics, unable to exercise his military talents for lack of a war, deprived of even the chance to engineer a major court intrigue because Pompadour so firmly held the strings, Richelieu wandered morosely off to his estate in Poitou in October. His interest in Thérèse had waned, now that he could visit her without the excitement of crawling through the fireplace, and he had formed no new intrigue that would keep him in Paris. The *Etats* of Languedoc, in disgrace at Versailles, were not summoned in December, so he did not make his annual visit to Montpellier. He was in an irritable, aggressive mood throughout the early months of 1751, supporting admiral Mahé de la Bourdonnais in his quarrel with Pompadour's protégé, Dupleix, openly repeating that the Treaty of Aix-la-Chapelle was "a masterpiece of stupidity, if not of corruption," and seeming not to miss a single opportunity of making himself offensive to Pompadour.

While their theatre was closed during Lent, the company of the Théâtre Française built three boxes on each side of the stage from which they hoped to get some extra revenue. Richelieu, on hearing this, was indignant that the First Gentlemen had not been asked for their permission (the censorship of the Paris stage was in the hands of the Lieutenant-General of police, but the administration of the theatres was the responsibility of the First Gentlemen, since the actors were the King's servants). He was enraged that the actors had been encouraged by La Vallière, who had himself rented one of the boxes. The duc de Gesvres was *en exercice*, but Richelieu persuaded him to let him handle the matter. At midnight on 25 April, he strode into the theatre at the head of a squad of workmen; there was a crashing of hammers and splintering of wood, and an hour or so later the offending boxes had been completely demolished.

The actors' reply was a play called *Les Sonnettes*, which appeared later in the year. Nobody dared try to stage it, but it was printed and circulated in Paris and Versailles to the accompaniment of much appreciative laughter. The central character was an aged *roué* who, his own powers having declined, let out rooms in his house to newly married couples. From each bed a wire ran to a bell in the landlord's room, and there he spent his nights listening nostalgically to the evocative jangling of the bells. There was no difficulty in identifying the debilitated Don Juan with Richelieu; and Richelieu, like many men who are very successful with women, had very little sense of humour. He was so enraged at the libel on his unimpaired virility that he made strenuous though unavailing efforts to have the author traced and put in prison.

He snarled his way through another unpleasant summer, this year so damp and windy that in August storms uprooted trees in the Bois de Boulogne. And in September he offered his most brutal affront to Pompadour. She had begun to plan the future of her seven-year-old daughter, Alexandrine d'Etioles, at first casting her eyes on Monsieur de Luc, Louis's son by Madame de Vintimille; but the King had unexpected scruples and refused his consent. She then revealed the admiration that underlay her opposition to Richelieu by suggesting that Alexandrine should marry Fronsac. It was a match that on the face of it was advantageous to both parties: Alexandrine would gain a great title; Fronsac would enjoy the immeasurable benefits of having the King's mistress as his mother-in-law, and there would be no position at court or in the government for which he might not reasonably hope.

Richelieu was horrified and outraged, suddenly conscious of the years that he had spent in trying to drag himself up from his Vignerot connection and recalling the sneers and jibes that had accompanied his progress at court and that he knew, even at the age of fifty-five, were still exchanged behind his back. With acid politeness he pointed out to the bourgeois mistress that his son was descended through his mother from the House of Lorraine, the House of Charlemagne, and of the Holy Roman Emperors, and he was bound to consult the wishes of that illustrious family before arranging a marriage for the boy. Did she wish him to make such inquiries? She did not. The matter was dropped. And she never forgave him.

The health of the royal children was a constant source of concern. Louis's second son, the duc d'Anjou, had died at the age of three, Marie-Louise at five, Thérèse-Félicité at eight. The Dauphin, now twenty-two, was vastly overweight, and Mesdames, his sisters, were as gluttonous as he; the cupboards in their private apartments were loaded with hams, mortadellas, cold stew, and Spanish wine, which they guzzled as the fancy took them. In February 1752, Anne-Henriette, the younger of the twin girls who had been the first fruits of Louis's marriage, fell sick of an unidentified disease which seemed related to the Bourbon family complaint of scabies. Despite dosing with root of wild patience-dock, iron filings, fumitory and tartared antimony, she died in the afternoon of 10 February, and, in accordance with custom, Louis at once left Versailles to stay at the Trianon until the body had been coffined and removed. Richelieu, not *en exercice* but still not to be prevented from interfering with the duties of Fleury (who had been very timid since his disgrace after Metz), escorted the sacrament to the dying princess and later attended the Dauphin when he went to scatter holy water on the coffin.

The struggle to snatch new privileges and to deprive one's rivals of existing ones, which increasingly absorbed the interest of the members of this sterile court, blossomed into scores of petty squabbles during the period of mourning for Anne-Henriette. Four dukes, not of royal blood, managed to have themselves officially announced when they went to pay their respects in the mortuary chapel, and the prince de Soubise lodged an eight-page complaint. Others fretfully tried to assess the importance and significance of the black bands that some wore instead of black cravats when they went in long black cloaks and weepers to offer their condolences to the King. And when the Dauphin, having led the procession on that occasion first to the Queen's apartments and then to his own, approached his wife's rooms, a desperate, brain-torturing problem arose.

The Dauphine, who had given birth to a son the previous October and had immediately become pregnant again, was so affected by her sister-in-law's illness and the bickering that accompanied it that she had a miscarriage and was taken to bed. Her bedroom had only one entrance, and her visitors would have to go out at the same door through which they came in. With the double doors open, this would not entail much jostling between those entering and those emerging; but it was quite impossible to open the double doors, for there might be some present whose position in society entitled them only to sidle in through a single door. The problem was both intractable and pressing; for the mob of courtiers, having tramped out of the Dauphin's quarters, down a corridor, through a small library and along the side of the little garden that had been specially made for the Dauphine, was beginning to cram her ante-room to overflowing.

Richelieu, fresh from a victory over the Grand Chamberlain, who had vainly protested at Richelieu's and Fleury's having the ends of their cloaks carried by Pages of the Bedchamber while he had to make do with a Gentleman Officer of the Order of Saint-Louis, went into urgent conference with the Dauphine's lady-in-waiting, the duchesse de Brancas. They found a brilliant solution: Madame de Brancas had the curtains at either side of the double doors brought to the middle and a bench placed at right angles to the curtains. Both doors were then opened, and the visitors, entering on one side of the curtains and bench and leaving on the other side, could be said to have used only one door at a time; if any claimed the right to have both doors open, well, both doors *were* open.

At the Tuileries, where the late princess's *dame d'honneur*, Madame de Beauvilliers, was on duty in the *chapelle ardente*, there were further crises. The counsellors of the supreme court, with a cunning worthy of their profession, tried to obtain three unwarranted privileges: to have Madame de Beauvilliers precede them, thus tacitly *introducing* them, into her dead mistress's presence; to have both doors opened for them; and to receive an aspergillum each from the herald-at-arms instead of sharing one between them. They were met with a firm refusal on each count; but Madame de Beauvilliers's troubles were not over. When she attempted to give the password to the captain of the guard mounted outside the chapel, he refused to accept it. Madame de Beauvilliers took her complaint to the duc de Biron, colonel of the guard, who replied with much gallantry and more duplicity that Madame de Beauvilliers's wish was his command and if it was her desire to give the password then he would issue the necessary instructions. Madame de Beauvilliers, too experienced a woman to be caught in this trap, pointed out that she was not asking for a favour but insisting on her right. It was eventually decided that she did have the privilege of giving the password, but only when she was actually in attendance on her dead mistress; and from then onward she took the precaution every evening of stepping across the threshold into the chapel before informing the guard commander of his duties.

After Anne-Henriette's death, the Dauphin fell ill, and, although the disease was the dreaded and infectious smallpox, Richelieu shared with the Dauphine the hours of waiting beside the prince's bed: a strange vigil in which the sick man, slow-witted and strait-laced, had only one bond in common with the immoral, mercurial Richelieu—their hatred of Pompadour. When the Dauphin had recovered, Richelieu amused himself with improvements to the estate at Gennevilliers. The house was, by his standards, small, with extensive kitchens and a few elegant salons decorated by Boucher and Vanloo, a pleasant retreat for a fastidious gourmet. But for two years in succession the ice that was sent out from Paris had arrived in poor condition, so now, in the park between the two ornamental lakes, he was having an icehouse constructed, buried in a huge mound of earth. Around the slopes of this sugar-loaf hill he planted trees, and on the summit he built a Temple of Love, with a gilt statue of Mercury on top of the cupola and pagan goddesses on the twelve pillars of the colonnade that encircled it. It made a remarkably pretty addition to the view but did little to cheer him up.

His mood was sour and pessimistic when he went down to Montpellier in October, the *Etats* having been recalled after two years of disgrace. To Voltaire he wrote: "Believe me, my dear Voltaire, it would have needed very little to have made this century greater than that of Louis XIV and to have given you many more things to adorn with your pen. I confess that we can no longer contemplate it—we are a thousand leagues away—and I should regret it less if there had been no remedy for the evil."

He received cordial greetings in Montpellier, for his compromise had saved the pride of the *Etats* and preserved some of their privileges. He made contact with the Protestants, against whom persecution had increased in recent years, and assured them that, although Versailles was pressing for severe measures, he would act with moderation if the Protestants would do the same, and so avoid arousing complaints from "those devils, the bishops." There was a larger proportion of Protestants in Languedoc than anywhere else in the kingdom, and their fanaticism was matched by that of the Catholic clergy, who constantly demanded the full penalties for all discovered at Protestant services: the men to be sent to the galleys, the women to be imprisoned for life, the children to be registered as bastards and compulsorily rebaptized as Catholics. Despite the penalties, the Protestants continued to hold their services and conduct marriages and baptisms "in the desert" —the gorges and barren places of the Cevennes and Vivarais. Some of them were urging a return to the methods of the *camisards*, trying to obtain justice by the sword. Although he was *en exercice* in 1753, his duties as First Gentleman were frequently neglected as he travelled backwards and forwards to Languedoc, trying to calm hotheads and forestall outbreaks of violence. By January 1754, he was a tired and rather dispirited man; it appeared unlikely that pitched battles between Protestants and Catholics could long be prevented, and he was sent reinforcements of thirty battalions of soldiers.

The year 1754 was disappointing for him. He began it with the highest of hopes, having found a young woman who seemed to have all the qualities necessary to replace Pompadour in the King's affections: Madame de Choiseul-Romanet, a twenty-year-old of dazzling beauty, described as *"tendre, sage et fidèle"* (though evidently not to her husband), who had already caught the King's eye. Richelieu undertook his familiar role as Mercury (there had been a great many witty remarks about the statue he had placed on top of the Gennevilliers Temple of Love) and arranged an exchange of letters between Louis and the pretty postulant. Everything was going well when Pompadour, who was well aware of the plot, called in the help of Madame de Choiseul-Romanet's cousin, Etienne-François de Choiseul, comte de Stainville, an ugly, amusing, charming, poor but very ambitious infantry colonel who had been seeking her patronage.

"The King will never confess his infidelity," she told him, echoing Madame de Châteauroux's words in similar circumstances. "I must confront him with proof of it—and I look to you to provide the evidence." Choiseul made love to his cousin—more *tendre* than *sage* on this occasion—and obtained the King's letters from her. Pompadour showed these to Louis; Madame de Choiseul-Romanet at once found herself out of favour. She died three months later.

No sooner had the Choiseul-Romanet affair collapsed than Richelieu's hopes were raised again by the discovery that Louis had taken to sleeping with teen-age girls in a private brothel that he had set up in the Parc-aux-cerfs quarter of Versailles. But here once more he was to be disappointed, for the direction of the brothel turned out to be in the hands of Pompadour. She had never derived pleasure from the royal embraces and for some months had been able to sustain them no longer, but she was willing to act as procuress. It was soon evident that, so long as she provided a succession of young prostitutes, some taken from the gutters of Paris, Louis was content to continue to accord her the place and privileges of *maîtresse déclarée*, and, unhappily for France, the power. She moved from her discreet apartments on the second floor to the rooms formerly occupied by the comte de Toulouse on the ground floor, where none but royalty had ever been lodged before.

Richelieu took opium to get to sleep, and spirit baths to tone up his system, and was daily plastered with fillets of veal in an attempt to cure an attack of scurvy. People said that the predictions of the author of *Les Sonnettes* had at last come true.

Triumph and Defeat

§ 1

In July 1755, the governorship of Languedoc became vacant on the death of the prince de Dombes; in the ensuing scuffle for places, Richelieu managed to take over the governorship of Guienne from the comte d'Eu, who succeeded his elder brother in Languedoc. As usual he was not satisfied; he had wanted the governorship of Languedoc, where he claimed he was well known and well liked (and where the governor's salary was nearly 160,000 livres as against less than 100,000 in Guienne). But his new post would bring him much honour even though there was little increase in his pay. And, as it happened, he was to draw his money for the next two years without performing his duties, for France was once more moving reluctantly towards war.

It was in the eighteenth century, not the nineteenth, that Britain established its wealth and power; it did this thanks to the boundless greed of its merchants, who forced an unwilling king into continual wars with France. The French fleet, which in 1706 had equalled those of Britain and Holland combined, had dwindled during fifty years of neglect to less than half of that of Britain alone. In the Orient, the French East India Company had lost its struggle against the British, and the riches of the subcontinent were about to slip from France's grasp; westward, the cordon that the French had tried to establish from the Great Lakes down the Ohio and the Mississippi was being raided by the British under George Washington and other local aristocrats; on the seas between, British warships were attacking French men-o'-war and capturing French merchant vessels.

When Parliament assembled in November, George II protested against the French "violation of the peace and . . . the faith of most solemn treaties" and told his loyal commons that to preserve his people from the calamities of war, "I have greatly increased my naval armaments, augmented my land forces . . . and concluded a treaty with the Empress of Russia and another with the Landgrave of Hesse-Cassel." The loyal commons, aglow at the thought of colonial expansion and increased trade, heartily applauded the King, whom they knew to be mightily scared of the war, which might lose him his Kingdom of Hanover to the French and, if he committed too many troops in Hanover, perhaps his Kingdom of Britain to the Jacobites into the bargain. It was at this point that Frederick of Prussia, who had frequently played his French allies false in the past, dismayed them with the ultimate betrayal by offering to enter into an alliance with Britain and guarantee Hanover from invasion, thus depriving France of the only real threat that she had been holding over George's head.

It would still have been possible for France to stay out of a continental war and use the money thus saved to build up her fleet and oppose the British encroachments in her colonies. But the King and the nobility were not interested in distant lands or maritime adventures; they were aristocrats, not merchants; cavaliers, not horse-marines. And even had all of them shown a passionate interest in France's imperial destiny, there would still have been Pompadour to cope with; for Pompadour had begun to take a hand in foreign affairs. In September 1755, the new Austrian ambassador to France, Starhemberg, had been invited to lunch at Bellevue, her new house which, constructed on a terrace overlooking the Seine, Saint-Cloud, and Paris, with the help of eight hundred workmen and the most expensive painters, sculptors, gilders, plasterers and cabinet-makers in the kingdom, had roused more resentment than any other of her extravagances. On the day it was ready for occupation and she invited Louis to supper, the fires smoked so badly that they had to have the meal carried down to the little house at the bottom of the garden that they called "the hovel." It was on the terrace of this *taudis*, screened from the château by winding sloping paths, and from the river by a long bower of hornbeams, that she introduced Starhemberg to her protégé, the abbé de Bernis, until recently ambassador in Venice. They discussed the proposals that Maria Theresa wished Pompadour to put to Louis for an alliance with Austria. After the announcement of the Treaty of Westminster between Britain and Prussia, Louis needed no persuading.

In order to forestall the expected British raids, maréchal de Belle-Isle was given military command of the entire Atlantic coast, from Dunkirk to Bayonne (thus including Richelieu's new province of Guienne) while Richelieu's successor as Lieutenant-General, the duc de Mirepoix, was to be responsible for the Languedoc coastline. Richelieu protested to the War Minister, Argenson, that he was senior to Mirepoix and should be given the honour of defending his old province; finding that Argenson showed very little interest in his arguments, he went off in a tearing rage to Pompadour's apartments, where he would probably have received even less sympathy had not Louis followed closely on his heels. He put his case so forcefully to the King that he emerged as commander-in-chief of the whole Mediterranean coastline: Roussillon, Languedoc, and Provence, and, with his usual preference for attack rather than defence, he suggested that he should be allowed to lead an expedition against the British-held island of Minorca.

First, however, there was his daughter's wedding, which he arranged and carried through with his habitual briskness. Septimanie was not quite sixteen; she had inherited her mother's elegant figure but was better looking and had a sharp pleasing wit. In recent years, Richelieu had taken her from his sister's convent of Le Trésor and brought her to Paris to be finished under the care of his distant relation, the duchesse d'Aiguillon; he had also bought himself a new mansion in the rue Neuve Saint-Augustin, the hôtel d'Antin, and it was here that he summoned Septimanie to inform her of the date of her wedding and the identity of her future husband: the comte d'Egmont-Pignatelli. Egmont-Pignatelli was twenty-nine, a widower, very rich and of ancient family, modishly vicious enough to neglect her almost at once for the dancers from the Opéra whom he entertained in his *petite maison* at No. 12 rue de Popincourt in the eastern suburbs; she disliked him at sight and continued to do so until her death. They were married on 10 Feb-

ruary in the chapel of the hôtel d'Antin and, after a brief honeymoon, the bridegroom joined Richelieu's staff in readiness for the
campaign that he hoped to fight in Minorca.

The wedding caused a deep rift between Richelieu and maréchal
de Belle-Isle, who had an estate near the abbaye du Trésor and
had for many years expected his son, the duc de Gisors, to marry
the attractive young Richelieu girl, who often came over from the
convent to visit them. Richelieu, however, had come to the conclusion that the Belle-Isles, descended from Louis XIV's famous
inspector of finances, Fouquet, were too plebeian to be allied to
his family, and the engagement between the two young people,
unwritten but assumed, had been broken off. "I am informed that
Belle-Isle is secretly working against you," his old friend the duchesse de Lauraguais wrote to him, discussing the chances of his
being given command of the Minorcan expedition. "And I have to
warn you that you are sometimes mistaken in your conjectures.
You told me that Madame de Pompadour was buttering you up;
but I know beyond question that even though she may treat you
well in your presence, it is far different when you are absent. They
were discussing with her whether the siege [of Mahon, the principal port of Minorca] should be undertaken and, if so, who should
be chosen for it. You were named among several others and she
exclaimed sarcastically: 'Monsieur de Richelieu! He is braggart
enough to want to be given the task. He would be as irresponsible
in taking a town as in seducing a woman; that would be very amusing! He needs a few good disgraces to teach him not to be so confident.' "

Diane-Adélaïde, even plumper now than when she had shared
with him and her sister Marie-Anne the tempestuous experiences
at Metz, was as faithful to him as ever and throughout the time
that he was away from Versailles she sent him long letters keeping him informed of everything that went on at court. She was
cultivating the abbé de Bernis, and hoping that, wittingly or not,
he would help Richelieu get the command that he so much desired. "It would perhaps be not altogether a bad thing to let the
marquise [de Pompadour] know, through you-know-who, that if
you are given the expedition you will fail. If she is badly disposed
towards you, that could help. . . . You must have this command,

take Mahon, and return covered with glory so as to make them
burst with rage. What a prospect! What a beautiful dream, my
dear duke! If only we can realize it!"

There was so much chatter about the French plans that news of
them had long ago reached London, where it was known that
Belle-Isle had been provided with a map of the English coast from
Portsmouth to Harwich and was forming an invasion force; and
that Richelieu was planning to attack either Minorca or Gibraltar.
The thought of invasion produced something akin to panic: the
government agreed to let George II bring his detested Hanoverian
and Hessian mercenaries over as reinforcements; and the citizens
of London sublimated both fury and fear by constructing a large
wickerwork effigy of Maria Theresa, surmounted with an imperial
crown and endowed with an even more imperial rump made of
flesh-coloured paper, which they paraded through the streets, halting at every crossing to give the perfidious queen a public whipping.

On 16 March 1756, a fortnight after Richelieu's sixtieth birthday, an order from the King established the composition of the
force which was to attempt the capture of Minorca and which
Richelieu was now appointed to command. He was to have 25
battalions of infantry, with supporting artillery and engineers, and
to be escorted and transported by a fleet commanded by the marquis de la Galissonnière. It was no great surprise to Richelieu to
discover that the Ministry of War had not a single detailed map of
Minorca, which had been in British hands since 1708. On his way
down to Marseille, accompanied by his new son-in-law and Fronsac
as aides-de-camp, he called on the comte de Bermond at Aix-en-
Provence. Bermond had visited Minorca some years before, and
Richelieu hoped he might provide some scraps of information to
supplement the meagre details on the map of Fort Saint-Philippe—
the fortress guarding Mahon—which was half a century out of date
and had been given him by the Spanish ambassador. None of the
fortifications built by the British was shown on it—which was just
as well, for they were so complex and well constructed that, had
the French Ministry of War known about them, the expedition
would never have been mounted.

He had no money with him to pay civilian workers or for any

additional equipment that he might need; the ministry had shown
no interest, and Louis was nursing a slight chill caught while chasing a fifteen-year-old prostitute round the bedroom of the house in
the Parc-aux-cerfs. The most that Richelieu had been able to do
was to get some of the Paris notaries to promise to raise 50,000
louis and send them on to him. At Marseille, where the transport
ships were to be fitted out, there were no stores or provisions and
not a single ship was fit to put to sea. He hurried on to Toulon
and found a similar lack of preparation and a conviction on the
part of the senior naval officers that the venture had no chance of
success. It looked as if the fiasco of ten years before, the expedition
in support of the Young Pretender, was to be repeated. "They intend to ruin you, that is certain!" wrote the disgusted Diane-Adélaïde, when he told her of all his difficulties.

But he did not intend that they should. When informed that
the crews were hiding because they would get only half pay while
the vessels were getting ready for sea, he persuaded La Galissonnière to promise them full pay as soon as their ships took up station in the roads. When this did not produce enough men, he
personally offered a bonus of six livres for every man who reported
for duty before 1 April; and when he found there were still shortages, he sent for sailors from the Atlantic coast. He bustled,
begged, and bullied. The naval experts had said that the convoy
could not be ready before late June, but on the morning of Thursday, 8 April, he went aboard La Galissonnière's flagship, the *Fou-
droyant*, to the roll of drums and with troops standing at the
present on each of the 17 warships and 198 transport vessels, their
faces turning paler and greener as the ships tossed in a strengthen-
ing breeze. With a good following wind, Minorca lay about thirty
hours' sail away, but as the breeze turned to a gale, it became evident that they would not be able to leave that day. The *Fou-
droyant*, dragging her anchor, collided with the *Triton*, and several soldiers fell overboard and were drowned; a few moments
later, there was another loud crash and the *Triton*, firing two
blank shots as a distress signal, disappeared from sight in the spray
and murk.

It was not an auspicious beginning, or even a beginning at all.

At five o'clock the next morning, they made a new attempt to leave, but one warship went aground, and the squadron hove to so that longboats could be sent to drag it free. By the time this had been accomplished, the wind had changed and the fleet had to return to Toulon. On the 10th the wind dispersed many of the transport vessels, and the others anchored in the shelter of the Iles d'Hyères, where they remained the following day and were grateful for supplies of fresh water brought out to them from Toulon. Torrential, blinding rain accompanied the wind, and, when they made a new start on the 12th, the transport vessels were again lost from sight. La Galissonnière spent the 13th in rounding up the stragglers, and as they once more moved forward on the 14th, they met a merchantman from Marseille who offered the disturbing news that a British fleet of 21 warships was on its way to the Mediterranean. Despite this, La Galissonnière had to give orders to shorten sail on the 15th to allow more time for the slower ships to catch up. On the 16th, to the relief of the 14,000 soldiers cooped up in the stinking holds, but to the dismay of Richelieu and La Galissonnière, the wind dropped, the rain ceased, the sun came out, and they found themselves in a dead calm, immobile on the deep blue, smooth water. At last, at dawn on the 17th, the wind freshened without turning into a raging tempest, and the ships began to scud along on their true course. At five o'clock that afternoon, the look-outs at the mastheads began to call the sight of land, and an hour later the mountains of Minorca were plainly in view. The thirty-hour voyage had taken a little under ten days.

They sailed around to Ciudadella, the capital of the island, and now had to decide where to land. La Galissonnière was unwilling to risk bringing his ships within range of any shore batteries, while Richelieu was equally reluctant to expose his men to a landing by ships' boats on an open beach. As the ships approached the land in the clear air and under a bright sun, Richelieu saw through his telescope long lines of the inhabitants, men and women, dressed in their Sunday best and presumably on their way home from mass, crowding the city walls, from which he deduced that there would be no opposition. The 250 British soldiers in the garrison had in fact begun to withdraw to Fort Saint-Philippe, across the island, as soon as the French force had been sighted, and the 250 grenadiers whom Richelieu sent ashore at an inlet a couple of miles down the coast met with no resistance. Almost at the same time, a boat flying a white flag brought out to the *Fou-droyant* the town magistrates, who gladly accepted Richelieu's conditions that they should put themselves under his protection and return to their homes in peace. Then, with typical swagger and foolhardiness, he ordered his barge into the port and disembarked with his staff and no escort at all. It was only later that he learned that a party of thirty British soldiers had not yet left the town and, with a little initiative, could have captured him and his headquarters. During the rest of the day and all through the night, he disembarked his troops and stores by the light of huge fires lit on the roof of the abandoned fort at the mouth of the harbour.

When the expedition had first been mounted, Richelieu had been allotted only one lieutenant-general: the comte de Maille-bois, a man treacherous with ambition, whose path was strewn with the tattered reputations of his superiors, all of whom he had secretly attacked and betrayed in turn. He was the son-in-law of the elder Argenson, had been appointed by the younger, and was deeply distrusted by Richelieu, who put him in charge of the troops protecting the base, while giving command of the column of grenadiers that was to lead the advance across the island to an old friend, the marquis du Mesnil. Du Mesnil made slow progress, in broiling sun over roads torn up and bridges broken down by the retreating British garrison, but met with no opposition. Richelieu followed with the main party and on 23 April was in front of Mahon. The British governor had retired to Fort Saint-Philippe, whence he sent a messenger to say that, since he had received no news of a declaration of war between their two countries, he must ask Richelieu what were the intentions of the troops that had landed on the island. To which Richelieu dryly replied that his intentions were precisely similar to those of His Britannic Majesty's warships in respect to the French ships that they were so constantly seizing.

It was in no joking mood that Richelieu took stock of the British fortifications and the solid rock that surrounded them, and of his own lack of transport. There was not a single cart or team of horses on the island fit to drag the guns up over the mountains from Ciudadella (the artillery officers estimated that it would take 400 days to get their batteries into position!) and it was difficult to see how even lighter supplies or food could be brought up by road. Du Mesnil solved the artillery problem by dragging the guns up behind the oxen that had been brought with them to provide meat, and the munitions were shipped round on the local lateen-rigged *tartanes* to the beach at La Mesquida, close to Mahon. On 24 April, La Galissonnière left Ciudadella, where he had finished landing the men and supplies, and began cruising up and down the coast, meanwhile sending anxious messages to Versailles, telling of his fears that he would be driven off by superior British forces and Richelieu would find himself trapped on the island.

The outlook was bleak in every direction. The French troops were encamped on a rocky plateau, criss-crossed with dry-stone walls and narrow sunken roads, burning hot by day and whipped by a chilly wind at night, the rock so naked and devoid of earth that it was impossible to drive in a tent peg. Richelieu sent urgently to Provence and Spain for straw for his men to lie on. In front of them squatted the great irregular rectangle of Fort Saint-Philippe, furnished with every type of defence work: counter-guards to prevent breaches in the walls, bastions to give flanking fire from the fortress itself, and ravelins to protect the deep ditches that had been blasted with immense effort out of the bleak rock. In front of the glacis for a mile around there stood lesser strong points and lunettes with walls eighteen feet thick, linked by trenches to cellars and mine galleries that contained food and ammunition and a cistern fed by rainwater.

It was a defensive position of great strength and depth, its approaches covered by 200 guns. It was impossible to dig approach trenches in the rock, and Richelieu would have to lead his men forward under increasingly heavy fire entirely in the open, using the houses on the outskirts of the town as his starting line. Maillebois wrote to his uncle-by-marriage, criticizing this decision, but it is difficult to see what else Richelieu could have done. It was certainly less open to criticism than the siting of batteries on the signal tower, which was Maillebois's suggestion. In none of Maillebois's recommendations to his superiors throughout his career is it possible to know whether they were made because he thought they would be militarily effective or, quite the reverse, helpful to his own career by making his commander appear incompetent.

The slopes leading to the signal tower, which was set on the top of the hill that faced the fort across the harbour, were completely dominated on the landward side by the British guns—as Fronsac, accompanying his father on a reconnaissance, discovered when he was almost bowled over by a cannon ball. Food and ammunition for the gun crews had to be carried down on wheelbarrows and stretchers to the shore and rowed round by sea to a point below the batteries and shielded from the fort. It was not until 8 May that the eight guns and six twelve-inch mortars were ready to open fire and then the balls and bombs fell short. The gunners doubled the charges and blew several of the guns off their mountings, and there were many more days of sweaty work in the grueling heat before the guns were at last ranging on the fort.

The first reliable warning that the British government had received of a probable attack on Minorca was at the beginning of February. They had then assembled a fleet under Admiral Byng to protect the island and to carry out reinforcements from the Royal Regiment of Fusiliers under Lord Robert Bertie. With Byng's squadron now on the way, and rumours that it was to be followed by another under Boscawen, Richelieu had serious fears that Machault, who was now *garde des sceaux* and Minister of the Marine, would order La Galissonnière back to the safety of Toulon. Richelieu had not enough artillery or engineers to deal with the massive fortifications of Fort Saint-Philippe. His subsidiary commanders, in Roussillon, Languedoc, and Provence, had stripped their own defences bare, and if La Galissonnière withdrew, he would be unable to get any further reinforcements of any kind. On 16 May, he and his staff officers attended the Corpus-

Christi celebrations in the cathedral of Mahon, grenadiers lining the route along which the sacrament was carried and riflemen firing a *feu-de-joie* during the benediction. Contrasted with the stolid protestantism of their predecessors, the visible and audible piety of the French commander-in-chief and his troops made a profound impression on the islanders, who no doubt saw a meed of heavenly recognition in the events of the following days.

For on 17 May the dreaded thing happened: the frigate *Gracieuse* reported sighting thirteen vessels off Palma, Majorca, which could only be Byng's squadron. La Galissonnière sailed to intercept them, and by the 19th the two fleets were almost within range. Darkness fell before they could engage, but on the 20th, after finding and losing each other in patchy mist, they encountered again, a few miles south-west of Minorca. The wind was in the British admiral's favour, but nothing else; the opening shots from the French ships did great damage and at six in the evening Byng broke off the engagement. La Galissonnière had instructions not to risk his ships, which represented the whole of the French Mediterranean fleet, and to withdraw if the action became too fierce. Byng, unhappily for himself, did not know this and, at a council of war held in his flagship that evening and attended by his captains and the infantry commanders, it was agreed that, even in the unlikely event of his defeating the French fleet on the following day, it would be impossible to land the reinforcements on the island, and that his primary concern must be not to leave Gibraltar unprotected. He accordingly sailed away—to disgrace, court martial, and a firing squad.

May burned into June; the troops complained that their letters were late in arriving and that the postal charge (fixed, like everything else, by a farmer-general who had bought the concession) was too high. Their ranks were thinned by fever, drunkenness, and the splinters from the rocky terrain, which made each British bullet twice as effective. Richelieu protested to the British commander, General Blakeney, that his artillerymen were winding brass wire round the cannon balls; Maillebois added that the infantrymen were filling their grenades with nails; both received indignant denials. The engineers, trying to construct battery positions, worked painfully slowly and perilously above ground, protected only by gabions and sandbags. The only real progress seemed to be made by one of Richelieu's cooks who, mixing eggs and vinegar and olive oil in an attempt to brighten up the maréchal's salad, lighted upon a *sauce Mahonnaise* which, distorted into *mayonnaise*, passed into culinary history. Richelieu, admiring the fine flavour and size of the local onions, had sacks of them sent back to Provence to be acclimatized.

There were rumours that a large British force under Hawke would be arriving in the Mediterranean before the end of the month with the intention of blowing La Galissonnière's fleet clean out of the water; bets of twenty-to-one were laid in London that Richelieu would be a prisoner before 15 July, and, although the two countries had been officially at war since 17 May, three Parisian bankers had no difficulty in taking up a hundred thousand crowns' worth of the bets, which they passed on to French punters. Voltaire, still addressing Richelieu as *"mon héros"* in his letters, though privately referring to him as "that babbler" and "that old swindler," loyally backed his protector to the extent of twenty guineas.

Richelieu had fired 34,000 cannon balls and 18,000 mortar shells at the fort; he had lost 2,000 men in killed, wounded, and sick; the expedition had cost 20 million livres; and he was scarcely any farther advanced than he had been a week after landing. From Versailles came reports that Louis was bad-tempered and that Argenson, who had already begun hinting that Richelieu had no stomach for his job, was openly discussing the possibility of sending an engineer "adviser," who would no doubt replace him in command. With the hot breath of Hawke and Argenson on the back of his neck, Richelieu ordered the assault to take place on 27 June, a night attack over the bald, bullet-swept approaches with no protection except the darkness.

One by one during the evening, the French batteries ceased fire. At 10 p.m. one cannon shot and four rockets from the signal-tower battery announced the assault. Richelieu took up his position in the centre of the main attacking force, which advanced with the harbour on its left; four other columns attacked from the landward side; two more detachments embarked in longboats behind the signal-tower to come in from the sea. As the French infantry emerged from the cover of the houses and walls of La Ravalle, they came under a withering fire, and it was here that Richelieu's personal qualities as a soldier were proven. He had a fearlessness and a habit of crediting others with as much courage as himself which won the hearts and confidence of those serving under him; he had already largely suppressed drunkenness by the remarkable expedient of announcing that any man found drunk would be "deprived of the honour of taking part in the final assault"; and now, as company after company marched into the bullet-torn night, he urged them fiercely on past mines and ditches to the redoubts where, their scaling ladders proving too short, they scrambled up the walls by standing on each other's shoulders and jabbing their bayonets into the cracks between the stones to serve as pitons. The fighting continued without respite through the night and when dawn came, at 5 a.m., Richelieu asked for a two-hour truce to remove his dead and wounded from the bleak battlefield.

During the night Lieutenant-Colonel Jeffreys, Blakeney's second-in-command, had been captured in one of the outlying forts; he had been the leading spirit of the resistance to the attack, and without him Blakeney, an old man long past coping with his responsibilities, gave up hope. The fighting began again at 7 a.m., but at midday Blakeney sent three *parlementaires* to ask for terms. The battle had been bloody, but much less prolonged than Richelieu had expected; loving the grand gesture and anxious to conclude an agreement before another British squadron appeared, he offered Blakeney the honours of war if he was prepared to capitulate before 8 p.m. Blakeney accepted and the British troops marched out of the fortress with colours flying and lighted matches, the soldiers carrying their muskets and twenty rounds of ammunition each, the officers retaining their swords and baggage. For 10 days they were fed and lodged by the French, until letters of safe-conduct were procured for the French ships that took them to Gibraltar: a motley collection of 132 officers; 3,167 soldiers; 38 officers' ladies and 32 officers' children; 390 soldiers' women and 351 soldiers' brats; 53 Greeks and 15 Jews.

As soon as the act of capitulation was signed, Richelieu sent

Fronsac off to court with the news and to collect the reward which he well deserved, for courage was one of the few laudable qualities that he had inherited from his father, and he had amply demonstrated it during the attack. Keeping good fortune in the family, Richelieu sent his son-in-law, Egmont-Pignatelli, after Fronsac with a more detailed account of the battle and was gratified to receive from Louis a letter of congratulation, telling him that Fronsac had been granted the reversion of Richelieu's post as First Gentleman, while Egmont-Pignatelli had been created a chevalier de Saint Louis and promoted *maréchal de camp*. The court was at Compiègne, where Louis ordered a *Te Deum* and fireworks; Pompadour gave a party at her *ermitage* in the château grounds; and the town fountains flowed with wine.

Richelieu, already savouring the triumph of his return, went aboard the *Foudroyant* on 8 July, leaving a garrison of eleven infantry battalions and a detachment of gunners in Fort Saint-Philippe. The weather was blustery again, and the winds contrary. It was not until 2:30 in the afternoon of the 16th that La Galissonnière led his ships in line ahead to anchor in the Toulon Roads. At five o'clock, the admiral's barge took the victorious maréchal into port to the accompaniment of five rousing shouts of "Vive le Roi!" from the ships' crews and a seventeen-gun salute, while the merchant ships in the harbour discharged whatever guns they had, and the garrison added another seven. He drove through cheering crowds to the Hôtel de Ville, where he was presented with addresses and listened to congratulatory verses. At Marseille there was another recital of celebratory odes and the ladies in the audience pelted him with flowers; at Montpellier he was presented with a laurel wreath which, with one of his happy gestures, he broke into many pieces and presented to the officers who accompanied him. But in all this there was one sour and sinister note: on landing at Toulon, he had been given a letter from Louis saying that the council feared that the British might attempt reprisals on the Mediterranean coast and that Richelieu was therefore ordered to remain there until he received further instructions.

Diane-Adélaïde had no doubt who was behind this, and when

Fronsac left Paris to rejoin his father, she entrusted him with a letter in which she told Richelieu that she had had a long talk with Machault, who "talked a great deal about the trick that Argenson is playing on you. . . . He has no doubt that it was he who prevented you from returning . . . and that despite the King's desire to see you he did not have the strength to resist Argenson. . . . All this is simply so that Maillebois shall arrive before you; he will be told to say just what Argenson wants said and to minimize as far as possible your difficulties and the glory that you deserve. . . . I am strongly of the opinion—and this is the *garde des sceaux*'s advice as well—that you should write a letter to Argenson, and another to the King, asking to return here for a week on urgent business; say that you would like nothing better than to go back again if that is in the King's interest; and do not appear to be suspicious of the slightest thing. . . . You know my interest, my adoration, my love for you. . . . M. de Fronsac leaves tonight; I would give much to be at liberty to go with him. . . . Farewell, sweetheart, I wish I could have news of you tomorrow."

In her next letter she was more wrought up than ever: "This monster Argenson, while praising your victory, takes great care to add that without M. de la Galissonnière everything would have failed, implying that he did more than you. . . . He says that you acted more as a warrior than a general and that you owe your success to luck and favourable conditions, rather than to your talents. . . . The *garde des sceaux* . . . has assured me that the King already seems less pleased with you than he was; he will let himself be persuaded and you will perhaps lose all the credit for your superb expedition. Madame de Pompadour, who seems delighted with you at the moment, may change by tomorrow. I know that Argenson spent some time with her yesterday and I fear that he is spitting his venom on everything he touches. You know from experience that she only likes you as the mood takes her: your friend today, she may be against you tomorrow. . . . I can see that on the whole they are annoyed to see you victorious; a good defeat would have made them all happy. . . .

"Come quickly; one must always strike while the iron is hot; I am very impatient to see you, more for your interests than for mine. Sometimes I have moments of despair when I would advise you to give it all up. My sister was right when she said that sometimes one was tempted to see it all as a dream, since it is impossible to put anything right with a master who is pleased to be nothing, is frightened to take an interest in anything, and leaves his ministers to do just as they wish. Really! I am furious with him for not appreciating all that you have done, and for being so feeble as not to resist Argenson. I hope you realize what he is like now and, although you say that we might have one who was worse, I would prefer, for your sake, to take that risk rather than see him where he is. Good-bye! Be here as soon as you can to clear out the swarm of reptiles who are leaguing against you in this madhouse. Burn my letter."

Richelieu did not obey her injunction to burn the letter, but he accepted her advice to write to Louis and to Argenson, asking for leave to return on grounds of health, since the dry, hot southern summer was too much for him. The royal permission was granted, and he arrived in Paris on 30 August to be greeted by cheering crowds outside the hôtel d'Antin. Despite Argenson's whispering campaign, France as a whole was generous in its praise; and the bishop of Saint-Malo went so far as to preach a powerful sermon on Ezekiel, Chapters 27 and 28, in which he likened Britain to proud, sinful Tyre, and Richelieu, quite unexpectedly, to the wrath of God.

After an absence of several months, and even with the help of Diane-Adélaïde's letters, it was difficult to identify all the cross currents of court intrigue. Everybody greeted him with bland courtesy, Argenson assuring him that Pompadour was the cause of his having been kept in Provence, and Pompadour telling him precisely the opposite. Louis was strangely ungracious, asking him boorishly, "Did you try the Minorcan figs?" and not offering him a word of congratulation.

On 9 September, an old friend, the marquise de Monconseil, gave a fête for him at Bagatelle, her delightful house in the Bois de Boulogne; among the many songs, ballets and playlets dedicated to the guest of honour, the most highly praised was a set of verses called *La Cheminée*, in which ladies of fashion pleaded with the victor of Minorca to come and sweep their chimneys. These gay indecencies must have been still in his mind the following month when he learned that Thérèse de la Pouplinière had died. During the last months of her life, she had become reconciled to "that animal" her husband and her once great passion for Richelieu had faded. He had sent her money when she needed it, and his physician to join in the hopeless attempts to cure the cancer from which she died; but for several years he had been too much occupied with other matters to call on her in person.

§ 2

The new year of 1757, his third as First Gentleman *en exercice*, was to be one of the most eventful in his life. It began with a disappointment. The chubby-cheeked little abbé de Bernis, Pompadour's protégé, was an old acquaintance of Richelieu, who had befriended the abbé's father, a gentleman with a long lineage and a short purse, who lived on his estate at Pont-Saint-Esprit. The son, after being educated at the seminary of Saint-Sulpice, scraped a living in Paris by his wits and charm and Richelieu secured his election to the Académie at the early age of twenty-nine; he also introduced him to the duchesse d'Aiguillon, who provided him with most of his meals, and to Madame d'Estrades, who in turn introduced him to Madame d'Etioles. For Madame d'Etioles he composed letters and little congratulatory odes to be sent to the King, and in general undertook the duties of her literary secretary. His immediate reward was a pension of 1,500 livres and a room in the Tuileries attics, which Pompadour and her friends furnished for him. Witty, flattering, effeminate or perverted—Casanova suggests that he was a *voyeur*—Bernis was always popular with the ladies of the court. After Pompadour had obtained the post of ambassador to Venice for him in 1752 and then used him in the discussions with Starhemberg three years later, she kept him close to her as a sort of foreign-affairs adviser, and he was a frequent visitor in most of the fashionable salons.

On the second day of January, Richelieu came upon him in the King's ante-room and, making himself agreeable, said: "Since you often have business with the King and his ministers, why do you not ask to be granted the *entrées de la chambre?* If you wish, I will propose it to the King myself." Bernis gave him one of his cherubic smiles and thanked him prettily. A few minutes later Louis came to the door of the council chamber, and Richelieu was thunderstruck to hear him say: "Abbé de Bernis, take your seat at the council." It was a bitter moment, to have to stand and watch this insignificant little man achieve the prize that he had so long coveted.

The rear staircase that led from the *petits appartements* down past the first floor to the smaller guardroom on the north side of the *cour de marbre* was the one that the King used on all except ceremonial occasions. When he was to travel by carriage, he customarily walked through the guardroom and beneath the oval room and his study to come out on the broad steps of the *cour royale.* This was the route that he followed on 5 January when he left Versailles to return to Trianon, where he was staying for a few days. It was six o'clock in the evening, very cold, with a full moon showing between the scudding clouds and the flames of the torches that the ushers held bending before a stiff breeze; the usual throng of idlers had gathered around the carriage and along the steps to watch the Captain of the Cent-Suisses lead the way for the King, who had the Grand Equerry and the First Equerry on either side of him, with Richelieu and the duc d'Ayen, Captain of the King's Guard, at his heels. They were half-way to the carriage when an indistinct figure pushed past two of the soldiers who lined the steps, sent an officer of the guard spinning, and ran up to Louis, who suddenly bent forward and then exclaimed: "Duc d'Ayen—somebody has hit me!"

It all happened so quickly, with some of the members of the royal party looking downward so as not to miss their footing on the steps and others dazzled by the glare of the torches, that the man who had dealt the blow was back through the line of guardsmen and into the crowd before anybody caught a clear sight of him. Richelieu, his sharp eyes immediately picking out the one incongruity in the scene, shouted: "Who is that man with his hat on?" At the same time Louis looked down at his hand, with which he had been gingerly feeling the spot where he had been punched, and called out: "I have been wounded! Arrest him and do not kill him!"

A footman who was holding the carriage door open began to shout, "The King is hurt!"; the man who had so foolishly drawn attention to himself by wearing his hat in the royal presence was seized by the scruff of the neck; and as Louis turned to go back up the steps, several courtiers hurried forward, eager for the honour of carrying him. He said in a feeble voice: "No, I have still enough strength to go up alone" and made his way slowly back through the guardroom and up the stairs. When he reached his apartments, he saw that he was still bleeding and, giving way to his natural panic, he moaned: "Oh, I have been struck down! Oh, I shall not recover from this!" Weakened by lack of courage rather than loss of blood, he subsided on the bed and began to clamour for a confessor and a surgeon. But the royal household was at Trianon, and there was neither confessor nor surgeon nor sheets for the bed nor even a clean shirt. He was undressed and wrapped in a dressing gown, while courtiers scurried in all directions. Some said that the wound should be left open and others that it should be bound up, while Louis grew more and more pale as he convinced himself that death was upon him. He repeated his demands for a priest, and at last the chaplain for the quarter was found. The King poured out a list of his sins; he then asked for absolution on the understanding that he would later confess at greater length, time and memory permitting.

A surgeon arrived and washed the wound but would not take the responsibility of probing it until a senior surgeon was present. La Martinière, who had succeeded La Peyronie as First Surgeon in 1747, was brought over from Trianon and, after examining the wound, announced that it was not deep and, in his opinion, not dangerous. It was, indeed, scarcely more than a scratch, having been delivered with a short-bladed penknife through the King's thick overcoat. Pompadour's doctor, reporting to her later, said: "If it had been any other man, he'd have been at the ball tonight." However, Louis now took it into his head that the blade had been poisoned, and, although the man in the hat had had his feet stuck in the guardroom fire in the hope of making him talk, nobody could discover whether this was so. He was a slow-witted creature, aged about forty and rather good-looking with sunken eyes, a big nose, and a feverish complexion now that his feet and ankles had been burned; he gave his name as Robert-François Damiens.

Louis, with rolling eyes and grievous moans, set the panic billowing again. His daughters arrived from Trianon and, seeing blood on the bandage that had been put on the wound at La Martinière's instructions, collapsed ponderously around the bed and lay unconscious on the floor for some moments, while the Dauphin, having allowed a few dutiful tears to well up, occupied himself with trying to restore order. The Queen suggested, from experience, that Louis was probably suffering from stomach ache, but on seeing the bloodstains, she too began to feel faint.

Amid all this swooning and shouting, Louis asked for a confessor again. His own, Père Desmarets, had not been found, but somebody proposed one of the household almoners who, the King was assured, was "well thought of." His services were accepted; Louis confessed for the second time and at very great length, and then begged for Extreme Unction. Orders were shouted along the line to bring the Holy Oils and the cardinal de la Rochefoucauld. They found the Holy Oils but fortunately, since the whole thing was degenerating into a rather blasphemous farce, not the cardinal; instead, Père Desmarets arrived, and Louis, who could not have enough of confessing, set off on his third recital.

The resemblance between his present pitiful panic and that at Metz a dozen years before, which had resulted in the disgrace of Madame de Châteauroux, was lost on nobody. The royal bedchamber buzzed with predictions about Pompadour's future, and there was joy when it was noticed that, although she had returned from Trianon, she had not risked entering the bedchamber. The Dauphin had already ordered Richelieu to eject her brother, the marquis de Marigny, who had been hanging about in the hope of obtaining news for her, and she now waited anxiously in her room on the ground floor, bitterly noting how many of her usual visitors were absent, and how many of her enemies were casually calling in to enjoy her uneasiness and savour the prospect of her approaching downfall.

In the crowded bedchamber, Louis was grovelling in an attempt to evade divine retribution. He made a public apology for his sins, begging his children to forgive him for the scandals he had brought upon them, and the Queen for the wrongs he had done her; he told the Dauphin that he was about to mount the throne and would be a more fortunate King—the realm would be in good hands. By this time almost everybody was in tears. It was nearly midnight, and, since nobody had been able to discover whether the knife was poisoned or not, the doctors decided to take the bandages off and see how the wound was progressing. It was at once apparent that there was no poison; and virtually no wound. The courtiers drifted off to bed, and Louis snuffled himself to sleep.

Next morning Bernis crossed Richelieu's path again. The little abbé, intent on ingratiating himself as quickly as possible with the Dauphin and working in his usual way through women, suggested to Madame Adélaïde that she should suggest to her sister-in-law, the Dauphine, that she should in her turn suggest to the Dauphin that he should call a meeting of the council to discuss what measures should be taken until the King was well enough to issue instructions again. The Dauphin accepted this advice and told Richelieu to have Lemoine, the Gentleman Usher, call a meeting of the council. Thus far, progress had been smooth though circuitous, but at this point Richelieu asked whether the meeting was to be of the *conseil d'état* or of the *conseil des dépêches* (the former, very limited in number and concerned with policy, was the true Cabinet; the latter, much larger, had administrative and executive duties).

The Dauphin replied that this was the *conseil des dépêches*, whereupon Richelieu, with an air of innocence, pointed out that an unusual problem had arisen: Bernis had been admitted to the *conseil d'état* on the previous Sunday, but the King had not yet officially summoned him to the *conseil des dépêches*. In these circumstances, would it be proper to call Bernis to the council meeting? The Dauphin was of the opinion that the King was the only judge of this, but the King was in no fit state to be worried by such problems. In the end, they put the problem to the Gentleman Usher, who said that he had frequently known people who were members of the *conseil des dépêches* without being members of the *conseil d'état*, but he had never known a member of the *conseil d'état* not to be a member of the *conseil des dépêches*. It was therefore agreed that Bernis should be invited to take his seat; but the abbé heard the story later and guessed that Richelieu had tried to exclude him—a silly little piece of malice for which he was to make Richelieu pay in full before the year was out.

Although it was now evident that no harm had befallen the King, the speculation about Pompadour's future continued. Louis kept to his bed for several days; then convalesced for a time in his room; and it was not until eleven days after the attack that he made his first trip out—to hear mass in the chapel. During all this time he neither spoke nor wrote nor sent any message to his mistress; those who hoped for her disgrace, or merely feared to be involved in it, pointedly stayed away from her apartments. Richelieu visited her when he had reason to do so, but showed no interest in the scheming that was going on around him: he did not believe that Louis had sufficient strength of will to get rid of his mistress, any more than he had done after Metz; on the other hand, her return would not be the occasion for any rejoicing. Pompadour's supporters finally persuaded Louis to go and pay her a call but, when she offered an affectionate greeting and told him how desolated she had been by the attack on him, he did not answer and soon afterwards returned to his study without having addressed a single word to her. Argenson was crowing in anticipation of Pompadour's imminent disgrace, but Richelieu, who knew the King much better, was not surprised to see that Louis stayed longer the next day and offered her a few words; on the third day, he had a meal with her and was shortly as dependent on her as ever.

Pompadour was in a position to ask for a head; and surprisingly she chose that of Machault, her own former favourite and an active Minister of the Marine whom the country could ill spare with a new war on its hands. He had offended her by staying away

XI Thérèse de la Pouplinière

by Maurice Quentin de la Tour, Musée de la Tour, Saint-Quentin

XII Septimanie, comtesse d'Egmont-Pignatelli

after Alexandre Roslin,
Musée de Versailles

XIII The maréchal duc de Richelieu (circa 1786)
by Auguste Couder, Musée de Versailles

during her dark hours; he was also disliked by court and clergy because of his attempts at tax reform, and would be a popular victim. Argenson heard the news in advance and was almost beside himself with joy. His own position was now doubly sure, since it would be unthinkable to dismiss the Minister of War and the Minister of the Marine at the same time. By what might almost be called a fortunate coincidence, his elder brother died at the end of January, and Argenson took this opportunity of demonstrating the strength of his new position by asking a special grace from Louis: that a Gentleman-in-Ordinary should be sent to offer him the King's condolences, an honour normally reserved for dukes and peers. Argenson put this request to Richelieu, who promised to present it to the King at the first convenient moment.

It was when Louis was going into the wig room to have his hair powdered that Richelieu mentioned Argenson's request; the King scowled without answering. Richelieu, seeing Argenson hanging about in the study, walked through to tell him that he had not been able to obtain a decision. Argenson pointed out that his brother had been dead for nearly a week and the compliment would soon be too late—and confidently pressed Richelieu to ask the King again. Louis's reaction was to scowl once more, but then he broke into a smile and said, yes, by all means, he would grant Argenson's request. When Richelieu asked Argenson to return to his room so that a Gentleman-in-Ordinary might be sent to him, the War Minister's delight was so unconcealed that the bitter thought flashed across Richelieu's mind that Argenson was now convinced of his ascendancy and must regard this mark of favour as setting the seal on his prospects of becoming First Minister, the goal that had become almost legendary, for nobody had held the title since Fleury died.

After the King's *coucher*, Richelieu went to his own room and was about to get into bed when one of the servants of the bedchamber brought him the usual notification of the time at which the King would hold his *lever*. He also told him that Machault's disgrace had now been announced, and he had surrendered his seals of office. Richelieu returned to the King's bedchamber to see if there was any information about Machault's successor in his two posts and found Louis still chatting with some of the officers of the household. As Richelieu entered, one of the servants whispered to him that Argenson had been dismissed. Richelieu told him he was mistaken—it was Machault who had gone—but the servant insisted that he had just come from Argenson's rooms, that nobody was being allowed to enter them, and that Argenson had disappeared. Richelieu asked him to go and make further inquiries and the man returned with the confirmation that Argenson had been handed a *lettre de cachet* ordering him to retire to his estate in Touraine within forty-eight hours.

Richelieu's mouth watered in anticipation; this was the moment that he had been waiting for. As he stood by the balustrade contemplating the brilliant political future that perhaps lay within his grasp, the treacherous Maillebois hurried across the room to him. "Machault's just gone!" he whispered gleefully to Richelieu. Richelieu, even more gleefully, whispered back: "And so has your uncle!" Maillebois gaped in astonishment and asked Richelieu what he was talking about. "I am only telling you what has happened," Richelieu said smugly. "You might be well advised to go and make sure for yourself." It was a perfect ending to an excellent evening.

Yet his hopes were to be dashed once more. In all the reshuffling of ministers that Pompadour dictated to Louis during her seventeen years in power, never once did she permit Richelieu to occupy even a minor seat on the council. The succession to Argenson's office had been given to his nephew, the marquis de Paulmy. Since Paulmy's qualifications were far from impressive, he was given the maréchal de Belle-Isle as an adviser—another blow to Richelieu, for now he had one of his most virulent enemies at the Ministry of War, determined to block any attempts at further progress in the army.

Throughout January another unhappy warrior, Admiral Byng, had been appearing before a court martial on board the *St. George* in Portsmouth harbour. Richelieu had written a plea in Byng's defence, which Voltaire copied and sent on to the president of the court: "Admiral Byng's position touches me deeply. I assure you that everything that I have seen and know of him redounds only to his credit, which should not be attacked when one has been defeated after having done all that could be expected of one. When two brave men fight there must inevitably be one who comes off worse, without that being a cause for blame. All Admiral Byng's manoeuvres were admirable, according to the honest opinion of our sailors; the forces were equal, since the English had thirteen vessels and we twelve, but our crews were fresher and more numerous. Chance, which rules over all combats and especially those at sea, was more favourable to us in sending more of our bullets into the English ships and it seems to me to be generally admitted that if the English had persisted, their fleet would have been lost, so that there can never have been a more crying injustice than that with which Admiral Byng is threatened, and every man of honour, and above all every military man, must be concerned with it." It was a gallant gesture but of no avail, and neither was the unanimous recommendation for mercy of the court. The government needed a scapegoat, and, while Blakeney, who had surrendered in much more dubious circumstances, was raised to the peerage and a public subscription opened to erect a statue to him, Byng was shot on the deck of the *St. George* on the 14th of March, *pour encourager les autres,* as Voltaire said.

In Paris, the protracted trial of Damiens had failed to discover any accomplices. It was held in the deserted Palais de Justice, for *parlement* was having one of its frequent quarrels with the King over taxes and had refused to conduct any of its normal business. Richelieu attended as frequently as his duties at Versailles would permit, to sit as a member of the court and be bored by the intricate arguments in favour of identifying the true instigators of the crime as Molinists or Jansenists or Jesuits or *parlement*. In fact, Damiens, who made several attempts to take his life in prison but showed little interest in his trial, appears to have been inspired only by the primitive logic of his small, clouded mind. He had worked as a servant in many houses and in one of them had heard somebody refer to the Metz affair and add that the only way to make the King behave decently was to frighten him with death and hell fire. From that moment, Damiens said, he felt it his duty to do something that would frighten the King, but not seriously harm him.

At 4 a.m. on 28 March the judges entered his cell to read him the verdict and sentence of the court, although he already knew what the atrocious details would be and in a dull, mocking way sometimes prompted the magistrates. At 7 a.m. began the *questions ordinaire et extraordinaire*, the full range of judicial torture; he added nothing to what he had previously said and, at 3 p.m., unable to stand as a result of the torture, he was dragged to a tumbrel and carted to Notre Dame, where he made the *amende honorable* and asked forgiveness for his sins. From Notre Dame he was taken to the Hôtel de Ville, jolting through dense crowds of sightseers, who showed interest in the condemned man but neither sympathy for his plight nor condemnation of his crime.

At the Hôtel de Ville he repeated that he had nothing to add to his confession, that he had no accomplices, and that nobody had been aware of what he intended to do. He was then taken out into the middle of the place de Grève and a ripple of excitement ran through the spectators, some of whom had been playing cards to while away the time at the windows that they had hired for 20 louis in the surrounding buildings, others standing behind the wooden barriers and the ranks of soldiers lining the square, and a few clinging precariously to roofs and chimneys. Damiens, fully conscious but showing no sign of emotion, helped the executioners to take off his clothes and was then pinioned to the table by iron hoops, which passed round his trunk, over his shoulders, and between his legs and were tightened by great screws. His head could move but the rest of his body was firmly clamped to the table.

One of the executioners clapped a handcuff over Damiens's right wrist and held it while another applied burning sulphur to the criminal hand that had been raised against the sacred majesty of the King. The man on the bench uttered terrible cries, which continued until his hand had been almost burned away; then the executioners tied cords to his arms and legs, attaching them high up on the thighs and biceps and winding them round and round, down to the ankles and wrists. The cords were fastened to the harnesses of four strong horses that had been led up to the corners of the table; the chief executioner gave the signal and his men set the horses tugging, with short, powerful, rhythmic jerks.

The man on the table began to scream again, but the too-strong flesh and sinew would not part. The horses were whipped into more vigorous action and the man's shrieks produced a mounting hum of comment and animation in the crowd. After an hour, the executioners took the two horses out of the shafts of the tumbrel to supplement the efforts of the original four and attached them to Damiens's thighs, pulling sideways. The only outcome was a momentary increase in the victim's screams. The executioners walked across the square to consult with the judges, but these merely repeated that the man must be executed in accordance with the terms of his sentence; although the horses were whipped up once more, it was soon evident that, despite the flogging that was being administered to them, they were becoming tired and discouraged. Dusk was approaching and the air was chilly; the crowd, accustoming itself to the horror and losing its sense of wonderment at the spectacle and the screams, was beginning to become restless; at last the judges agreed that the condemned man should be dismembered with the aid of knives.

After the horses had been tugging for a total period of one and a half hours, the left thigh parted from the body. There was handclapping from the crowd. But it would be wrong to think that, in this age of sensibility, none of the onlookers was touched by pity: one noble lady, unable to contain her feelings any longer, exclaimed: "Oh! one feels so sorry for those poor horses!"

Further incisions were made in the other thigh and this was successfully pulled apart from the trunk. Amazingly, the man's screams still seemed as strong as ever. But after one shoulder had been slashed round and the arm torn off, the screams diminished, although he continued to rock his head from side to side. It was only when the second arm was severed and dragged away that his head at last fell back on the slab and all sound ceased, although some said that the body still pulsed as they removed it from the iron hoops and threw it, together with the arms and legs, on to the stack of wood at the side of the square. The chief executioner set light to the pyre and for the second time that afternoon there was the stench of burning flesh in the place de Grève. The outrageous assault on the person of the King had been avenged.

§ 3

Richelieu's suspicions that the appointment of Paulmy and Belle-Isle to the War Office would do nothing to help his military career were soon confirmed. During the autumn of 1756, Frederick of Prussia had overrun Saxony, and Louis—to avenge the Dauphin's father-in-law, to help Maria Theresa, and to pursue his own plan of attacking George II by land—recalled his ambassador from Berlin and began to prepare the invasion of Hanover. On 24 February 1757, he created the comte d'Estrées a Marshal of France and gave him command of the army that was being assembled on the Lower Rhine, with the duc d'Orléans as deputy commander and the comte de Maillebois as quartermaster-general. Richelieu at once protested at having been passed over and was not at all mollified when he was given command of one of two armies that were being formed to defend the Upper Rhine. The other was to be commanded by one of Pompadour's nominees, the prince de Soubise, and neither his command nor Richelieu's was comparable in strength to the 100,000 men of Estrées's Army of Hanover.

But now court intrigues came to his assistance and from 28 June, when the foreign minister, Rouillé, was replaced by the plump, ingratiating Bernis, events moved very quickly. Estrées had disappointed Louis by the cautiousness of his advance into Germany against the numerically inferior forces of the Duke of Cumberland; he had annoyed Pompadour by complaining about her friend Pâris-Duverney, the millionaire army-contractor. And he had the misfortune of numbering among his senior officers the comte de Maillebois who was busily composing criticisms and sending them off to the War Office, where the minister was now not his uncle-by-marriage but his brother-in-law. Pompadour planned to increase the importance of Soubise's command by giving him some of Richelieu's troops and sending Richelieu off with the rest to supersede Estrées. Looking farther ahead, it was reasonable to suppose that Richelieu would commit a sufficient number of errors—all of which Maillebois could be counted on to report and exaggerate—for her to be able to replace him with Soubise, who would thus certainly qualify for a marshal's baton.

Richelieu was overjoyed when he was told in confidence on 11 July that he was shortly to take over Estrées's command, and he celebrated this unexpected turn of fortune in the massive, faithful embraces of the duchesse de Lauraguais, whom he took with him to Strasbourg, where he marshalled the reinforcements that he was to take with him. Belle-Isle, meanwhile, had been sending urgent messages to Estrées, warning of plots against him at court and urging him to bring Cumberland to battle as soon as possible instead of expending so much time and energy on complaints about supplies, the disloyalty of his officers and the lack of discipline among his troops. "If you want to continue to command the King's army, make haste to cross the Weser, to give battle and to win." On 26 July, Estrées fought Cumberland at Hastenbeck and forced him to retreat, leaving the whole of Hanover open to the advance of the French army; two days later he received notification that he was to hand over his command to Richelieu.

Richelieu joined his army at Oldendorf on 3 August. He had been placed in a delicate situation, for if he failed to achieve a decisive victory, he would be accused of having thrown away the opportunities created for him by Estrées; if he succeeded, it would be said that he had merely profited from Estrées's efforts. The enemy swept the countryside clean of provisions as he retreated, and the unusually wet summer and the fatigues of much marching and countermarching before Hastenbeck had produced an alarmingly high incidence of sickness in the French army: an average of 100 men in each battalion. Yet Richelieu, always eager to attack, urged his troops on through the torrential rain in the hope of forcing Cumberland to face him near the city of Hanover.

Cumberland refused the challenge; continuing to keep himself three or four days' march away, he went northward towards Stade, on the Elbe, where he hoped to receive reinforcements from Britain for his mixed force of Hanoverians, Brunswickians, and Hessians. Richelieu halted to rest his men and form depots of food and munitions, and on 22 August he received from Cumberland a proposal for an armistice, which he promptly rejected. On the 24th he set his army on the move again, but the next evening, after a hard day's marching under a hot sun, a fierce storm descended on the camp, the wind and hail ripping tents from their pegs and sending the horses panicking among trees that came crashing down in the tempest. It was two days before the army had dried and sorted itself out, and it continued its advance through a desolate countryside, the roads winding through marshes. Lacking stores for the winter and finding himself in a terrain which offered little freedom of movement, Richelieu was more than ever anxious to force a decision. He had sent a detachment as far south as Halberstadt to guard against a surprise attack by the Prussians, and another group had captured Harburg, preventing Cumberland from retreating round to the other side of the mouth of the Elbe; on 4 September he set up his headquarters at Kloster-Seven and, without waiting for the rest of the army to join him, made a dash with 1,000 men to try to drive in Cumberland's outer defences around Stade. The force was ludicrously small and, but for the lack of spirit of the Hanoverians and his own dashing leadership, he might well have suffered serious losses, but the raid served to rattle Cumberland's nerve.

Although Stade was a natural fortress, dominating the approaches from the westward and guarded by the Schwinge on the south and the Elbe on the east, Cumberland, possibly remembering Richelieu's victorious onslaught on Fort Saint-Philippe, did not relish the prospect of a siege, and he had been left in no doubt about Richelieu's aggressiveness. On 5 September he again asked for an armistice. Richelieu was now more ready to consider the proposal than he had been a fortnight earlier; his forces were dispersed and he did not have enough artillery with him to reduce Stade if Cumberland put up a fight. The task of bringing up guns through the marshes would be long and risky; pride urged him to dispose of the lesser German armies as quickly as possible so that he could match himself against the one man whom he considered to be a worthy opponent: Frederick of Prussia. He told Cumberland that he was willing to talk, and wrote to Paulmy and Bernis, informing them that he was opening negotiations.

Bernis agitatedly replied that the council had received no previous hint of these proposals and that an armistice would simply mean that the French, having failed to press home their advantages, would be forced to keep their army on the alert all through the winter lest Cumberland resume operations. He instructed Richelieu not to take any decisions on suggestions that had not been submitted to the King. It was a sharp reproof and Bernis was rather pleased with himself when he showed a copy to Louis, who deflated him by commenting: "You don't know the maréchal. What he refers to as a proposal is quite possibly an accomplished fact. Send a second courier to tell M. de Richelieu from me not to enter into any negotiations at all, and to refer to Fontainebleau at once any that may already have begun."

Louis was right; four days later he received a dispatch from Richelieu saying that he had signed an agreement with Cumberland at Kloster-Seven on 8 September, and that it had been guaranteed by the King of Denmark. Cumberland undertook to send back to their native states all his auxiliaries from Hesse, Brunswick, Saxe-Gotha, and Lippe, with passports issued by Richelieu and orders to disperse to their homes; to withdraw his own Hanoverian troops beyond the Elbe, with the exception of a garrison of 6,000 in Stade, who were not to be reinforced and were not to venture beyond limits laid down by the French; and to accept the occupation by the French of all the territory which they at present held until the conclusion of peace between the two countries. Richelieu, on his side, accorded Cumberland the honours of war and allowed his troops to retain their arms.

This was not the armistice that Bernis had feared; it was a capitulation, and news of it was received in France with an outburst of joy. Richelieu sent Fronsac, who had already collected French honours for the news of Fort Saint-Philippe, to Vienna with the tidings of Kloster-Seven, hoping that he would reap an Austrian reward; to the French court he sent the duc de Duras, whom many believed to be his illegitimate son. Duras was the luckier of the two: three days after his arrival, the duc de Gesvres died, and, unlike Fronsac, who had merely received the reversion of his father's post, Duras was at once appointed to the vacancy as First Gentleman of the Bedchamber.

On every front the prospects were good: the Austrians had defeated Frederick of Prussia at Kolin in June; the Russians had routed another Prussian army at Gross-Jaegersdorf in August; the Swedes were at Stralsund, intent on winning back their former territories in Pomerania. Leaving a token force to ensure the observance of the treaty, Richelieu set off on 10 September by forced marches to Halberstadt, whence he would be in a position to menace Magdeburg and, beyond it, Berlin. He drove off an attack by Prince Ferdinand of Brunswick; signed an agreement with him on the lines of demarcation to be observed while both armies went into winter quarters; sent twenty battalions of infantry and eighteen squadrons of cavalry to reinforce Soubise, who thought that Frederick of Prussia might attack him in the defensive position he had taken up at Eisenach; and then distributed his army in depth through Brunswick and Hanover, while he himself looked forward to a triumphal return to Versailles until the spring.

He had failed to allow for the intrigues of Bernis and Pompadour and the bad faith of Cumberland. Bernis, enraged at Richelieu's contemptuous disregard of the foreign office, and Pompadour, annoyed that Richelieu's success had frustrated her plans for Soubise's advancement, both found fault with the treaty. Bernis insisted that the Hanoverian troops that were allowed to cross to the right bank of the Elbe must undertake not to serve against France or her allies; and that the Hessian troops should be disarmed before they were allowed to return to their homes; and he warned Richelieu that George II and his government had no respect for even the most solemn undertakings: "It observes them only when it thinks it cannot violate them with advantage and impunity." It was not until 8 October, four weeks after the treaty had been signed by Richelieu and Cumberland, that Bernis informed Richelieu that Louis was ready to ratify it as soon as the King of Britain had done so. "Henceforward," Bernis wrote smugly to the French ambassador in Vienna, "M. de Richelieu will do well, in any matter of politics, to wait until I have communicated the King's commands to him."

Bernis's concern that the Hanoverian troops should undertake not to serve against France's allies was unnecessary, for George II and Maria Theresa had been discussing signing a separate armistice and deserting Prussia and France respectively. If Bernis really believed that the British would try to dishonour the agreement, it would have been wiser for France to have ratified it at once. There had, indeed, already been signs that Cumberland was preparing to welsh on the bargain, for on 23 September he had written as "votre ami affectionné" to Richelieu: "Having been informed by the Landgrave of Hesse-Cassel that you have told him that the Hessians who formed part of my army are to be disarmed on return to their country, although you did not desire this to be put *positively* in the *Convention* that we have made: I find myself obliged to inform you that, notwithstanding my firm resolve to keep *in good faith* not only the *Letter* but the *Spirit* of the *Convention* guaranteed by His *Danish* Majesty, I find myself obliged to halt all the columns of troops which were on the march, until you shall have explained yourself on this article." The Hessians remained halted, neither disarmed nor in the areas to which the treaty confined the garrison of Stade; Cumberland was recalled and another general, Zastrow, given command of the Hanoverian troops. Zastrow informed the French that instead of dispersing his troops he was having to keep them together because of difficulties in arranging food supplies; shortly afterwards, Richelieu learned that the Hanoverians were bringing in remounts for their cavalry and building up other military stores.

It is significant, in the light of what happened later, that, although Bernis had tried to discipline him and assert his own authority by tinkering with the clauses of the treaty, none of Richelieu's critics had yet spoken out against the convention as such. Indeed, Pompadour in a letter which she ended, in her typically patronizing style, "rest assured that your enemies cannot do you any harm so long as you remain my friend and have confidence in me," told him on 2 October that "I think as he [Bernis] does about your capitulation, I find it good and indeed excellent." But the whole picture changed on 5 November when Soubise, with 50,000 men, met Frederick of Prussia, with little more than 20,000, at Rossbach and was out-generalled and crushingly defeated. Simultaneously with this news, Richelieu learned that the Hanoverians were concentrating troops up and down the Elbe and that Zastrow refused to discuss the terms of the convention until he had heard

from George II, who had not yet ratified it. Richelieu counter-
manded the orders for his army to disperse into winter quarters
and hastened to Brunswick, ready to move either left against the
Hanoverians or right to prevent Frederick pursuing Soubise, and
then sent detachments to Luneburg and Soltau. Before the end of
the month, he received official notification from Ferdinand of
Brunswick that he was adding the armies of Hanover and her allies
to his own and that the "truce" of Kloster-Seven was ended.

Richelieu was genuinely appalled at his opponents' conduct, at
once dishonest and dishonourable. He was also in an extremely
difficult position, for he now faced a numerically superior enemy;
his troops were still dispersed; some of them—the garrison at Harburg, for instance—were already besieged. He was short of supplies
in a country that had been stripped bare by both sides. True to
his nature, he decided to attack. He had been marching north,
through Brunswick, Wittingen, and Luneburg, to relieve Harburg
and threaten Zastrow; now he turned south again, racing back
through Ulzen to Celle, on which Ferdinand was advancing with
his Prussian contingent. On Christmas Day he flung bridges across
the Aller and chased Ferdinand from the town, but lack of supplies prevented him from continuing the pursuit. He withdrew his
men behind the Aller and established his own headquarters in
Hanover, reasonably confident that there would be no further attacks before the spring. But although the enemy in front of him
was quiescent, those at the rear were more active than ever.

Belle-Isle had been more than ready to join forces with Bernis
and Pompadour. "M. de Richelieu tells us nothing, except when
and how it pleases him," he wrote to Vienna. Bernis claimed that
Richelieu could have prevented Soubise's defeat at Rossbach if he
had advanced beyond Halberstadt and threatened Frederick; Bernis even suggested that Richelieu had deliberately refrained out of
dislike for Pompadour. Belle-Isle, writing to Soubise, added the
final smear—and the one that clung the longest: "The disorder, in-
subordination and brigandage of M. de Richelieu's army have been
carried beyond all bounds. I have never seen anything that even
begins to approach it in all the fifty-seven years that I have been a
soldier. It is undoubtedly the fault of the general, for it is his duty

to be the master; otherwise he is not fit to command. Though it is true that one must begin by having clean hands oneself and set an example of the most exemplary probity."

There was a little truth and a great deal of injustice in these accusations. Richelieu had taken a risk in allowing his enemies to retain their arms, but he had some right to expect that a son of the King of Britain would have standards of honour at least as high as his own; and the auxiliary troops would have been safely dispersed to their homes if Versailles had not delayed the ratification of the treaty. He had moved on to Halberstadt with all possible speed; his orders had been to remain there, ready for an advance in the spring, and the army contractors had even been instructed not to supply him with any more bread if he went beyond the town during that year's campaign. The reinforcements that he had sent to Soubise had been greater than he had been asked for, and, despite a gruelling march over the snow-covered Hartz Mountains, they arrived ten days before Soubise, by his incompetence, ruined Richelieu's plans as well as his own at Rossbach.

The complaints about looting were no doubt well founded (and Richelieu had in fact told Zastrow that he would feel himself at liberty to sack the territories he occupied if the convention was broken); but this was the custom of the time, each nation accusing the others of it while denying the guilt of its own troops. The wars of the eighteenth century were the seed bed for the fine old traditions of the most famous regiments of Europe, when officers and men set for their successors an example of unflinching courage, looting, rape, and wanton destruction. It was still the practice for senior officers to share the hazards of war with their juniors, and they also shared with them the pillage and the sexual and sadistic pleasures of campaigning in another land. When Richelieu took over the Army of Hanover, complaints were already coming in about looting under Estrées; there had been looting under Saxe and Lowendahl; Berwick had been reproved for it while Richelieu was with him at the siege of Philippsburg. The greatest looter of the eighteenth century was the greatest French general of his time, Villars, under whom Richelieu served his apprenticeship at Denain. Yet, because Richelieu's enemies were so active and successful in spreading scandalous stories about him—that his troops had nicknamed him *le petit père La Maraude*, or even that he had taken bribes from Cumberland and Frederick—Richelieu gained the reputation among his contemporaries of being more corrupt than most. When, on his return, he built a sumptuous *salon* at the bottom of the garden of the hôtel d'Antin, his critics mockingly named it the *pavillon de Hanovre*.

Soldiering for Richelieu was interesting only when battles were taking place; the prospect of three months in winter quarters in Hanover, far from the delights and excitements of Paris and the court, filled him with gloom. He sent to Louis an appreciation of the position, a forecast of the possible lines of attack open to the enemy in the spring and his plans for combating them. He added that, because of the need to discuss these plans and also to restore his health, he begged permission to be allowed to return to the court for the remainder of the winter. He was restless, embittered by criticism; Pompadour had succeeded in laying the blame for the whole disappointing campaign on his shoulders, Soubise's mistakes as well as his own. He may have been genuinely ill; certainly the skin disease from which he previously suffered had broken out again. Bernis persuaded Louis that Richelieu's second-in-command, Villemeur, was incapable of exercising command in his absence and the duc de Clermont was sent to Hanover. It was clear that this was a permanent replacing of one general by another and that Richelieu would not be returning to the army in the spring.

He arrived at court on 20 February and was received in a friendly way by Louis, much more affably than after the Minorcan campaign, for there were now no successes to forgive. Richelieu tried to justify his conduct of the campaign and particularly the Convention of Kloster-Seven, but nobody was interested now, and certainly nobody was willing to be convinced. The pleasures of court life, which had been so seductive when viewed from Hanover, turned sour. He decided to take up his governorship of Guienne, which the military expeditions of the past two years had prevented him from assuming officially. He let it be known that he intended to spend as much as half of every year in his new capital, Bordeaux; there were many who believed and hoped that he would settle there permanently.

§ 4

The burgesses of Bordeaux were well aware of their new governor's taste for vice-regal splendour, and they received him with the mixture of obsequiousness and bombast that his rank and their pretensions dictated. Early in the morning of Saturday, 3 June, two aldermen, in the new white and red satin robes lined with red taffeta that had been expressly made for the town dignitaries and had cost the town purse more than 1,000 livres apiece, left Bordeaux for Blaye, the port twenty-five miles down-river on the opposite bank of the Gironde, accompanied by the officer of the watch, twelve constables, and two trumpeters. They took with them the *Maison Navale*, the richly gilded ceremonial barge, glittering in the bright sunshine and bouncing across the waves under a gusty wind as they towed it behind the municipal brigantine.

At midday on Sunday, Richelieu came down the steps of the citadel at Blaye, boarded the *Maison Navale*, and seated himself in the gilded armchair that had been placed behind a gilt balustrade in the large cabin, whose walls were decorated with crimson velvet, gold lace, and the arms of Richelieu. The barge got under way, drawn by four longboats manned by twenty men apiece, each man dressed in a red and white cloak with cap to match; while a fifth longboat towed a smaller vessel containing an orchestra whose puffs and squeaks, now that the wind had subsided, drifted clearly across the intervening water as refreshments were served to the voyagers: the guests accounting for 264 livres' worth although the governor took no more than a bowl of soup. As they approached the outskirts of the town and rounded the long curve from the quai des Chartrons to the quai Sainte-Croix, the great merchant vessels moored on either side fired salutes, and more gunfire cracked out from the shore batteries. The governor disembarked to receive the keys of the town from the senior alderman and then to be escorted to the tribune—of timber, paper and canvas, painted to resemble marble and gold—where he received addresses from other officials. From there he progressed to a triumphal arch (of imitation greystone and yellow marble) near the porte de Cailhou, and then on horseback, at the head of a great procession, to the cathedral for a *Te Deum*. It was evening before he took the final salute at the entrance to the Hôtel du Gouvernement. It had been a successful day, with only one cloud to mar it: the representatives of the *cour des aides* (the board of excise and revenue) and of *parlement*, forbidden to address him as "Monsieur" as they had intended, had equally refused to give him the title of "Monseigneur" that he had demanded.

The battle over privileges was joined again within the week. On 7 June, Richelieu made his first visit to the Palais de Justice, preceded by forty guards and all his household and followed by the provincial nobility. The guards halted at the head of the grand staircase, and the nobility left their swords outside the *grande salle*, where Richelieu was met by two ushers and conducted to the doors of the audience chamber. Here four councillors and the president greeted him; and the president, boldly taking his stand on the procedure recorded in the *parlement*'s register for the year 1644, manoeuvred himself into the right-hand position and sped through the doors a fraction ahead of the governor. Richelieu restored the balance by taking a place above the *doyen* and having a *carreau* on the seat of his chair as well as under his feet. But he lost the final round when, having addressed the *parlement* and sat down again, he found that the warm and respectful reply was delivered by the president *with his cap on*.

That evening Richelieu gave a dinner in the Hôtel du Gouvernement for the local aristocracy and their ladies: 400 guests in all, of whom 196 sat down at a single table. As time went on, his dinners became more intimate and the guests largely restricted to women; but he threw open the *salons* almost every night to any of the Bordeaux gentry who wished to come and play the dice games that were forbidden elsewhere in the town. Richelieu was often wrongly accused of having corrupted the King, but he could with some justice be held responsible for a marked falling-off in the moral standards of Bordeaux. He converted much of the governor's residence into a gaming house, and used the rest of it for his private assignations, though without showing any gratitude to the ladies who granted him their favours. Some years later, when the *intendant* complained that prostitution was rife and the conduct of some of the women so scandalous that only locking them up in prison would cure them, Richelieu smilingly answered: "Why make exceptions? Treat them all the same. I'll have the town gates locked."

On 17 July, the Jesuits invited Richelieu to hear a philosophical thesis which they had dedicated to him. Representatives of the *parlement* were invited, but the president learned in time that Richelieu was insisting on a dais as well as a *carreau*. The parlementarians did not attend; neither did Richelieu. The thesis was delivered to his empty chair, which had been placed not on a dais but on a carpet. The implications of all this were closely studied and the general verdict was that Richelieu had scored. But in October, at a *Te Deum* in the cathedral, he discovered too late that he had been given a seat behind the president, and then— even more vexatious—somebody noticed that members of his bodyguard were inside the choir, and he had to order their removal, since his privilege extended only from the choir to the church door.

The *Te Deum* was in honour of a great victory gained by Richelieu's kinsman and Marie-Anne's one-time lover, the duc d'Agénois, who had succeeded to his father's title of duc d'Aiguillon in 1750 and was now military governor of Brittany. British raiding parties had been bringing much havoc and shame to the coast of Normandy and Brittany, and Aiguillon had at last caught a large force near Saint-Cast, where he inflicted a crushing defeat on them. He was the hero of France, which was again smarting under the defeat of the army of Hanover at Krefeld, where Ferdinand of Brunswick attacked just as the comte de Clermont was sitting down to his dinner; by the time he had finished his leisurely meal, he had lost 4,000 men. "The comte de Clermont," remarked one of his officers, "dined at one, had lost a battle before six, reached Neuss [twelve miles from Krefeld] at ten, and went to bed at midnight. He had accomplished a great deal in a short time."

Aiguillon's victory, and the possibility of raids along his own coastline, prompted Richelieu to look to his defences and during the next twelve months he made continual tours of inspection, travelling in his *dormeuse* and insisting, even in the smallest towns, on the same sort of regal reception that he had been given at Bordeaux. There was nothing lackadaisical about his methods; he prodded and pried and was not to be put off with excuses or glib assurances. In April 1759, during a visit to Bayonne, he went down to the Spanish border and admired the lively paces of the Basque girls who performed a folk dance for him; but his staff remarked with surprise and admiration that for three whole days in Bayonne itself he found no time for *les belles dames*.

For the smaller towns, a visit from Richelieu was as bad as a plague of locusts, and the departmental records groan with the doleful accounts of the expenses they were put to. Perigueux, for example, on which he descended in October 1759, had to employ 350 workmen for a whole day at six sous a head to cart away the heaps of rubbish that had accumulated at the town gates; messengers and look-outs had to be hired to give warning of the governor's coming; and a scribe had to copy out details of a visit by the prince de Conti so that it could be consulted for precedents. There were 15 livres to be paid to carpenters for chopping down a tree in the main square and carting away the pieces, 80 livres to the joiners who worked on the *tribune des harangues* that went up in its place, and 84 livres to the painters who decorated the tribune.

There were materials as well as wages: 134 livres' worth of stakes and joists and planks, 30 livres for iron rope and nails, 14 livres 17 sous 3 deniers for canvas and 50 livres 15 sous for paint. There was the hire of a carpet for the town hall and the purchase of candles for the men who worked late; 120 livres for the volunteer band and two supplementary hautbois; and 12 livres for the four drummers of the company of artisans. And then the presents: gloves for the officers of the guard; two pairs of silk stockings for the lieutenant of the maréchal's guard; gifts of money to the guardsmen and the valets, and candles for the footmen.

There were travelling expenses for the two councillors who went to meet the governor; and 15 livres' worth of gunpowder for the volunteers and men with falconets who gave him a welcoming volley. On top of this there was a calf to be presented to the bishop at a cost of 25 livres; and partridges and truffles for the bishop too: another 38 livres. What with the blacksmith and two pounds of candles to light the town hall and unspecified "sundries" to the amount of 15 livres, the town had to find almost 1500 livres for the pleasure of having the maréchal tell it how inefficiently it was preparing to withstand the British. For Richelieu's criticisms were sharp and to the point.

In Guienne, as in Languedoc, the Protestants were a problem to him; their religious sympathies with the British and their continued denunciation by the priests and repression by the government made them an obvious risk to the security of the country. They were loyal Frenchmen and would not give direct aid to France's enemies; but they were also victims of persecution and might well take advantage of attacks from outside to begin an uprising within. In January 1760, the Protestants of Guienne wrote to their co-religionists in Switzerland and Holland that there had been a slight relaxation in government pressure, but later in the year they reported that Richelieu "has taken it into his head to try to abolish all public worship, even meetings in houses, and to have the children re-baptized. We cannot tell what will result from this move; these are newly founded parishes, consisting of timid and fearful souls. God, no doubt, and J.C. will give them strength to find glory."

In March 1761, another correspondent wrote bitterly of Richelieu as an "old sinner who thinks he can attain Paradise by dint of persecutions . . . but it seems that the court does not approve of his vexations." He could not have been more mistaken; Richelieu had never shown any belief in God or an afterlife and would probably have considered that, if such a life existed, it would come to him as his natural due. He was as incapable of understanding the proselytizing zeal of the Catholics as he was of approving the Protestant determination not to be converted. The orders came from the King's council and he carried them out—that was all.

For exactly the same reason, he was meticulous in carrying out his instructions to force through legislation in the *parlement*, which demanded the right to debate the taxes whose volume increased with the continuing costs of war and royal debauchery.

From 1761, when he overrode all protests and had the new taxes entered in the parlementary registers without a word of discussion, to 1771, when he filled the streets with troops, dissolved the recalcitrant *parlement* and set up a new and docile one in its place, he was constantly quarrelling with the province's representatives. But as he had a stack of blank *lettres de cachet* at his elbow and the readiness to use them on the slightest pretext, there was nobody who could stand against him. "No other governor," said one commentator, "made such a wide use of his authority." Nor, probably, so much enjoyed doing so.

The cares of office did not divert his attention from the ladies for long. At Montpellier he had a permanent mistress named Madame Capon, the wife of a local *syndic*; in Bordeaux he renewed acquaintance with her daughter, Madame Rousse, and established her openly as his mistress despite the scandalmongers who whispered that he was her father. She presided over his dinner parties in the Hôtel du Gouvernement while another young woman was installed in the new house that he built on his estate at Fronsac, a few miles away. The low, rectangular building in the Italian style stood on a hill above the village, approached on foot by a magnificent flight of broad marble steps or by carriage along the curving drive that swept round the hill and up to the terrace. On the ground floor, besides a dining room and study and bedroom, there was an oval salon, 36 feet long and 30 feet broad, whose walls and ceiling, and even the floor, were entirely covered with mirrors, and from whose windows the eye roved over the long loop of the Dordogne, across to the vineyards of Entre-deux-Mers on one side and of Saint-Emilion on the other. Bordeaux was constantly buzzing with stories of the orgies over which Richelieu presided there; no woman of reputation could afford to be seen within its walls, and no woman of fashion could afford not to.

The intimate parties were held at Fronsac, the elaborate ones at Bordeaux. There he lived in vice-regal splendour, admitting the common people on high days and holidays to wander in and out of his dining room and watch him at dinner as if he were the King himself. After dinner he would take his guests to the theatre, where the plays, which he chose himself, were frequently improper. In winter he would give a ball after the theatre, but in the summer the performance did not begin until the heat of the afternoon had passed. To ensure that the air remained fresh, nobody was allowed into the theatre before the governor arrived, and the rest of the audience had to wait outside locked doors until it pleased Richelieu to make his appearance.

§ 5

He kept to his resolve of spending at least half of each year in Guienne, and sometimes it was longer, for when he grew piqued with life at court or in Paris, he would go back to comfort himself with the pomp and circumstance of Bordeaux. In Paris he was often reduced to seeking his mistresses in low company and entertaining them in houses of assignation, such as the fashionable gambling hall kept by the comte Jean du Barry in the rue de la Jussienne. Louis Marais, the police inspector who had taken over the supervision of the Paris brothels from Meusnier (and was not sure of the spelling of a name that was to become famous), reported in 1759 that "on 22 April, La Gourdan [a well-known bawd] sent the demoiselle Martin at eight in the evening to the comte du Bary, who introduced her to M. le maréchal de Richelieu, and he left them together in his room. M. Dubary told her: at any time that you have need of 50 louis, you can find them here or at M. le maréchal's. M. le maréchal has promised to pay her frequent visits."

Richelieu was as malicious and high-spirited as ever and delighted in the discomfiture of others. One evening early in May 1763, he went down to the Seine to bathe at Poitevin's floating baths just above the pont Royal. It was dusk when he arrived, and he was followed shortly afterwards by two people who entered the adjoining cubicle in the men's section. One of them was the archbishop of Lyon and the other, though Richelieu did not yet know it, was the new inheritor of the title of duchesse de Mazarin, dressed in man's clothing. As soon as they began speaking Richelieu pricked up his ears.

"He listened more closely and thought that he recognized Mme. de Mazarin's voice. He sought and found a crack in the partition through which he verified with his eyes that it was she. He equally clearly recognized M. de Montazet, archbishop of Lyon. This spectacle interested M. le maréchal immensely. . . . Eventually the prelate got into Mme. de Mazarin's bath and, burning amid the waters, set about giving proof of his love. He was on the point of a successful conclusion when the maréchal struck up a saucy song which put our lovers off; and the archbishop got out of the nymph's bath furious at not having executed his project. The maréchal found the incident so diverting that he has written to Favart, asking him to compose some verses on it."

But these days it was Richelieu himself who was sometimes mocked in love. More and more he was having to buy his pleasures, and more and more he was beginning to fear the diseases which promiscuity might bring—and from which he had suffered enough in the past. In the hope of avoiding them he made use of a professional procuress, Madame Surville, who had learned her trade as an attendant at the Opéra. She was soon fobbing off on him an all-too-experienced young woman named Le Blanc, whom she represented to him as a virgin. "How easy it is to trick even the greatest men when they are obsessed!" Marais commented at the end of a long report on how the maréchal had been fooled.

In August of that year Richelieu decided to take the waters at Bagnères-de-Luchon and then go on to Saint-Gaudens to open the *Etats* of Nebourzan, for he included within his governorship both *pays d'élection* and *pays d'états*. He took Madame Rousse with him, and there was a great scurrying round and exchange of letters among local officials anxious to curry favour and avert wrath. "M. le maréchal expects to arrive between the 10th and 12th September, but you will understand that you should announce his arrival for the 1st, so that everything may be ready sooner rather than later—lodgings, roads, provisions and the rest. . . . You must not forget to put the road from Bagnères-de-Luchon to Montrejean in good repair, and from Montrejean to La Bigorre, as well as Montrejean to Auch and Auch to Layrac. . . . Do your best to see that Madame Rousse is lodged comfortably. . . . Try to think of some little things that you can procure for Madame Rousse. . . ."

It was at Montrejean, where the road began to climb into the

Pyrénées, that difficulties arose, and at Cierp, fifteen miles farther on, a traveller usually had to dismount from his carriage and decide whether to continue on horseback or to get into a bullock cart, furnished with a canvas tilt and some chairs, which took five or six hours to cover the remaining ten miles to Luchon. Sometimes a narrow carriage for two persons, drawn by a hand-led horse, could make the journey; in doubtful weather it was followed by the peasantry, ready to push when the vehicle stuck or right it when it toppled over. Richelieu, however, found the roads tolerably well repaired and, in lieu of starving peasants, took with him a squadron of the maréchaussée and a company of infantry from the militia. The owners of the houses that had been set aside for him and Madame Rousse borrowed the best furniture that their friends could provide, and he was not deprived of the customary crimson silk curtains or the crimson counterpane on his bed, or a two-gun salute from a couple of cannon borrowed from the seigneur de Barbazan.

He returned to Bordeaux via Nérac, attended by the usual confusion and expense: cockades for the trumpeters, drummers, pipers, and town-sergeants; 36 livres for a yard and a half of the inevitable crimson velvet; 32 livres for gloves for the maréchal; more than 200 livres for the supply and preparation of part of the supper—not a very large part, to judge by the separate bills for meat, wood and coal, bread and biscuits, salad and pot herbs, sugar, spice, anchovies and olives, a hired *maître d'hôtel* from the nearest town that boasted one, and 25 livres' worth of fish from the *chasse-marée*, the express cart that carried fish from the coast inland and happened to pass that morning. There were torches and candles and a tip for the women who got up the linen for the tables, and the hire of the tables themselves and glasses and goblets, and jugs and bowls, and tapestries to hang in the great hall of the college, and 8 livres' worth of nails to hang up laurels and metal decorations on the main gate; to say nothing of gratifications for the drummers and pipers and trumpeters and town-sergeant, and the hire of horses and the cost of filling holes in the road. It all came to more than 870 livres, in return for which the inhabitants at least had the pleasure of seeing the maréchal wearing the badge of the Saint-Esprit on the *cordon bleu* across a suit covered with diamonds, which was said to have cost him 150,000 livres.

In Paris and Versailles his great interest now was the theatre. This undoubtedly arose in part from the fact that the actresses were pretty and frail, and so ready to be overtaken that their pursuit did not place too great a strain on a man now far advanced into his sixties; but he had always been fond of the drama: Voltaire, Marmontel, and Favart were among his close acquaintances, and their plays were often performed in his private theatre at the hôtel d'Antin; the only material memorial that Richelieu left behind him is the magnificent municipal theatre that he had built in Bordeaux despite the opposition of the inhabitants. During his year *en exercice* he was responsible not only for the *menus plaisirs* at court but also for the administration of the Opéra, the Comédie-Française, and the Comédie-Italienne. Unfortunately, as with everything else, he was not willing to restrict his activities to his own period of office and was constantly interfering with the other three First Gentlemen: Aumont, Duras, and Fleury, and harassing the miserable Papillon de la Ferté who, as *intendant* of the *menus plaisirs*, was annually confronted with the task of balancing an unbalanceable budget.

It was with Duras, Richelieu's former protégé and putative son, that his quarrels were fiercest, usually precipitated by rows between their respective mistresses. In 1763, Aumont suggested that duties and spheres of influence should be agreed between the four of them, and they finally arranged that Aumont should be responsible for the accounts, the staff, and the stores, Fleury for music and funerals, and Richelieu and Duras for the theatres. There was an unwritten understanding that Duras should have the Comédie-Française and Richelieu the Comédie-Italienne, but within a few months Duras was in a fury because Richelieu had been poaching on his ground and had taken as his mistress Mademoiselle Pinet, who was a member of the Comédie-Française but not, to judge by a police report, its most brilliant star: "One must hope that M. le maréchal has found her more lively in their *tête-à-tête* than she is on the stage; otherwise he runs the risk of catching a cold."

Richelieu was unpopular with the actors, who were restive under his autocratic hand, and in April 1765, a storm broke. He had become very friendly with an actress of the Comédie-Française named Dubois, who had first lost her innocence to his son, Fronsac, and whose father, also a member of the troupe, had received treatment from a surgeon for venereal disease and then refused to pay the surgeon's bill. The surgeon complained to the company of actors, and these, seeing an opportunity to embarrass the favoured Mademoiselle Dubois, referred the dispute to Richelieu, who replied that it was a matter of honour for their own jurisdiction. Delighted, the actors expelled Dubois from their company; but his daughter demanded Richelieu's intervention, and he ordered the troupe to take Dubois back and to continue with the projected performance of Le Siège de Calais, in which the elder Dubois played Sir Walter de Manny.

The actors determined on a trial of strength. At half past four in the afternoon of Monday, 15 April, the actor Le Kain arrived at the theatre and asked who was to play Manny; on being told that it was Dubois, he handed in his script and left. He was followed by another of the leading players, Molé, who did the same thing. Finally, Mademoiselle Clairon, queen of the Comédie-Française, at whose home the whole plot had been rehearsed, arrived saying that she had left her sickbed to appear because it was her duty to her public. "And who is playing Manny?" she asked. She was informed that it was Dubois, whereupon she was taken ill again and had to return to her bed. It was now nearly time for the curtain to go up. One of the actors went on the stage and announced that, since some of the players were missing, it was not possible to present Le Siège de Calais and Le Joueur would be performed instead. At this, there was such an outburst of shouting and whistling that the actors were unable to make themselves heard, money had to be refunded and the theatre closed. The King's players had disobeyed the orders of the King's First Gentleman and were in a state of mutiny; at Richelieu's instigation, the Lieutenant-General of police, Sartines, ordered Clairon, Le Kain, and Molé to be taken to For l'Evêque, the old prison on the quai de la Mégisserie.

Clairon, for whom a room was specially furnished, went there in style in the carriage of Madame de Sauvigny, wife of the *intendant* of Paris, and, amid applause from the crowd, seated on Madame de Sauvigny's lap; though her pleasure was somewhat alloyed by the attitude of the exempt of police who escorted her. When he read her the order for her arrest, she declaimed in her grandest manner that she was obedient to the King's commands, that she was entirely at the King's disposal, that her possessions, her person, and her life were his, but that her honour remained untouched. "That's true enough," said the exempt. "Where there's nothing, the King has no rights." Clairon was released, on grounds of ill health, on 22 April, but the men were kept in prison, brought out to play their parts, and then taken back again. They too began to plead illness, and in the first week of May performances had to be suspended for lack of players. The Parisian playgoers, always a very vocal group, began to protest against Richelieu's tyranny. It was Fronsac who found the solution to the problem: through Mademoiselle Dubois he persuaded her father to offer his resignation from the company in return for a pension of 1,500 livres a year and a lump sum of 4,000 livres to pay his debts.

Richelieu, seeking a less tempestuous mistress, left Mademoiselle Dubois and found an eighteen-year-old Provençale, Rosette, *"belle comme une ange,"* whom he set up in his *petite maison* in the rue de Clichy. She shared his favours with several others, for in January 1766, Marais reported that he had picked up the former Madame Surville, since widowed and married to a man named La Mule, and had forced her to tell him all the details of her practice. Her principal customers included Richelieu and Duras and four others "but M. de Richelieu was the best and that same day, the 6th of this month, she was due to take to his *pavillon* [at the bottom of the garden of the hôtel d'Antin] the demoiselle Sainte-Foy, formerly mistress of the duc de Duras. In fact this was done, and the maréchal gave her ten gold louis. The said La Mule also admitted to me that over the past six months or more, and at least twice a week, she has taken to him the demoiselle La Blanc [with whom she had tricked him three years before] and that each time he gave her six louis."

On 14 March, Marais reported: "Last Tuesday the woman Surville, called La Mule, took to M. le maréchal duc de Richelieu's *pavillon* a girl aged eighteen, named Clauze, who lives at the porte Saint-Denis in the house of a flower-seller. She is very pretty and has for six months had an understanding with a hat-maker named Dubois, living in the rue pavée Saint-Sauveur. The maréchal, after disporting himself with her in his usual fashion [here follows an unrepeatably frank statement of Richelieu's sexual habits] gave her eight gold louis and three louis to the woman La Mule, whom he greatly saddened by telling her that he was leaving immediately for Bordeaux."

He had just passed his seventieth birthday.

Sunset and Evening Star

§ 1

Richelieu at seventy, although his enemies described him as a little monkey with a face as wrinkled as a roast apple, was sprightly and full of life. He had outlived most of his contemporaries, and even the next generation had begun to die around him. Pompadour, worn out by the tuberculosis that began to show itself almost as soon as she arrived at court, fell seriously ill in April 1764. She settled her affairs, chose the carriage in which her dead body should be conveyed from her apartments at Versailles to her hôtel in the rue des Réservoirs, just outside the palace grounds, and then asked her friends to leave her "to my confessor and my women." She met death confidently and with a gracious smile. In the afternoon of Palm Sunday, as her confessor was tiptoeing out of the room, she opened her eyes and said: "Just one moment, *monsieur le curé*, and we will go together." At half past seven in the evening she was dead; a few minutes later, the duchesse de Praslin, looking out of one of the château windows, saw two men emerge from an archway by the chapel and make towards the rue des Réservoirs, carrying a stretcher on which was the body of a woman "covered with so flimsy a cloth that the shape of the head, breasts, belly and legs showed plainly through it." The all-powerful mistress's corpse was not allowed to remain under the same roof as the King, even for the little time needed to fetch the carriage that she had ordered.

A few years earlier, Richelieu would have seized the opportunity to renew his claims to a place on the council and one of the ministries of state; but Pompadour had kept him out too long; he was soured and particularly discouraged by the rise of Choiseul, whom Pompadour had called "my pretty little monkey." Etienne de Stainville, duc de Choiseul, a squat, carroty-haired, spade-faced man, with a pug nose, wide, thick lips and a pointed chin, was quick-witted and full of thrust; he had many of Richelieu's characteristics: courage, extravagance, conceit, and a whirlwind success with most of the women he met, but he also had qualities that Richelieu notably lacked: patience and caution, besides being twenty years younger. For his services in betraying his cousin, Madame de Choiseul-Romanet, Pompadour had made him successively ambassador to Rome, ambassador to Venice, and Minister of Foreign Affairs in succession to Bernis; then Minister of War in succession to Belle-Isle, and Minister of the Marine turn and turn about with his cousin, the duc de Praslin.

When the Seven Years War ended in 1763, France lost India, Canada, Louisiana, and most of Senegal; the wealth and honour of the richest and most civilized nation in Europe had been tossed away by a royal booby and a pink porcelain whore. Choiseul set about rebuilding the army and navy, although it was by now too late; he remained the strong man of the government for ten years, while Richelieu sniped at him with lampoons and caricatures but without any real hope of success.

A common hatred for Pompadour and Choiseul had nourished the strange friendship between Richelieu and the dull, fleshly, puritanical Dauphin; but the Dauphin died in December 1765, Richelieu sitting at his bedside for whole nights together, sending to Papillon to have lighter sheets made in the *menus plaisirs* wardrobe so that the prince might lie more comfortably, and perhaps sensing that this was the beginning of the end of the House of Bourbon. Two months later, Stanislas Leczynski died of burns, his lighted pipe having sent his dressing gown up in flames. In 1767 the Dauphine died, whom Richelieu had brought back from Dresden, mother of the last three Bourbons to sit on the throne of France; and in the same year Fronsac's wife, after three years of marriage; and in the following year the poor, devout, much-sinned-against Maria Leczynska.

Though he had renounced his claims to power as a politician, Richelieu still retained the weapon of the bedchamber. For four years after Pompadour's death, Louis was without a *maîtresse dé-claree*, satisfying himself with casual women brought to him by his *valets-de-chambre*. In 1768 the new mistress who was to occupy Pompadour's position appeared at Versailles, and Richelieu later denied having had anything to do with the plot to plant her in the King's bed, or even having known her before her arrival at court. But from the reports of the very busy Inspector Marais, it is clear that Richelieu was not only lying but had himself been sleeping with the future royal mistress at various times over the preceding three years.

On 18 March 1765, Marais noted briefly that a "demoiselle Beauvarny" had become the mistress of Richelieu's acquaintance, the comte Jean du Barry. On April 12, with the variations in spelling that came from receiving reports by word of mouth from illiterate bawds, Marais recorded that "the demoiselle Beauvarnier and the sieur Du Bary are still living peaceably together, though it would be more accurate to say that Du Bary is using this young woman as a property that he farms out to anybody in a position to pay well. He leaves the daytime entirely to her, provided that she listens to his advice and so long as the returns are proportionate to the outlay, and certainly in such matters he ranks as the best pimp in Paris. At present he has sublet her charms to M. le duc de Richelieu and M. le marquis de Villeroy, during the daytime only. The former had her come to his home and has found that this young pullet rekindles a spark of natural warmth in him; the marquis, on the other hand, goes to her, usually in the afternoon. Du Bary takes care not to be there and they spend several hours together. . . . It is difficult to resist her pretty looks, her air of sweetness and honesty; the marquis has swallowed the hook, and the pair of them shower her with presents every day. She is currently well supplied with diamonds, expensively dressed, has a carriage *à la grecque*, Du Bary keeps a good table and lives well, and everything is fine."

Marais himself, despite the cynicism that his professional duties must have bred in him, appears to have fallen a little under the spell of the demoiselle Beauvarnier's "pretty looks and air of sweetness," for on 27 September a note of indignation creeps in. "The life that the comte du Bary leads with the demoiselle Beauvarnier is infamous. She is nothing more or less than his milch-cow. In order to get himself protection and money he lets her out to all comers, provided, of course, that they are men of quality or wealth. She has often been seen going in the mornings to the *pavillon* of M. le duc de Richelieu and often, too, M. le duc de Fronsac goes to visit her at Du Bary's—who has the civility to go off on his own affairs at such times. Recently the little vicomte de Sabran opened his purse wide and Du Bary granted him a whole day. What an abominable life!"

Within three months, the demoiselle Beauvarnier had arrived at the same conclusion, and on 6 December, Marais recorded that she had "at last left the sieur Du Barry. She got tired of acting as bait at his clandestine gambling parties and, after a brief liaison with M. le duc de Richelieu, for which he paid her fifty louis, she handed the money to an upholsterer, who discreetly furnished an apartment for her in the sieur de la Planche's house, rue Montmartre. When everything was ready, she had all her effects carried there without Du Barry's knowledge and settled herself in. Du Barry did not show any regret; she was beginning to be a little too frayed for his type of business. They say that the lack of concern that he has shown on this score has keenly wounded the young woman's pride. She is trying to console herself by accepting the attentions of the foppish sieur de Lestorières while satisfying her temperament with the young sieur Vernier. These two individuals provide her with warm companionship but that does not bring much into the kitchen. I shall not be surprised to see her at any moment apply for the protection of La Brissault [a procuress]. She is undeniably a pretty woman; it is a pity that she should be a little too sure of it: she is always smirking."

Marais was right: the economics of her new venture defeated her, and in February 1766, she returned to Du Barry "on condition that he tolerates not only all the affairs that she may fancy, but also all her caprices, and that he accepts that she shall not have to sleep away from home unless there is a considerable sum of money involved (which she will have to pay into the common funds) and to prove her enthusiasm and talent for business she is amusing turn and turn about M. Brissard and M. de Cramayel [both farmers-general] and has enlisted M. le marquis de Lignerac to satisfy her own whims. But this young woman is going a little too fast; her health is not robust enough to support such heavy work; her eyes are beginning to redden and she will soon have a very tired look."

Incredibly, her looks survived. Concurrently with a large group of protectors-in-chief, she served innumerable passing lovers. Surrounded by debauchery, and steeped in it, she still preserved the look of innocence in her deep blue eyes (which, perhaps through myopia, gazed so steadily and frankly at the person she was addressing), the angelic halo of golden hair whose colour was so striking that she frequently left it unpowdered, and the pretty childlike quality in her small mouth and delicate nose. Uneducated but intelligent, affectionate and guileless, totally lacking in any ambition other than to enjoy more and more of the luxuries that the exploitation of her body brought her, she was as near as fact has ever come to reproducing the fictitious character of the sweet-tempered, golden-hearted whore.

She was born at Vaucouleurs in August 1743, the illegitimate child of a woman named Bécu; nobody, with the possible exception of her mother, knew the identity of her father, but the child herself favoured the theory that it was a certain Father Angel, a monk whose name before he took his vows had been Vaubernier, and it was Jeanne Vaubernier or L'Ange that she called herself in her early years. She obtained a position with the widow of a farmer-general but was dismissed after the son of the house had been found in her bed; she then became a shopgirl and nominally followed other occupations that at that time were used as a cover for prostitution. Before joining the comte Jean du Barry in his gaming house in the rue de la Jussienne, she changed her name to Beauvernier or Beauvarnier, its earlier form having become too ribaldly apt. (Vaubernier, with only slight mispronunciation, would mean "worth tossing in a blanket.")

For more than two years after the affair in 1765, the police reports make no further reference to any association between Mademoiselle Beauvarnier and Richelieu. During this period he brought up from Bordeaux and edged into the Ballets-Italiens a Mademoiselle Durfort, whom Marais describes a little patronizingly as "a big pleasant girl," and enjoyed the favours of another young actress, popularly known as *La Belle ou la Bête*. Mademoiselle Beauvarnier meanwhile remained the mistress of Jean du Barry, although it was noted in January 1768 that "at the moment it is M. de Sainte-Foix, treasurer of the Ministry of the Marine, whom she is engaged in tapping, by kind permission of the said sieur Du Barry."

Some months later, about the time that the unhappy Maria Leczynska lay dying, somebody introduced the twenty-four-year-old prostitute to Le Bel, the *premier valet-de-chambre*, and Le Bel, after, it was said, enjoying a foretaste of the delights that awaited his master, slipped her into Louis's bed. Her youth and seeming innocence, allied with zeal and great experience, completely captivated the King. If Richelieu was the unnamed person who first took her to Le Bel—Richelieu claimed that he was in Bordeaux at the time and even put round a nonsensical story that he had never met her until the King one day invited him to her apartments to take a cup of coffee "made with almond milk" —he never dreamed that she would be of more than passing interest to Louis, who often amused himself with girls of the lower classes. That the King should select such a woman to be his acknowledged mistress would have gravely offended Richelieu's sense of decorum; it had been difficult enough for him to swallow his disgust at having to pander to the rich, middle-class Pompadour; he would not willingly have replaced her with this creature from the gutter. Yet it turned out, thanks to her lack of interest in anything but her own comfort, that he was to get on better with the immoral little Jeanne Bécu than he had ever done with the stylish and cultured Pompadour.

First she had to be *décrotté* sufficiently to get even a toehold in Versailles society, and for this the first essential was a title. Jean du Barry, whose title was genuine, would have married her— and, indeed, on the strength of their common relationship to

Jeanne, he was in the habit of referring to Louis as "my brother-in-law"—but he already had a wife. So, to keep the honours in the family, he fetched his brother, the comte Guillaume, up from his estate in Languedoc, married him to Jeanne, and then sent him back home without the reward of a honeymoon, an unexpected nicety in view of the bride's profession. As comtesse du Barry, Jeanne was now qualified to be presented at court, and her sponsors were rumoured to include Richelieu, his kinsman, Aiguillon, and Bertin, the Minister of Mines and Agriculture.

All three were declared enemies of Choiseul, who now had to decide whether to fight, to run, or to ask for a partnership. As a man of spirit, he decided to fight; he refused the comtesse du Barry's attempts at friendship; he lobbied the ladies of the court, urging them to boycott her official presentation; he offered first his sister and then the young and charming wife of a doctor friend as worthier objects of the King's affections. He was so energetic and confident, and the thought of Louis's elevating such a woman to the status of *maîtresse déclarée* was so monstrous, that bets were offered at court and in Paris that the King would not in the end demean himself so far; he might receive her in her *robe de chambre* but never *en grande toilette*.

There was some delay in finding an eligible lady willing to present the comtesse du Barry, but after several postponements, the comtesse de Béarn agreed to take on the shameful task, in return for spot cash and the promise that a lawsuit would be rigged in her favour. On 22 April 1769, the royal apartments were packed with the nobility of France, come to witness the first official appearance of the little slut who was to be set in authority over them. It was a glittering occasion, the eyes dazzled with jewels, the air resonant with great names and the rustle of heavy silks; among all these superior people there was not one with sufficient self-respect to protest or even to take the risk of staying away, though there were many who watched eagerly in the hope that the cheap little strumpet would bungle some part of the ceremonial and give them the opportunity of assuaging their envy and humiliation with a condescending snigger. Richelieu moved busily and contentedly among them—it was his year *en exercice*—while Choiseul maintained a brave face and a stream of confident, witty conversation.

As the moments ticked on, the hum of talk grew louder, and an excited note crept into it, for the new mistress was nowhere to be seen. There was a rumour that she was not even at Versailles. Within the compass of the crowded *cabinet du conseil*, stuffy despite the cool spring air outside, it was possible to feel the scales of fortune adjusting themselves; the sullen, bilious look that indicated displeasure began to appear on Louis's face; Choiseul's supporters exchanged excited looks, elated glances; Richelieu crossed to the window embrasure and concealed his agitation by staring stony-faced into the distance. The noise of gossip had ceased. All sound and movement were dying away; the great looking glasses on the walls reflected infinite perspectives of glittering *parures*, brilliant gowns, coats trimmed with gold and waistcoats slashed with ribbons of the chivalric orders, all as still as if they were worn by wax figures; and in the settling silence the pendulum clock, mockingly adorned with figures representing "France governed by Wisdom and crowned by Victory," ticked louder and louder.

The silence was almost complete when Richelieu caught sight of a flurry of movement at the bottom of the *cour royale*, and, as a carriage clattered and rocked over the cobbles towards the *cour de marbre*, he recognized with relief the newly acquired livery of the comtesse du Barry. He swung round and hastened over to the King, smiling, deferent, elated; he whispered in his ear and the onlookers saw the jaundiced, peevish expression drain from Louis's face. The buzz of conversation began again, irritated, frustrated; presently the comtesse de Béarn swept in, leading the comtesse du Barry, who had been delayed in Paris by her hairdresser, in the short, mincing steps and deep curtsies that they had so industriously rehearsed. Halting, sinking to the floor amid billowing skirts, inclining her golden head with an infinitely graceful curving of white arms and shoulders and neck, she looked as delicate and virginal and unattainable as a fairy princess.

"You could never see anything as pretty as she," an eyewitness recorded, "and both friends and enemies are forced to agree that she eclipses all the beauties of the court. The next day, which was a Sunday, Madame du Barry was present at the King's mass in the chapel of the château, in the place formerly occupied by Madame de Pompadour. She was superbly dressed and covered with diamonds."

Louis had lost the last shred of respect in his court, as he had long since lost it in the nation as a whole. The country seethed with discontent, some of it inspired by the philosophies of liberty and egalitarianism that were discussed in many of the richer bourgeois homes and a few of those of the aristocracy, but most of it motivated by poverty, pride, and ambition. The lower members of society yearned for a life that would be above the level of beasts; the middle classes craved the power and privileges of those above them; and those who held the power and privileges were determined not to let them go. The malcontents were not looking for a new society, but for a better place in the existing one; and their aspirations were most clearly expressed in the struggle between the *parlements* and the government, although this was just as selfish a quarrel as the rest. Choiseul, who had favoured the *parlements*, was dismissed in 1770; and the government then consisted of three reactionaries: the abbé Terray, Richelieu's kinsman Aiguillon, and René-Nicolas Maupeou. Aiguillon, who took over the Ministry of Foreign Affairs, had been involved in a bitter quarrel with the *Etats* of Brittany, and when the King refused to allow this to be brought before the *parlement* of Paris, *parlement* declined to continue to carry out its duties.

On the night of 19 January 1771, Maupeou sent musketeers to the home of each member of *parlement* to ask him whether he was prepared to resume his seat. Those who refused—the majority —were ordered to leave the city at once, and Maupeou set up new courts of law, the judges paid and appointed by the government instead of living on their fees and buying and selling their offices, while the jurisdiction of the old *parlement* of Paris, which had covered half the country, was shared among six new *parlements*. All these reforms were for the good and might even at this late date have done something to save the people from the worst horrors of the revolution that came twenty years later. But since they were prompted only by the desire of the King and the peers to preserve their privileges, and were strenuously opposed by the former magistrates unwilling to give up their own, they did not last.

The *parlements* were supported by the *cour des aides*, and the nation was threatened with a fiscal as well as a judicial strike. On the night of 8 April, each member of the Paris *cour des aides* received a *lettre de cachet* ordering him to attend a session the next morning; as soon as they were assembled, Richelieu entered at the head of a body of armed men. He held himself erect, and the wrinkles and creases of seventy-five years deepened as he puckered his face with enjoyment of the task before him. He made towards the chair of the First President and was greeted with cries that only princes of the blood were allowed to sit there. "In view of the function that I have come here to perform," he replied in his thin, crisp voice, "it is not worth while for me to insist."

He read an edict from the King, suppressing the *cour des aides* for reasons of economy; the members were instructed to return to their homes. They rose from their seats but refused to leave the hall, shouting protests and gathering into knots to debate what they should do next. "Gentlemen," Richelieu rapped out, "you may stay here for eight days, if you wish—I shall remain for nine." They went. In September he performed a similar duty at Bordeaux, travelling in from Fronsac with an armed guard to inform the *parlement* that its functions were suspended; after ordering the members to their homes, he locked and sealed the doors of the council chamber.

In December, his most loyal mistress died: the gross, garrulous Diane-Adélaïde, last survivor of the five Mailly-Nesle sisters, for whom Madame du Deffand wrote a typically acid epitaph: "She was the most stupid, the most haughty and the most impertinent of women; she was overwhelmed with debts; never in her life had she paid servants or tradesmen or workers; she borrowed from the lowliest people and never paid a thing back; she had already had 50,000 écus' worth of debts paid for her; as her perquisites as *dame d'atour*, she had had all the silver, jewels, etc., on the deaths of two dauphines. She has a great deal of furniture but not

enough to cover all her debts; she had the baseness to prefer bor-
rowing rather than getting rid of a single one of her jewels. In
short, a dreadful woman."

It was the verdict of the emergent, self-complacent class on
those who had been their rulers for too long. But these rumblings
beneath his feet did not disturb Richelieu. Age had not mellowed
him; unless provoked in some way, he made a point of being polite to his inferiors, but he never permitted politeness to degene-
rate into consideration; and he made it quite plain that their
personal qualities, even their names, were of no interest to him at
all. In May 1771, he presided at the reception into the Académie
Française of the abbé Arnaud, and for the rest of his life he never
referred to him other than as "that fellow Renaud."

His arrogance sometimes verged on irritability, and he was often at odds with his children as well as with his colleagues. Fronsac, who irritated him by stealing his mistresses, was a courageous
but singularly unsympathetic little man, brutal and a bully, of
whom Richelieu once said: "He has inherited all my vices and
none of my virtues." The son, cheated of his inheritance by his
father's longevity, took every occasion to make fun of him and,
alluding to the veal fillets that Richelieu used as a treatment for
scurvy, described him to Louis XV as "ce vieux bouquin, gilt-
edged and bound in calf"—an unfilial jibe that does not completely translate, since vieux bouquin can mean both an old book
and an old buck.

With his daughter, Richelieu had hitherto been on the best of
terms, approaching as near as his character would permit to the
role of doting father. At the sound of his carriage wheels outside the house, identifiable as Richelieu's because of their excessive speed, Septimanie would leap to her feet and, crying "Here's
papa!" run to meet him as he came skipping up the stairs like a
young man of thirty: surely the most un-papa-like papa in Paris.
After five or ten minutes of enchanting the company with his
witty and malicious chatter, he would bound into his carriage
again and rattle off on one of his endless errands and intrigues.

Unfortunately, Septimanie was deeply attached to the dowager
duchesse d'Aiguillon, who had brought her up after she left her

aunt and the abbaye du Trésor; and she shared the old woman's dislike of her son, the present duc d'Aiguillon, and of the new mistress whom Aiguillon and Richelieu had helped to power. There was trouble in 1769 when Septimanie and her friends, the comtesse de Brionne and the duchesse de Grammont (Choiseul's sister, whom he had unsuccessfully offered as mistress to Louis), did not receive their usual invitations to join the royal party at Compiègne because they had too plainly shown their dislike of Madame du Barry. And when Aiguillon was appointed Minister of Foreign Affairs, Septimanie and the dowager refused to accompany Aiguillon's wife on the customary round of visits to give thanks to the royal family, because they believed they would be required to include Du Barry in the list. The refusal provoked a minor scandal and seemed to set Septimanie in opposition to her father. Richelieu was so enraged that he ceased visiting her and forbade the dowager to see or even write to her.

There was renewed trouble when the young Gustave of Sweden visited Paris, and Septimanie, who had never been in love with her husband, formed an attachment for him. Gustave thoughtlessly sent her a letter in which he commented favourably on Choiseul's policies; it was intercepted and opened in the *cabinet noir*; and Aiguillon showed a copy to Richelieu, reproaching him for letting his daughter plot against them. The old man's heart grew harder, and in October 1773, when the tuberculosis that had killed her mother ended Septimanie's short life, she died alone. Fronsac attended the funeral, but her father was away on one of his visits to Bagnères-de-Luchon.

He returned to Fontainebleau at the beginning of November, apparently untouched by his daughter's death but greatly occupied with preparations for the marriage of one of Louis's grandsons, the comte d'Artois, with Marie-Thérèse of Savoy. It was again his year *en exercice*, and he was determined to make the plays, balls, and firework displays a record in royal magnificence; he harried Papillon unmercifully, bombarding him with suggestions, instructions, requests and reproaches and finally demanding a chorus of four hundred mounted grenadiers for one of the operas. The celebrations began in mid-November and continued until the last week of December. At the end of them, the new Dauphin (later to be Louis XVI), who heartily disliked Richelieu and referred to him as "that dried-up old mummy," grunted: "Well, that's the end of your famous spectacles—now we can go and amuse ourselves." Since Richelieu was just as unpopular with the Dauphin's young wife, Marie-Antoinette of Austria, his prospects during the next reign were none too bright, but the King was only sixty-four—fourteen years younger than Richelieu—and there was plenty of time before he need worry about that.

His own health was as reliable as ever. George III and his ministers were doing their best to lose the American colonies, and it seemed likely that France might find some rewarding fishing in these troubled waters, so in March and April 1774, Richelieu, as senior Marshal of France, presided over a series of conferences to discuss the reform and re-embodiment of the coastal militia, which had been disbanded at the end of the Seven Years War, more than ten years earlier. The committee included nine provincial governors or military commanders and five *intendants*; he kept them hard at work for upwards of seven hours a day, gave them a splendid dinner afterwards, and then showed them round the treasures of his mansion, the paintings and sculptures under superbly decorated ceilings, the magnificent furniture, the lacquered walls, the gleaming gilt and bronze, and the mirrors which, even in old age, he loved to have about him. In the garden there were more sculptures, including two by Michelangelo, and—the object of the greatest interest to all his visitors—at the end of the alley of chestnut trees that flanked the terrace facing the rue Louis-le-Grand, the famous *pavillon de Hanovre*, the scene of so many of his intimate triumphs, and still surprisingly often put to use.

He was paying a great deal of attention to Mademoiselle Colombe, a pretty, plumpish newcomer at the Comédie-Italienne, ("I'm just running over her lines," he explained to Papillon, who found them closely closeted one day). One evening when he took supper with Fronsac at Gennevilliers, he met two of his son's recent actress acquaintances: the brilliant young tragédienne, Raucourt, and her friend, Mademoiselle Virginie. Richelieu invited Raucourt to inspect the elegant Temple of Love with which he had crowned the sugar-loaf hill that contained the icehouse. It was a steep slope, but he skipped lightly up it, nimble with anticipation; when the pair returned half an hour later, it was evident that he had once more given proof of his eternal youth: a feat which brought him all the more applause because Mademoiselle Raucourt was already famous not only as one of the theatre's brightest young stars but also as one of its most enthusiastic lesbians. No sooner had he reached ground level than he was proposing to show Mademoiselle Virginie around the Temple and was only with difficulty persuaded to postpone that task until another day.

§ 2

That spring of 1774 the King was tired and querulous. His laggard body responded only fitfully to the aphrodisiacs with which he provoked it; he was conscious that he was fast becoming an old man. He complained to Richelieu one day that he felt his strength flagging, although he made fewer demands on it than the maréchal did on his. Richelieu, who had occasionally experienced similar doubts during his seventy-eight years, assured him confidently: "A little rest will restore everything that you lack. It will be as sure a remedy for you as it has always been for me."

On Tuesday, 26 April, Louis went to spend a few days at the Little Trianon; he woke on Wednesday morning with a headache, tremors, and a feeling of stiffness but resolved to go hunting as he had arranged the night before. He drove out into the forest but then decided not to mount his horse and sat shivering and disconsolate in his carriage, watching the rest of the party hunt until mid-afternoon, when he returned to the Little Trianon and shut himself up in Du Barry's rooms. He ate no supper, went miserably to bed at an early hour, and during the night sent for the First Physician, Le Monnier, to whom he complained that he had a backache. Le Monnier diagnosed a slight fever, and Louis had Du Barry brought from her bed to sit with him.

Neither she nor the doctor believed that this was anything more than a minor ailment exaggerated by the King's habitually terrified reaction to any hint of ill health; but she was glad of the opportunity to fuss over him, and she easily persuaded the First

Gentleman—that year the weak-willed duc d'Aumont—to stay out of the sickroom and block the *entrées* on Thursday morning. The Little Trianon had no accommodation for any but the most intimate of Louis's attendants, and when Du Barry sent word of the King's indisposition to Aiguillon at Versailles, he agreed that she should try to persuade Louis to remain where he was, thus scoring off the detested Dauphine and other members of the royal family, who would be committing a breach of etiquette if they visited the invalid uninvited and could be accused of callousness if they did not. Louis was groaning heavily, but Le Monnier held to his opinion that this was another of the King's bilious attacks and would clear up within a day or two.

When the royal family heard that the King had not left his bedroom by three o'clock on Thursday afternoon and had been seen only by his mistress and the First Physician, they asked Pichaut de la Martinière, the First Surgeon, to pay him a visit. This was a shrewd move, for La Martinière had held his post for more than a quarter of a century and was one of the few men around the King who was prepared to speak his mind. He was also a known opponent of Du Barry. Ignoring the mistress's protests, he pronounced the Little Trianon too inconvenient a place for the King to be ill in, from both a medical and a ceremonial point of view, and had Louis bundled up in a cloak over his night-gown and driven back to Versailles, a distance which was covered in three minutes with the King, terrified of catching cold, screaming at the coachman to flog on his horses.

As he was carried out to the carriage at the Little Trianon and in from it at Versailles, he kept up an uninterrupted wail, complaining of pains in his head, his back, and his heart; but the courtiers who saw him for the first time for two days came to the same conclusion as Du Barry: that he was making a great fuss about nothing. Le Monnier prescribed opium and, after a visit from the royal family which Du Barry managed to keep extremely short, the King was put into a newly made bed, where he moaned through the night. At the suggestion of Du Barry and Aiguillon, he had told his children and grandchildren not to return until they were sent for.

At nine the next morning Le Monnier found no improvement

in the King's condition and came to the conclusion that he needed to be bled; but this was a decision that he did not intend to take on his own responsibility, and he asked Louis's permission to call in the Dauphine's physician, Lassonne; whereupon Du Barry and Aiguillon proposed their own physicians, Bordeu and Lorry, to restore the balance. But these were not satisfied with the morning's cupping and agreed to perform another one at three o'clock if the fever had not subsided—a piece of news that set Versailles in an uproar; the Barryists and Aiguillonites maintained that the King's illness was only a passing indisposition, while their opponents protested hopefully that it was a malady of the utmost gravity. The doctors were puzzled. They knew that Louis had had a grave illness, believed to be smallpox, at Fontainebleau when he was a youth; the great scare at Metz might have been caused by a serious fever or simply a mild bout of liver trouble; but otherwise the King's health had always been good. They decided to try to reduce the fever that day and agreed that if a second bleeding did not achieve this they would subject him to a third. On hearing this, Louis began to exclaim excitedly: "A third bleeding! Then this is a serious illness? A third bleeding would bring me very low! I do not *want* a third bleeding! *Why* must there be a third bleeding?"

The doctors pacified him, assuring him that there would not be a third bleeding, and instead made the second one very copious. After this, the King broke into a light sweat and was moved to a camp bed while his bedclothes were changed; here he continued to urge the doctors to feel his pulse and look at his tongue. There were now fourteen of them: six physicians, five surgeons, and three apothecaries, and Louis kept them circulating briskly, sticking out his tongue and ordering, "Now you, Lassonne," "Now you, Bordeu," "Now you, Lorry," and so on. Examination of his pulse and tongue was alternated with inspection of his belly and, although he derived great comfort from all this attention and desired it to continue, he complained that the light of the candle hurt his eyes. A *garçon-de-chambre* was accordingly detailed to shield the candle with his hand.

During the course of the evening, it having been decided that an enema might usefully be administered, the patient was suitably placed at the side of the bed and the doctors formed a double rank through which advanced a small procession composed of Forgeot, the Master Apothecary, carrying the nozzle, his assistant, carrying the body of the syringe, and the *garçon-de-chambre* with a candle. On arrival at the bedside, Forgeot fitted the nozzle to the syringe and was about to apply it when the *garçon-de-chambre* realized to his horror that the light of his candle was shining full and unveiled upon the royal posterior. A man of instant action, as well as unquestioning obedience, he snatched a hat from under the arm of the nearest doctor and clapped it over the candle. Forgeot, finding himself suddenly in almost total darkness and terrified lest he should commit some unheard-of assault upon the royal person, dropped the syringe with a clatter and a volley of oaths, while the rest of the distinguished company did their best to suppress their laughter.

At about ten-thirty that evening, one of the doctors was giving the King a drink when he detected an unusual flush on his face; wishing to see more clearly, but without frightening the patient, he called: "Bring a light here, the King cannot see his glass." The other doctors gathered round, nodded to each other, but said nothing; and a quarter of an hour later, on the pretext of examining His Majesty's tongue, which he readily protruded for them, they confirmed what they already suspected: whatever illness the King had had at Fontainebleau, it had not been smallpox, for that was unmistakably what he was suffering from now. They notified the royal family, asking them to stay away from the sickroom, and the true nature of the illness was soon being whispered throughout the château.

This was the drama of Metz repeating itself: the fear of death, the scurry to confess, the banishment of the mistress. At this point Richelieu, veteran of that famous affair, moved in to the attack as confidently as he had done thirty years before. He conferred with Du Barry and Aiguillon and then took up his station in the sickroom and began to conduct affairs with such an assumption of authority that it seemed as if he, and not Aumont, was on duty that year. For three days he persuaded the doctors to tell Louis that the spots that he saw on his hands were merely symptoms of a miliary fever, and his daughters, who knew the truth, bravely sat with him during the day, while Du Barry kept vigil at night.

The doctors were unwilling to let him lose consciousness without his having had an opportunity to ask for the sacraments; on the other hand, Richelieu talked them into believing that they might literally frighten the King to death if they told him he had smallpox. Eventually they asked Madame Adélaïde what she thought they should do (it was significant that, although they were discussing the possibility of the King's death, it did not occur to them to consult his successor, the lethargic Dauphin); and she, whether because it was her true opinion or, as many suspected, because she was an admirer of Aiguillon, replied that she was sure the situation was not yet serious enough to warrant taking the risk of telling him.

On Monday, 6 May, the archbishop of Paris, himself a sick man, drove out to Versailles to inquire whether his ministrations or advice were needed. Before he could get out of his carriage, the news of his arrival was passed to Richelieu, who hurried down the back stairs and intercepted the archbishop in the guardroom, where he sat him down on a bench and assured him that it would be quite impossible for him to see the King that day, since the hour of the *entrées* was past, and the archbishop did not have the right to be admitted at other times. The archbishop, an experienced old churchman with no desire to get himself unnecessarily involved in other people's affairs, went off for a chat with Madame Adélaïde, who confirmed the general opinion that she had been won over to the Aiguillon-Du Barry camp by replying, when the archbishop asked whether she thought he ought to mention the sacraments to the King: "That is your business." To which the archbishop responded: "In that case, I will wait, since I am told there is no danger." But the Dauphin unexpectedly asserted himself at this point; fearing that his grandfather might die unshriven, he ordered that the archbishop should be admitted to the sickroom.

Richelieu could not refuse to obey the Dauphin's orders, but before the archbishop was admitted to the King's bedroom, he took him aside once more and pleaded with him not to jeopardize Louis's life by mentioning so frightening a thing as confession; the shock would be as fatal to him as a pistol shot. "If you are so eager to listen to that sort of thing," he added with irrepressible irreverence, "come into a corner and *I* will confess. And I take my oath that my confession will amuse you a great deal more than the King's." So when the archbishop was conducted to the King's bedside, he made no attempt to have a word with him in private and was only too happy to spend the time discussing his nephritis, in which Louis took a fellow-patient's interest and considerately ordered his cohort of doctors to examine the archbishop's tongue and feel his pulse.

When the archbishop returned to his carriage to jog painfully back to Paris, Richelieu was relieved to see that the King appeared more comfortable and a little less frightened. He looked doubtfully at his hands from time to time and once said, "If I had not had smallpox when I was eighteen I might have thought it was that," but it was clear that such an idea was still far from his mind, although those around him now noticed that his head was "scarlet and as big as a bushel."

On Tuesday the archbishop returned to Versailles and let it be known that he intended to stay there but made no other move towards bringing the King to confession. The Grand Almoner, cardinal de la Roche-Aimon, who more than any other priest was responsible for ensuring that Louis expired in a state of grace, had been under great pressure from the anti-Aiguillonists and his own clergy to broach the question of confession and had promised them that he would do so, but whenever he spoke to the King, it was in such a low voice that nobody else could hear what he said, and he was able to assure all parties that he had done as they wished. Nobody, it seemed, was going to take the risk of mentioning the matter to the King, for fear of the vengeance of Aiguillon and Du Barry if he recovered; but during the afternoon, while he was talking to Bouillon, the Grand Chamberlain, Louis again peered at his hands and said, "That is smallpox!"; and again "But that's smallpox!" Bouillon hastened off to set the opposition's hopes soaring; but again the joy was premature.

Bordeu, Du Barry's doctor, persuaded Louis that he was wrong and, since he felt so well and frightened himself every time he talked about it, the King did not return to the subject for several hours.

Night and the return of his fears made him doubt Bordeu's assurances. He was unable to sleep and, at a quarter to midnight, turned to Du Barry and said: "I am ill. I know what I must do. I do not intend to repeat the scandal of Metz. We must part. You must leave tomorrow. Go and stay at Aiguillon's house at Rueil—and tell him to come and see me at ten tomorrow morning." Du Barry went out weeping. Louis continued to move restlessly in his bed, and a few minutes later La Borde, the *premier valet-de-chambre* on duty that quarter, announced that Aiguillon wished to see him. Louis, showing his first sign of firmness since the beginning of his illness, snapped: "Let him come at the time I told him to!"

Richelieu held a conference with Aiguillon and the tearful Du Barry and convinced them that they had no reason to be greatly downcast; sending Du Barry to Rueil, only two leagues away from Versailles, was certainly not disgrace or exile. Others shared this opinion, for at the midday mass in his bedroom, when Louis said to the archbishop, "I have smallpox," the cautious prelate merely bowed. To the Grand Almoner, however, Louis said, "I will speak to you this evening," and when La Roche-Aimon bowed and whispered in his ear, Louis was heard to reply, "Yes." As the cardinal left the room, he found Richelieu at his elbow, repeating the arguments against administering the sacraments; but this time La Roche-Aimon replied that, since the King knew the nature of his illness, confession would bring him comfort. Richelieu continued to protest that the shock might well kill him, but the argument had now lost a great deal of its force.

At a quarter to four Du Barry drove off to Rueil with Aiguillon's wife, but by nine o'clock that evening the King's health seemed to have taken a marked turn for the better: the blisters that the doctors had applied very lavishly for several days had apparently taken effect, and confession appeared as far away as ever. Among the whispering groups in the ante-rooms, there was a new rumour: that at six that evening Louis had told La Borde to fetch Du Barry and had been surprised to learn that she was already at Rueil. They discussed it endlessly: a change of heart? a flash of his old cunning, suspecting that she had not gone at all? Each faction read into it its own hopes and fears. Late that night Louis got out of bed, put on his breeches and tried to walk over to his armchair, but the pain from the eruptions on his feet forced him to get back into bed again.

Quietly, unobtrusively, the King's confessor, the abbé Mondou, had taken his place among the waiting crowd in the ante-room; he waited all day, but the summons did not come. The First Gentlemen were now taking turns to stand watch in the sickroom, and during the night of 5 May, it was Duras's turn, unluckily for his two enemies, Richelieu and Aiguillon; for at 3:45 in the morning, Louis asked for Mondou to be brought to him, and Duras, far from trying to dissuade him, at once sent a messenger to find the priest. Mondou talked with the King for more than an hour. When he left, Louis had Aiguillon brought in. He told him that Mondou had refused to give him absolution until Du Barry had been sent farther away, and he ordered Aiguillon to see that she went immediately to an estate that Richelieu owned at Chinon, a hundred and fifty miles away. Aiguillon, realizing that he would be the next to go, protested that there must be some misunderstanding: he would speak with Mondou and La Roche-Aimon about it. With Richelieu's support, he easily persuaded the diplomatic Grand Almoner to allow Du Barry to remain at Rueil, but the abbé was a far more difficult proposition, and he appears to have agreed only on condition that the King's disavowal of his scandalous life should be made in public.

At 6 a.m. the cardinal entered the bedroom with the sacraments. The clergy formed a semicircle round the bed; Mesdames knelt at the door of the bedchamber—the Dauphine and the comtesse de Provence in the *cabinet du conseil* beyond—and the Dauphin on the stairs that led down to the guardroom. As soon as the rite had been completed, La Roche-Aimon turned towards the door as if to leave, but Mondou caught him by his rochet and whispered something in his ear. The cardinal, apparently reminded of his promise, again went towards the door, where he halted and proclaimed in loud tones: "Gentlemen, the King has charged me to tell you that he asks God's forgiveness for having offended against Him, and for the scandal that he has given to his people; that if God shall restore him to health, he will devote himself to penitence, to the upholding of religion, and to the relief of his people." Whereupon, as the Grand Master of the Wardrobe noted in his diary, "the maréchal de Richelieu, in a voice loud enough to be heard by everybody, bestowed on him the most insulting epithet."

Richelieu refused to accept that the game was up. To one who knew the King's character so well it was clear that if he recovered, his promise to renounce Du Barry would be as worthless as the one that he had sworn about Madame de Châteauroux. But this time the King did not have a second chance. By Sunday he had taken a decided turn for the worse, his pulse and temperature were up, and there were bouts of delirium; on Monday he talked a great deal with his confessor, probing for grains of comfort upon what might lie in wait for him beyond the grave. On Monday evening he asked for Extreme Unction.

All through the night the priests knelt around his bed, holding candles whose light, now that the curtains of the four-poster had been drawn back, shone full upon him as he lay open-mouthed and scarcely stirring, his head so swollen and discoloured that it resembled a huge bronze Negro mask. The bishop of Senlis, standing at the foot of the bed, recited prayers, and a chaplain held a crucifix, which from time to time he lowered to Louis's lips. From the outer rooms came the sound of politicians arguing, surrounded by courtiers whose faces, long with misery or bright with the thought of rewards almost within their grasp, plainly revealed which camp they belonged to. The windows were thrown open and a thin breeze drifted in from the *cour de marbre*; a few inquisitive locals had gathered there, but for the most part the people of Versailles, as of Paris, had shown little interest in the events of the past ten days.

A little after 3 p.m. on Tuesday, 10 May, he died. An usher went into the *oeil-de-boeuf* and announced, *"Le Roi est mort"*; then the bedroom was locked and the rest of the royal family hustled into carriages to take them away from the house of death.

By a quarter past five the new King was driving towards Choisy, accompanied by shouts of *"Vive le Roi!"* while in the locked death-room nobody remained but the Grand Almoner, the First Gentleman of the Bedchamber *en exercice*, the Grand Master of Ceremonies, and the Captain of the Scots Guard. Under the gaze of these four, the body was hastily bundled into a double leaden coffin, which was still not staunch enough to prevent the stink of decay from creeping out. Two days later, at eight o'clock in the evening, the coffin was put into a large and rather gaily decorated coach. For some reason, nobody had succeeded in finding a black one. The coach, followed by La Roche-Aimon, Aumont, Ayen, and the curé of Versailles, with an escort of twenty pages carrying torches and fifty troopers from the bodyguard, rumbled ponderously down to the crape-covered railing at the bottom of the *cour royale* and then, the horses breaking into a smart trot, set off for Saint-Denis to the accompaniment of jeers and cheerful, obscene songs from the bystanders.

§ 3

Aiguillon was dismissed; Du Barry was handed a *lettre de cachet* exiling her to the convent of Pont-aux-Dames, near Meaux, whose abbess was ordered to hold her incommunicado; Maurepas was recalled from a quarter of a century of disgrace to head the new government. Richelieu, at seventy-eight, found himself with neither influence nor standing at court. As First Gentleman, he would be in attendance on a young king, not yet twenty, who detested him only a degree less than did the eighteen-year-old Queen. It was reasonable to expect the old reprobate to retire from the scene and spend what few years were left to him in decent obscurity and even repentance, and he did in fact leave for Richelieu in June, planning to go on to Bordeaux from there. But he had no intention of fading into the background, and almost immediately reappeared in the limelight with an unsavoury lawsuit that entertained Paris and the whole of France for several years.

The central figure was the marquise Julie de Fauris de Saint-Vincent, a great-granddaughter of Madame de Sévigné and estranged wife of a *président à mortier* of the *parlement* of Aix-en-Provence. Richelieu had met her twenty years before, at the time of her marriage to a husband who was middle-aged and neglectful, and who shortly obtained a *lettre de cachet* to commit her to a Benedictine convent at Millau to put an end to her infidelities. Six years later she wrote to Richelieu to ask him, in his capacity as governor of Guienne, to favour the brother of one of the nuns; Richelieu kept the correspondence alive and was soon sending her a letter every week, addressing her as "dear cousin" on the strength of a very remote relationship through his second wife's family.

Almost ten years passed before Julie suggested that Richelieu should help her with a small loan because she had exceeded the allowance that her husband made her. Richelieu sent her a draft for 3,000 livres; she added a nought at the end, but did not need to take the risk of cashing it—the mere sight of so handsome a loan from "her cousin, the governor," was enough to calm her creditors' fears and prompt them to offer further advances. She used their money to entertain her latest lover, François de Védel-Montel, adjutant of the Dauphin regiment, which was quartered in the town; and when the regiment was moved, Julie persuaded Richelieu to have her transferred with it, first to Tarbes and then to Poitiers, where she was elegantly lodged in the convent of the Little Sisters of Saint Catherine.

Poitiers is on the road from Paris to Bordeaux, and Richelieu visited Julie there at least four times during 1771 and 1772. It is evident from his letters to her that they were on terms of very playful familiarity: "I shall lose no time in throwing myself at your feet and kissing at least your hand. . . . I am told that you came here yesterday evening, which was very wrong of you; I shall give you a whipping for your naughtiness." When she gave birth to a son in the convent, she seems to have had no difficulty in persuading Richelieu that he was the father, though her letters show clearly that the child was Védel-Montel's.

Védel-Montel, now second-in-command of his regiment, was posted to Paris, and Julie once more used Richelieu's influence to have herself transferred, this time to the convent of the

Daughters of Mercy in the rue du Vieux-Colombier. But she was beginning to suspect that Védel-Montel's interest in her was declining, and she searched desperately for some means of obtaining the money which she knew would hold him. Years before, when she had added the nought to Richelieu's draft, she had also amused herself by tracing his signature. The copy had been remarkably accurate, and so it proved to be again when she forged a series of bills in his name, none of them for a very large amount, but in all totalling some 350,000 livres. These were hawked around Paris by Védel-Montel and two new lovers whom she had acquired since her arrival: a swindler named Bénaven, and the convent chaplain, the abbé Froment. In so large a city, and with the reasonable assumption that Richelieu might be dead within the three years before the bills matured, Julie felt safe from detection. But she had made one miscalculation; Richelieu was known to be erratic almost to the point of dishonesty in recognizing and redeeming this sort of debt. One of the purchasers consequently called on the maréchal's steward to make sure that the bill would be met.

As soon as he learned of the forgery, and before discovering that Julie was the perpetrator, Richelieu ordered his steward to begin criminal proceedings. But when the Lieutenant-General of police, Sartines, opened his investigation, it became clear that Julie was prepared to wash a great deal of Richelieu's dirty linen in public, and Sartines asked Richelieu if he wished to withdraw the charges. Richelieu replied that he would do so if Madame de Saint-Vincent would withdraw her countercharges that he was the father of the child born in Poitiers and that the bills were not forgeries but genuine notes in repayment of money he had borrowed from her father before the Minorcan campaign. Julie, either through natural wildness or because she did not trust Richelieu to keep his side of the bargain after she had virtually confessed to forgery, refused.

Now began an extraordinary series of arrests, enquiries, releases, and rearrests in which Richelieu nonchalantly challenged and thwarted the authority of the police, *parlement,* and even the King. Julie and Védel-Montel, who had been released from the

Bastille by Sartines while Richelieu considered whether to press his charges, were taken back into custody and confined in the Châtelet. Bénaven, who had a criminal record, was sent to For l'Evêque, the prison on the quai des Mégisseries. None of them was yet seriously worried, for *parlement* had been recently recalled by Maurepas in order to win favour with the upper bourgeoisie, and it was known that the Recorder of the Grand' Chambre had remarked: "We shall have no difficulty in discovering the guilt of the man who suppressed the *parlement* of Bordeaux." Indeed, it was rapidly clear that *parlement* was trying not the forgers but the maréchal.

Encouraged by this, Julie spent the night before her official confrontation with Richelieu in composing "the most licentious songs about the witnesses and the examining magistrates," as one observer recorded. He added that "she has large, well-proportioned features but there is something lascivious in her face and the sight of a man seems to animate her suddenly and inflame all her senses." That she had not lost her wits was clear when, during the questioning, she claimed that one note for a very large sum had been given to her by Richelieu in return for her favours. "Take a look at your face, madame," said Richelieu caustically. "Could that command so exorbitant a sum?" "I would never venture to claim that," Julie replied modestly, "but take a look at your own, Monsieur le Maréchal, and consider whether it would ever be tolerated for less."

But though Richelieu might be defeated in repartee, he still had the use of the *lettres de cachet*, which it was his right to issue as senior Marshal of France. Julie soon discovered that her witnesses and relations were being committed to prison without a shred of evidence against them, as Richelieu scattered his *lettres de cachet* with a recklessness that trebled the spate of pamphlets and protests against him. The unfortunate Bénaven was transferred from For l'Evêque to the Conciergerie in order to appear before *parlement* in March 1775. *Parlement* decided to set him at liberty provisionally, but the gaoler at the Conciergerie had no sooner received this order than he was informed that Richelieu had issued a *lettre de cachet* for Bénaven to be committed to For l'Evêque if he were released from the Conciergerie. The gaoler referred this conflict to a judge in chambers; but the judge failed to persuade Richelieu to withdraw the *lettre de cachet*, and Bénaven remained in prison. *Parlement*, enraged at this flouting of its authority, sent its First President to appeal to the King, and the King declared his royal will that *parlement* should be obeyed and Bénaven released. Bénaven was consequently set free and had no sooner set foot outside the Conciergerie than he was arrested under a new *lettre de cachet* issued by Richelieu, and taken to For l'Evêque. It was not until August that the combined efforts of *parlement*, the King's council and the King got him out again.

In January 1776, the Palais de Justice caught fire and many of the documents in the case were destroyed; in March, *parlement* met for what was expected to be the final hearing, but adjourned until the autumn without arriving at a verdict. It was not until April 1777 that a decision was reached, preceded by a new tide of Résumés, Reflections, Mémoires, Précis, Postscripts, and Responses that brought the grand total of pamphlets to more than one hundred and sixty. Notable among them was Madame de Saint-Vincent's plea to *parlement* to declare all Richelieu's proceedings "nugatory, iniquitous, tortious, and inimical to the authority of the court, the laws and ordinances of the realm, the liberty of citizens, the safety of families, and public order . . . and to restrain him from disregarding the rules of justice, abusing his influence, making armed nocturnal excursions into convents and the homes of private individuals, searching their pockets, desks and cupboards, pillaging, purloining and suppressing their titles and documents, imprisoning the occupants and holding them in illegal custody without due warning and authority . . . preferring charges without sufficient evidence of the alleged offences, obtaining committal warrants against witnesses in a position to give evidence against him, harassing them, criminally prosecuting them, threatening them, persecuting them, and transforming into his own witnesses those of the accused whom his representatives succeeded in corrupting by promises and money." It was a fairly moderate picture of the usual legal procedures of any member of the upper aristocracy.

Amid all the excitements of the closing days of the trial, Richelieu received a visit from a notary of Compiègne who informed him that a certain Madame de Gaya, an eighty-year-old widow whose lover Richelieu once had been, had cut all the members of her family out of her will and had made the maréchal her sole inheritor of a sum of 50,000 écus. Richelieu was charmed by this tribute. "You know," he said to the notary, "if all the women I ever slept with had left me their property, I should be richer than the King."

He was in need of this windfall when, a few days later, *parlement* delivered a judgement that was as fantastic as any of the proceedings that it had listened to. The notes were found to be forgeries; but all the accused were declared innocent. Seven of the defendants were awarded damages of 65,000 livres and costs against Richelieu; *parlement* claimed 60,000 as its own costs. It was by only a few votes that it decided against compelling him to reimburse all the holders of the forged notes.

§ 4

In February 1778, Voltaire was allowed to return to Paris after living abroad for a quarter of a century, and Richelieu, who had kept up their friendship by letters and visits to Ferney, went round to greet him in the rooms that the marquis de la Villette had lent him. They went together to the Comédie-Française for the rehearsals of Voltaire's new tragedy, *Irène*, and many onlookers claimed that the poet, two years Richelieu's senior, looked the better preserved. But Voltaire was soon in bed, presenting a sorry sight in nightcap and dressing gown, in contrast with the dapper maréchal, still able to mount and sit a horse like a young man, and forever strutting around in expensive satins with the blue sash of the Saint-Esprit across his chest.

His good looks had disappeared. "It was not possible to recognize in him the hero of so many gallant adventures," said the duc de Levis, "for he did not possess those noble features which time erodes without effacing; deep lines furrowed his face in every direction; and he sought in vain to conceal the dwindling of his height, which even in his youth was only average, with excessively high heels. His mind had not undergone the same process of decay and no doubt he no longer had the vivacity and sprightliness of youth, but his memory was excellent; he took an interest in the affairs of the day and would talk with as much simplicity as grace of those of the past. He judged men and matters with admirable discernment and his jokes were spicy without being unkind."

For years he had used a mixture of opium and brewer's yeast as a remedy against sleeplessness, and the ailing Voltaire asked for some to be sent to him. But either because he took too much of it, or, a more likely story, because the servant who brought the bottle to him from Richelieu dropped it and prepared a substitute in which he used too much opium, the physic did the poet more harm than good. He took to his bed permanently and died on 30 May 1778.

Backstage rivalries continued to embroil Richelieu in squabbles with Duras and with Fronsac, whom he also suspected of over-eagerness to inherit his title, but now and then his aged ears still pricked to the sounds of martial glory. Ever since the outbreak of the American War of Independence in 1775, France had been drawn, by popular clamour and against the inclination of the King and his ministers, closer and closer to war. Her recognition of the new American republic in 1778, and her alliance with Spain against Britain in the following year, made the long-continued but undeclared hostilities official. Minorca had been returned to Britain at the end of the Seven Years War, and Richelieu stumped round to the King's study with a map of the island in his hand, demonstrating to everybody how simple it would be to capture Fort Saint-Philippe again, and how shameful it would be if that honour were allowed to fall to the Spaniards. Members of the council told him rather unkindly that the King wished him to keep quiet, whereupon he thrust his way into the study and declared: "Sire, I have the honour to be one of your old soldiers. I thought I had the right to express my opinions. But since Your Majesty does not approve of that, will he at least permit me to take action?"

The King did not allow his 83-year-old soldier to take up arms again, but it was noticeable that there was a change of attitude of both Louis and Marie-Antoinette towards the man whom they once treated with disdain. It is not without significance that this reversal followed closely on a change in their relationship to each other. For seven years Marie-Antoinette, first as Dauphine and then as Queen, underwent the humiliating experience of having her husband shun her bed. It was not until August 1777, when her brother came to Versailles and had a heart-to-heart talk with Louis, that the King agreed to have the minor operation which freed him from his painful disability. The outcome of the royal pair's marital adjustment was that Richelieu, who had hitherto personified in an extreme form the delights that were denied them, was no longer an irritant. His naughty stories could be laughed at without a bitter aftertaste, and, as soon as he had been accepted into the royal intimacy once more, he became outspoken on other subjects and often addressed the King with the frankness of an elder statesman.

In 1779 he had a sharp attack of indigestion that turned into something resembling a small stroke, and Louis, congratulating him on his recovery, remarked: "You are no longer a young man. You have lived in three centuries."

"Not quite, Your Majesty," said Richelieu, "but at least in three reigns."

"And what do you think of them?" Louis asked.

"Sire, under Louis XIV one did not dare to say a word; under Louis XV one muttered; under Your Majesty one speaks out loud."

It was a saddening thought for him; seldom amenable to discipline himself, he nevertheless remained convinced of the sanctity of authoritarianism and privilege, the complete reactionary. He was alarmed at the extent to which the King was making economies and reducing ceremonial. "He foresaw nothing good in this new state of affairs and said that, in a monarchy, the high nobility should set the nation an example of respect and devotion to the ruler; that not only his household but all the great lords should be constantly in attendance on him."

But though the mild, reforming views of Voltaire were too wild for him, and the more advanced theories of Rousseau no better than anarchistic madness, Richelieu remained young in heart and kept up with the fashion in dress if not in thought. And now, to his boast of having lived in three reigns, he added a new one: of having married in each of them.

His bride was the widow of Edmond de Rothe, a descendant of an Irish Catholic family that had served the kings of France for a century, although Edmond himself was in the East Indian trade. Jeanne-Catherine-Josèphe de Lavaulx de Sommercourt was de Rothe's second wife. When he died on his way back from China in 1772, she was left with their four young children and a fifth, a boy, from his first marriage. Richelieu is said to have met her a year later when her carriage overturned on the way to Versailles, and he gave her a lift in his own, but it is just as likely that their paths crossed because of his continuing links with the Jacobites, or through their common friend, the comtesse de Marbeuf. He met her frequently, she remained loyal to him throughout the Saint-Vincent scandal, and at the time of his illness in 1779 he began to realize that he needed rather more attention than he was getting from the only permanent female guest in his house: Madame Rousse, whose association with him was more notable for its duration than for its fidelity.

Matters came to a head early in 1780, when he had another frightening experience. He awoke feeling a little out of sorts and, after drinking some whey, had an attack of indigestion, which, like his illness of the year before, developed into a kind of seizure. "I tried to take my opium, but it turned my stomach. I was in an extraordinary state: I could see; I could hear; but I could neither move nor speak. Misfortune is useful in some ways, for this decided me to get married: I intended to put a protective barrier between my senility and M. de Fronsac. I saw him act as if he were master of the house; he wanted to have me bled, and, but for my surgeon valet-de-chambre who opposed it and swore that they could kill him before he would bleed me, I should have been dead. My senses gradually returned; I could move before I could speak, but I remained all the time in possession of my wits. My first thought, as soon as I could make myself understood by signs, was to write to Madame de Rothe and ask her to give me proof of her friendship by marrying me as quickly as possible."

She was almost forty and he was not quite eighty-four. Her fortune was small: a pension of 6,000 livres a year from her husband's estate, the income from 40,000 livres in trust for her children, 10,000 livres' worth of furniture, silver and jewelry, and some 50,000 livres owing to her husband from his brother and from the King's agent in Mauritius. She was, if the malicious Madame du Deffand is to be believed, "neither beautiful nor ugly, neither young nor old, neither stupid nor witty: it would be impossible to be more commonplace." She accepted Richelieu's proposal; he was in such a hurry to get married that he obtained the archbishop's dispensation for the wedding to take place during Lent. It was celebrated in his private chapel at the hôtel d'Antin on 15 February 1780 and followed by fireworks and a ball. As for the subsequent events, conflicting stories were put about: one to the effect that the bridegroom had acquitted himself much better in his eighties than he had at his first marriage in his teens; the other version was that he left the bride at her bedroom door, slipping into her hand a set of verses that he had composed for the occasion, one quatrain of which ran:

> Conceal your charms as soon as midnight's past,
> Lest I should Love dismay.
> My joy, since I've Love's lusty weapon lost,
> Does not survive the day.

Certainly the marriage brought little joy to many of his old acquaintances. The new duchesse was a vigorous new broom; Madame Rousse was ordered out of the hôtel d'Antin and followed by the many pimps, procurers, and shady hangers-on who had haunted the great mansion for years. When Fronsac showed his disapproval too openly, Richelieu told him: "I warn you that despite my eighty-four years I count on having a child who will be a better man than you." The gossips chuckled that this was more than possible, since the new duchesse was said to have a soft spot for the comte de Coigny. Fronsac, perhaps hoping to give weight to the rumour, picked a quarrel with Coigny at a ball given by the prince de Guémenée some days later and in the resultant duel Coigny received two slight wounds.

It was in the early days of the marriage that one of the farmers-general who had long been a friend of Madame de Richelieu called to present his newly married daughter to her, and found her talking to the duc de Crillon. Richelieu entered the room shortly afterwards and with his usual charm offered to show the young woman round the splendours of his home. The duchesse continued to chat with her two male visitors, but after a time they perceived that her attention was straying from the conversation and that she was evidently worried by her husband's long absence. Crillon assured her that nothing ill could have befallen him, but she was not content until he offered to go and make certain. He withdrew in the direction of Richelieu's private apartments, only to reappear within a few seconds, pursued by the maréchal, who was dancing with rage, swearing and belabouring Crillon with his clenched fists. Crillon had entered one of the rooms just in the nick of time, to find Richelieu in full possession of his youthful humours and the young woman, whether through admiration or disbelief, so hypnotized that she was in imminent peril of having her name added to Richelieu's roll of dishonour.

Madame de Richelieu, to avoid any further adventures of this kind, insisted that he should discontinue his habit of taking every day before dinner a teaspoonful of the aphrodisiac which he concocted from a secret recipe: a brown liquid of the consistency of honey and with a strong smell of saffron. Some of his friends suggested later that this interruption of a régime that he had followed almost all his life was the indirect cause of his death; but that it had no immediate effect was proved in April when it appeared that Richelieu had successfully carried out his threat to Fronsac. These hopes ended with a miscarriage (and the rumour that Fronsac had bribed one of the duchesse's attendants to give her a drink containing an abortive substance). Some time later, the Queen playfully, and a little unkindly, asked Richelieu if it were true that Madame de Richelieu was pregnant again. "I think not, madame," Richelieu replied. His eyes twinkled as he continued: "Unless it is as a result of last night." He paused a moment and then added: "Or this morning."

On most Sunday evenings in summer he could be seen proudly

escorting his wife through the Tuileries gardens at the fashionable hour of six, tottering a little on shoes whose heels grew slightly higher every year. His wife was tender and solicitous, striving to prevent him from slipping out through the garden gates on the furtive expeditions that still called to him from time to time; barring the door to his less reputable friends; and feeding him on newly hatched pigeons, which were considered to be the most nourishing and easily digested of foods.

His skin disease bothered him occasionally, and the neighbours, believing that he bathed in milk and that his servants sold his bath water, were careful in their choice of dairies. Others thought that the milky substance in his bath was diluted almond juice, or even some new ingredient in that most distrusted of eighteenth-century commodities: soap. He continued to soak himself in scent, but there was little else that he could now do to improve his appearance, though one witness claimed to have been present at a daily ritual of stretching the skin of the maréchal's forehead upwards and backwards under his wig in an attempt to get rid of some of the countless wrinkles.

He still presided over the Tribunal of the Marshals of France, which met in his house and had extensive powers. It was concerned with matters of military honour, and, since most of the nobility and a great number of the bourgoisie held commissions in the army at one time or another, the Tribunal's jurisdiction could conveniently be stretched to cover a great variety of disputes and offences. In addition to conferring on Richelieu the honours of the Constable of France, with the right to have armed guards in his ante-rooms, the presidency also provided him with an inexhaustible supply of *lettres de cachet*, on which he had so lavishly drawn during the Saint-Vincent case.

His increasing deafness handicapped him and was on one occasion the cause of his defeat by an officer to whom he was giving a severe reprimand. As the officer did nothing but bow and smile in return, Richelieu grew testy and threatened him with severe punishment. When he had finished, the officer bowed again and replied: "I am most put out at not being able to hear all the obliging things that Monsieur le maréchal has been kind enough to address to me, but I am a little deaf." Richelieu, not doubting for a moment that the officer's hearing was perfectly sound, sat with a ferocious scowl while this was being shouted into his ear.

But it was never safe to take liberties with the old man; he had behaved with sufficient insolence throughout his life to know how to recognize it, and deal with it, in others. Some young officers who had been involved in a brawl with the police at one of the boulevard theatres were brought before him, and, remembering his own boisterous youth, he was inclined to deal gently with them. Sensing this, and hoping to gain a reputation for daring by twisting the deaf old lion's tail, one of the young men asked leave to speak and then informed Richelieu, with an expression of shocked disapproval: "Monsieur le maréchal, one of the constables had the impudence to say he didn't give a —— for you." The words echoed round the room as they were repeated *fortissimo* in the maréchal's ear. "That may well be, sir," he answered sweetly, "but since he did not ask you to convey that message to me, you will please have the goodness to take yourself off to the Abbaye."

It was customary for officers to report themselves to the Abbaye, one of the three prisons to which the Tribunal committed people under *lettres de cachet*, and not to be sent there under escort. Once inside it was not always easy to get out again. One lieutenant-colonel, imprisoned for contempt, sent a plea to the Tribunal which he thought might particularly appeal to Richelieu: he claimed that "he could no longer live separated from his wife; that he was tormented by the most violent desires; and that in him nature spoke with too strong a voice for him to be able to silence it."

"Ah!" said Richelieu. "Then tell him that he won't get out of prison until he has imparted his secret to me." And the impatient husband stayed there.

It was not only in his capacity as *doyen* of the Marshals of France that Richelieu could send people to prison. As First Gentleman, he could commit any actor or actress to For l'Evêque under an *ordre anticipé*. This was a temporary measure, requiring confirmation by an *ordre en forme*, signed by the secretary of state for Paris; but so much time was taken up by the minister in deciding whether to issue the order that in practice Richelieu had the power of arbitrary imprisonment for several days at a time and did not hesitate to use it.

Despite his own experiences, he was a great believer in the efficacy of imprisonment. When Champville, one of the actors at the Comédie-Italienne, sang out of tune, Richelieu clapped him into For l'Evêque for five days, though this action was not so much for his faulty singing as for challenging to a duel another member of the company who criticized him for it. Mademoiselle Rosalie, of the same troupe, playing the part of the boy who guides Blondel in *Richard Coeur-de-Lion*, fell out with the singer who played Blondel and stuck her sleeve so full of pins that the unfortunate Blondel severely scratched his hand when he leaned on her arm. Rosalie then carried the dispute into the wings, where she screamed at Blondel with more truth than politeness that he was only a jumped-up barber's boy.

The theatre director was so incensed that he asked Richelieu to fine Rosalie 100 écus. "Nonsense," said Richelieu. "She'll go to bed with somebody for 50 louis, show a profit and come back and give us another 100 écus' worth of insolence. Into prison with her. I know what I'm about. Into prison!"

In 1783 he had another small stroke while taking his stroll through the Tuileries gardens; feeling a little fatigued, he bent down towards a chair and was suddenly overcome and would have fallen had not somebody caught him. He refused to acknowledge his weakness in public and rested only a few minutes on the chair before getting up and resuming his walk. But he could not continue and had to get into his carriage and, on arriving home, went to bed and stayed there for a fortnight, while the gossips sniggered that his illness was caused by his having "deceived himself into believing that he could give his wife a demonstration of truly vernal love."

He was very far from finished. In February 1784, he celebrated his 88th birthday, a month early, with a magnificent ball in the hôtel d'Antin; two days later, in Bordeaux, he began the last of the scandals associated with his name. It fittingly epitomized the arrogance of his character and his class. It arose from his interest in the theatre at Bordeaux, where, although he was no longer able to make the journey, he maintained his right to allot the seats of honour in the boxes and at the sides of the stage. He gave instructions that these were not to be occupied except by the aldermen who were on duty to preserve order in the theatre; this was at once contested by the whole body of aldermen who claimed that the policing of the theatre was a municipal affair and the governor had no right to make regulations.

The argument became so heated that the mayor, the vicomte de Noë, decided on a personal protest; accompanied by aldermen who were not on police duty, he presented himself at the door giving access to the wings and demanded entrance. A door porter, especially despatched to Bordeaux by Richelieu and dressed in the royal livery, refused to let them pass, whereupon Noë had the man taken to prison, having first stripped him of his uniform so as not to offer an affront to the King. The municipal officers reported the matter to Vergennes, the Foreign Secretary (who was also responsible for the provinces), and a week later Vergennes notified them that the King would inquire into the dispute and that the porter should be released.

This did not satisfy Richelieu. Since Noë held the rank of lieutenant-colonel in the militia, Richelieu was able to summon him before the Tribunal of the Marshals of France, accused of impeding a sentry in the course of his duty. Richelieu presided at the trial at which Noë was found guilty, and Richelieu then condemned him to make a public apology to the Governor of Guienne (Richelieu) and to be suspended from his office of mayor for a year.

Noë, who had wisely not appeared at the trial, refused to accept the decision of the Tribunal on the grounds that it was improperly constituted, that it had no jurisdiction over him, and that no recognizable offence had been shown in the charge. He appealed to the *parlement* of Paris, which gladly accepted the opportunity to order both parties to appear before it. Richelieu's reply was to send an armed escort to conduct Noë to prison, a duty which it failed to perform because he had escaped over the border into Spain. Richelieu then appealed to the King's council.

Council, *parlement*, Tribunal, each as archaic, unrepresentative and corrupt as the other, juggled the permutations of this unfunny farce. The council referred the affair back to the Tribunal. The Tribunal declared Noë's appeal to *parlement* null and void. *Parlement* assembled and rejected the ruling of the Tribunal. Each reached a different conclusion, but Richelieu remained undefeated. Not until after the maréchal's death did Noë dare to set foot in Bordeaux again.

The Queen, who had a candidate of her own for Richelieu's post, used the uproar over this latest of his exploits to suggest to his wife that the time had come for him to resign from the presidency of the Tribunal; but Madame de Richelieu replied that she would not dare even hint such a thing to him. At this, the Queen had Ségur, the Minister of War, write a semiofficial letter to the duchesse, saying that he understood that Richelieu was subject to fits of eccentricity which made him incapable of continuing in his office, and he strongly advised that he should voluntarily give up the presidency before he was dismissed from it.

Madame de Richelieu was now at her wits' end. She was frightened of her husband's wrath if she showed Ségur's letter to him but was even more worried at the effect that dismissal without warning might have on him. In the end she decided to let Richelieu see the correspondence, and the maréchal sent the minister a reply which left no doubt that he had not lost his wits or his caustic tongue. "I habitually see people," he wrote, "who retain their posts despite the fact that they drivel all day long. I therefore consider myself quite entitled to continue in my own office since I drivel only intermittently—in the morning or the evening."

Perhaps to give proof of his fitness he visited the Bastille on 25 August 1786, and an astonished clerk in the prison governor's office recorded that "he climbed up to the top of the towers—at the age of 90 years, 5 months 12 days." From the summit of the ugly building that loomed so menacingly over the life of Paris, he looked back over a longer stretch of history and personal adventure than most men would ever know. He looked back over three reigns and, in a moment of lucidity or despondency, he may have realized that they were about to end in the total destruction of the world that he had known. Louis XIV had bank-rupted the nation financially; Louis XV had bankrupted the monarchy morally; Louis XVI was not the man to restore either.

The world in which he had spent his ninety years was about to disappear, abruptly and irrevocably, suddenly becoming the *ancien régime,* defunct as the dodo. Over the middle fifty years of the eighteenth century, the years of his own maturity, the tawdry court had cast a pall of shoddiness, yet some figures stood out from it, for good reasons and for bad. Richelieu was one of those out-standing figures—bright-eyed, sharp-tongued, egocentric, blazing with vitality and second to none in courage, but with so many dreams unfulfilled, so many projects undertaken and left incom-plete: so little to have done in ninety years, except to have slept with more women than he could count or remember, and never to have known love.

The giddy attacks became more frequent, and he was compelled to agree to the Marshals' holding the Tribunal at the maréchal de Contades's home, though he still kept the armed guards in his ante-rooms and the Constable's drawn sword and the Senior Mar-shal's lily-strewn baton on his coat of arms. In December he took to his bed after a particularly severe attack; but when Fronsac—himself nearly as shrivelled as his father and crippled with gout—came to pay his compliments and size up his chance of inheritance, Richelieu said: "Not this time—I'm counting on reaching a hundred."

He was overconfident. On 8 August 1788, he died of congestion of the lungs, at the age of 92 years and 5 months. His timing was excellent, for on that same day summonses were issued in the King's name for the *Etats-Généraux* to meet for the first time in 175 years. Richelieu's world had died with him.

APPENDIX:
PEOPLE
BIBLIOGRAPHY
INDEX

People

In this list, some families are dealt with together, in the groups into which they fall in the book; but the nobility of France was so intricately linked by marriage and adultery that, were this the biography of some other person, the same families might be reassembled in quite different but equally close relationships.

ARGENSON; PAULMY

Marc-René de Voyer de Paulmy, marquis d'Argenson, *garde des sceaux*, was father of (1) René-Louis, marquis and *ministre des affaires étrangères*, author of the *Mémoires*; (2) Marc-Pierre, comte and *ministre de la guerre*. Marc-Pierre's son, Marc-René, marquis de Paulmy, was founder of the Bibliothèque de l'Arsenal.

BACHELIER, François-Gabriel

Succeeded his father as *premier valet-de-garde-robe*, 1703; bought post of *premier valet-de-chambre*, 1707; appointed inspector of the château de Versailles, 1730; died as governor of the Louvre, 1754.

BOURBON; ANJOU; BERRY; BOURGOGNE; BRETAGNE; DOMBES; DU MAINE; EU; FOULOUSE

Bourbon, the family name of the kings of France, was also borne by Louis XIV's legitimized children: the duc du Maine (and his sons, the prince de Dombes and the comte d'Eu), the comte de Toulouse, and their sisters. Of Louis's three legitimate grandsons, the youngest, the duc de Berry, married his cousin, Marie-Louise-

Elisabeth, daughter of the duc d'Orléans; the second, the duc d'Anjou, gave up his French titles in 1700 on becoming Philip V of Spain; the eldest, the duc de Bourgogne, was father of two successive ducs de Bretagne, who died at the ages of two and five, and of Louis XV, who as a child was given his uncle's former title of duc d'Anjou.

BOURBON-CONDÉ; CHAROLAIS; CLERMONT; ENGHIEN; NANTES

Louis-Henri, 1692–1740, head of the house of Bourbon-Condé, was the son of Louis III de Condé and Marie-Françoise de Bourbon, "Mademoiselle de Nantes," daughter of Louis XIV and Madame de Montespan, and sister of the duc du Maine. He was prince de Condé et d'Enghien as well as duc de Bourbon, but was customarily referred to simply as "Monsieur le Duc." His brothers and sisters included Mademoiselle de Charolais and the comte de Clermont, the original owner of the duchy of Châteauroux, who was abbot of Saint-Germain-des-Prés and whose mistress was the ballet-dancer, Camargo.

BOUFFLERS; LUXEMBOURG; VILLEROY

Madeleine-Angélique, duchesse de Boufflers, who was the mistress and later the wife of the duc de Luxembourg, was a granddaughter of the maréchal duc de Villeroy, Louis XV's governor. Another of his grandchildren was the marquis de Villeroy who married Marie-Renée de Montmorency-Luxembourg, whom Richelieu visited at the abbey of Jouarre. Marie-Renée's brother was the same duc de Luxembourg whose first wife, Marie Colbert de Seignelay, was the mistress of his second wife's first husband, the maréchal duc de Boufflers.

CLAIRON (stage name of Claire-Joseph Léris)

One of the most famous of eighteenth-century actresses; made her début at the Comédie-Française in 1743 at the age of twenty; retired in 1766 after the Dubois scandal.

DAUPHIN

The title of the heir apparent to the throne of France. During Richelieu's lifetime there were six: the Grand Dauphin, 1661–1711, son of Louis XIV; his son, formerly duc de Bourgogne, 1682–1712; his son, formerly duc d'Anjou, later Louis XV, 1710–1774; his son, Louis le Dauphin, 1729–1765; his son, formerly duc de Berry, later Louis XVI, 1754–1793; his son, Louis-Joseph-Xavier, 1781–1789. The Dauphin who is counted as Louis XVII was born in 1785 and is presumed to have died in captivity in 1793.

DUBOIS (stage name of Louis Blouin)

Made his début at the Comédie-Française at the age of thirty; after his resignation, Richelieu found him an engagement in the theatre at Bordeaux. His daughter, Marie-Madeleine, made her début in 1759 at the age of fifteen.

DURAS; AUMONT; DURFORT; MAZARIN

Jean-Baptiste de Durfort, maréchal duc de Duras, married Angélique-Victoire de Bournonville, one of the three women with whom Richelieu celebrated his election to the Académie Française. His daughter, Victoire-Félicité, married first the duc de Fitz-James and then the duc d'Aumont. His son (whom some believed to be Richelieu's), Emmanuel-Félicité, married Charlotte-Antoinette, daughter of Guy-Paul-Jules, duc de Mazarin, and Louise-Françoise de Rohan-Rohan. Their daughter, Louise-Jeanne, inherited the duchy of Mazarin from her mother and was the archbishop of Lyon's companion at Poitevin's baths. She married her cousin, Louis-Marie-Guy d'Aumont, marquis de Villequier, who took her title as duc de Mazarin. (See MAZARIN.)

LA GALISSONNIÈRE, Roland-Michel Barrin, marquis de

Governor of Canada from 1745 to 1749, he died shortly after his victory over Byng. The Mémoires Authentiques say that Richelieu's adjutant, di Lorenzi, discovered Byng's signal code in a house at Mahon and this enabled La Galissonnière to forestall all of Byng's manoeuvres. I can discover no confirmation of this and it is not mentioned in the Admiralty records of Byng's court martial (which include Voltaire's copy of Richelieu's plea for Byng).

LA MARTELLIÈRE, Claude-Louise de Lory, Madame de

Her husband was *conseiller, secrétaire du roi, de la maison couronné de France et de ses finances.* Gossip said that Richelieu was the father of her son, Charles, who served as one of his aides-de-camp during the Hanover campaign.

LA POUPLINIÈRE, Alexandre-Jean-Joseph le Riche de

This is his own usual spelling of his name, though others used varying forms, including La Popelinière, which is possibly how it was pronounced.

LE KAIN (stage name of Henri-Louis Kaïn)

The most powerful dramatic actor of his time, he made his début at the Comédie-Française in 1750 at the age of twenty-one.

MAILLY; CHÂTEAUROUX; FLAVACOURT; LAURAGUAIS;
NESLE; VINTIMILLE

Louis de Mailly, marquis de Nesle (and, from 1710, Prince of Orange, a title that Louis XIV had then taken away from William III of England) married Armande-Félice de la Porte-Mazarin, daughter of Paul-Jules, duc de Mazarin, and Félice-Armande-Charlotte de Durfort-Duras. Their five daughters were: Louise-Julie, who married the marquis de Mailly, her second cousin and brother of Françoise, duchesse de Mazarin; Pauline-Félicité, who married the marquis de Vintimille; Diane-Adélaïde, who married the duc de Lauraguais, son of Marie-Angélique de Brancas, duchesse de Villars (known as the duchesse de Brancas or Villars-Brancas, and not to be confused with Jeanne-Angélique de la

Roche-Varengeville, who was wife of the maréchal duc de Villars and has been rather improbably identified as the duchesse de —— of the *Vie Privée*); Hortense-Félicité, who married the marquis de Flavacourt; and Marie-Anne, who married the marquis de la Tournelle and was created duchesse de Châteauroux. (*See* Du-ras *and* MAZARIN.)

MAZARIN; MAUREPAS; POLIGNAC; SAINT-FLORENTIN; LA VRILLIÈRE

Françoise de Mailly de Rubempré, 1688–1742, first married Louis Phélypeaux, marquis de la Vrillière; their eldest son held several offices of state, as comte de Saint-Florentin until 1770 and there-after as duc de la Vrillière; their elder daughter, Marie-Jeanne, married her cousin, Jean-Frédéric Phélypeaux, comte de Maurepas; their younger daughter, Louise-Françoise, married Louis de Bréhan, comte de Plélo, and became mother-in-law to the duc d'Aiguillon. (*See* RICHELIEU.) Her second marriage was to Paul-Jules de la Porte-Mazarin, duc de Mazarin, whose daughter by his first wife had married the marquis de Nesle (*see* MAILLY) and whose son, Guy-Paul-Jules, passed on the Mazarin title to his daughter, Louise-Jeanne (*see* DURAS). Her younger sister, also named Françoise, married the marquis de Polignac, was mistress of the chevalier de Bavière, the duc de Bourbon and the prince de Conti, and fought the duel with Madame de Nesle.

MOLÉ, François-René

The son of a Parisian painter and sculptor, he became the most popular comic actor of his age.

ORLÉANS, ducs de (*Also* ducs de CHARTRES, MONTPENSIER, BEAUJOLAIS, and VALOIS)

Philippe, son of Louis XIII and brother of Louis XIV, married first Henrietta-Anne of England, second Charlotte-Elisabeth de Bavière, author of the *Correspondance*; their son, Philippe, later Regent, married Françoise-Marie de Bourbon, illegitimate daughter of Louis XIV; their son, Louis-Philippe, married Jeanne-Marie-

Auguste de Bade-Bade; their son, Louis-Philippe, married Louise-Henriette de Bourbon-Conti; their son, Louis-Philippe-Joseph ("Egalité"), married Louise-Marie Adélaïde de Bourbon; their son, Louis-Philippe, became King of the French in 1830, the literally crowning achievement of generations of treachery.

PARABÈRE; ROTHENBURG; ROTTEMBOURG

Marie-Madeleine, comtesse de Parabère, the Regent's mistress, was a daughter of the duc de la Vieuville. Her son-in-law, Friedrich-Rudolph, comte de Rothenburg, was Frederick the Great's emissary to Louis XV, and is not to be confused with his uncle, Conrad-Alexandre Rottembourg, French Ambassador to Berlin and Madrid.

RAUCOURT

(stage name of Françoise-Marie-Antoinette-Josèphe Saucerotte)

Made her début at the Comédie-Française in December 1772 at the age of sixteen; went bankrupt four years later and fled to Germany where she is said to have been whipped and branded for swindling. Taken back into the Comédie-Française in 1779 at Marie-Antoinette's request, she appeared as a man in a play written by herself in 1782, and was posthumously the occasion of a riot outside the church of Saint-Roch in 1815 when the curé refused to allow her body to be brought in for her funeral service.

RICHELIEU; AGÉNOIS; AIGUILLON; BELLEFONDS; CHINON; DU CHÂTELET; FRONSAC

Armand-Jean, duc de Richelieu, grandson of the Cardinal's sister, had four children by his second wife, Anne-Marguerite, daughter of Jean-Léonard de Grandbois d'Acigné and Marie-Anne de la Roche-Jagu. They were Catherine-Armande (Mademoiselle de Richelieu), who married François-Bernard du Châtelet and was mother of the marquise de Bellefonds; Elisabeth-Marguerite-Armande (Mademoiselle de Fronsac), *prieure perpetuelle des réligieuses bénédictines de la Présentation;* Marie-Gabrielle-Elisabeth (Madame de Richelieu), *abbesse des Cisterciennes du Trésor* and later *abbesse de l'Abbaye-aux-Bois;* and Louis-François-Armand, later maréchal duc de Richelieu.

The maréchal's son, the duc de Fronsac, married (1) Adélaïde de Julhac, by whom he had a son, the comte de Chinon, who became *ministre des affaires étrangères* under Louis XVIII; and (2) Antoinette de Gallifet, by whom he had Armande, who married the marquis de Montcalm-Gozon, and Simplicie, who married the marquis de Jumilhac, whose family have inherited the Richelieu titles. Another grandson of the Cardinal's sister, Louis-Armand Vignerot du Plessis, became father of Emmanuel-Armand, comte d'Agénois, later duc d'Aiguillon, who married Louise-Félicité de Bréhan-Plélo. (*See* MAZARIN.)

SAXE, Hermann-Maurice, maréchal comte de

His mother was Aurora, countess of Koenigsmark. Probably the best known of his mistresses was the actress Adrienne Lecouvreur; his illegitimate daughter by another actress, Marie Rintaut (known as Marie de Verrières), was the grandmother of George Sand. He died in November 1750 but was not buried until February 1751: at Strasbourg, which was the nearest town to Paris with a Protestant cemetery.

SOISSONS, François de Fitz-James, évêque de

The son of Jacques de Fitz-James, duc de Berwick, who was the illegitimate son of James II of England and Arabella Churchill, Marlborough's sister. Appointed bishop of Soissons in 1739 at the age of thirty; First Almoner to the King 1742; resigned 1748.

TENCIN, Claudine-Alexandre Guérin de

After taking vows at the age of sixteen, she remained in the Augustine convent of Montfleury for eight years and during that time is said to have had two children by Arthur Dillon. She wrote several historical novels. In her letter of 5 November 1742, *"la gimbarde"* has been taken by P. M. Masson (following Soulavie) to be her code name for Louis XV; but she would not have ventured—nor would Richelieu have accepted—other expressions in the letter if she had been referring to the King.

Bibliography

Between 1790 and 1793 the abbé Jean-Louis Soulavie published the *Mémoires du maréchal de Richelieu* in nine volumes: a collection of sparse facts copied or remembered from documents that he had been allowed to examine in Richelieu's library and a great deal of fiction invented and spiced to suit the current revolutionary palate, and so wide-roving that it was much more a history of the Regency and the reign of Louis XV than a biography of Richelieu. In 1791 *La vie privée du maréchal de Richelieu* appeared in three volumes; this is usually attributed to Faur, Fronsac's* secretary, but was possibly the work of Jean-Baptiste de la Borde, formerly *premier valet-de-chambre* to Louis XV, who knew Richelieu well.

In 1789 Fronsac announced that Soulavie's projected biography was based on only a small portion of his father's papers and that he had asked Sénac de Meilhan to write an official biography. Sénac emigrated, however, leaving behind him the masses of documents that Fronsac had lent him. After Fronsac's death, the comte de Chinon also emigrated and was unable to take the remainder of the family papers with him. Both collections were impounded by the Revolutionary authorities, but parts of them were returned to Chinon and his two sisters during the Directory and the Consulate. Chinon, who returned to France at the Restoration and died in 1822 after a distinguished and honourable career, left no direct heirs; it was from the Jumilhac family, descendants of his younger stepsister, that A. de

---

* To avoid confusion, I refer to Richelieu's son and grandson by the titles they held during his lifetime. Fronsac was duc de Richelieu for less than three years, his son, the former comte de Chinon, succeeding him on 4 February 1791.

Boislisle obtained in 1868 the brief fragments of biography, dictated by Richelieu, which were published fifty years later as the *Mémoires authentiques du maréchal de Richelieu*, and which are to be found in Volume XL of the Fonds Richelieu.

It is on the unreliable *Mémoires* of Soulavie, the uncertain *Vie privée*, and the meagre *Mémoires authentiques* that subsequent biographers of Richelieu have based their work, and it is only in recent years that it has become known that the University of Paris possesses more than a hundred volumes of papers of the Richelieu family, presented in 1933 by the comte de Jumilhac, duc de Richelieu, and housed in the Bibliothèque Victor Cousin. I am extremely grateful to the Rector of the University for having permitted me to consult them.

The forty-six volumes devoted to the affairs of the maréchal duc de Richelieu contain letters, dispatches, reports, and legal documents and deal with all his interests, financial, political, and military, as well as amatory. They confirm Boislisle's opinion that La Borde (or Faur) worked from original documents when compiling the *Vie privée*. They contain, for example, the letter from Madame de Goesbriant inviting Richelieu to send for her in the Kitchen Court and the rude reply written in his own hand (*Vie privée*, I, 466–68), as well as letters from persons whose existence has sometimes been doubted: Madame de Valois' lovelorn confidante, for instance, and the tragic Madame Michelin.

There are letters from Mesdames de Châteauroux, Pompadour, and Tencin on matters of court intrigue; and others—usually upbraiding him for his inconstancy—from Mesdames de Nesle, Polignac, Charolais, Valois, Parabère, La Martellière, Villeroy, La Pouplinière, and that mysterious duchesse de ———— to whose memory and honour Richelieu was so unaccountably—and untypically—true that even in these letters which he kept locked up in his library, her name has been scratched out with a penknife so that her secret remains undiscovered. To some of these *lettres galantes* he affixed, with his own seal, locks of the writer's hair, and it is a strange experience to turn the pages and be confronted with these trophies: with, for instance, the dark brown curls, still shot with gold, of the comtesse de Parabère, who was born in Paris in October 1693 and died in 1755.

The accuracy of the *Vie privée* can be judged from the fact that in fifteen letters from Mesdames Charolais, Du Châtelet, and Goesbriant, I found only one discrepancy between the originals and the versions printed in the *Vie privée*—and that was the omission of a sentence of no significance.

In addition to the Rector and Conservateur en Chef des Bibliothèques of the University of Paris and the Directrice of the Bibliothèque Victor Cousin, I have to thank the directors and staff of the following libraries for help and permission to consult their books and manuscripts: The British Museum; the Archives Nationales, the Bibliothèque Nationale, the Bibliothèque de l'Arsenal, and the Bibliothèque Historique de la Ville de Paris; the Archives Départementales de la Gironde and the Bibliothèque de la Ville de Bordeaux; the Archives Départementales de Lot-et-Garonne; the Bibliothèque de la Ville de Rouen.

This bibliography lists only those sources from which I have drawn material for the book.

MANUSCRIPTS

Archives Nationales: K.143; o(1), 845: T.473, 1093, 1256, 1663, 1677, 1686.

British Museum: Add. mss. 15,945; 21,385; 21,386; 23,102; 23,736; 24,024; 29,760; 32,750; 32,752; 32,873; 32,875; 35,895; Eg. 39.

Bibliothèque de l'Arsenal: 2267; 3270; 3271; 4041; 4518; 7590; 10016; 10067; 10117; 10158; 10159; 10238; 10252; 10253; 10598; 10672; 10730; 10927; 11317; 11565; 11594; 11680; 11774; 11846; 11914; 12306; 12437.

Bibliothèque Nationale: Ff.6944; 10364; 10681; 10864; 11248; 11301; 11311; 11907; 11357–60; 13703; 22158; 22798; n.a.f. 5273; 6574–78; 9726; 11222.

Bibliothèque Victor Cousin: Fonds Richelieu XXII–LXVII.

Archives départementales de la Gironde: C.193; 418; 511; 513; 575; 612; 1047; 1048; 1052; 1057; 1082; 2179; 3614; 3633; 3666; 3729; 3764; 3783; 3796; 4256; 4449; 4698; G.305; 306; 307; 477; 542.

Bordeaux, Bibliothèque de la ville: 828 (XXXVI); 1696 (II); 1696 (XVII).

Paris, Bibliothèque historique de la ville: 610; 670; 703; 707.

Rouen, Bibliothèque de la ville: Collection Leber 3334 (5815); 3335 (5816); 3344 (5825); 3357 (5838).

PRINTED MATTER

Allonville, Armand François d', *Mémoires secrets* (Paris, 1838).

Argenson, René-Louis Voyer de Paulmy, marquis d', *Journal et Mémoires* (Paris, 1858).

Armaillé, comtesse La Forest d', *La comtesse d'Egmont* (Paris, 1890).

Bachaumont, Louis Petit de, *Mémoires secrets* (London, 1777).

Barbier, Edouard-Jean-François, *Journal* (Paris, 1857).

Barras, Paul-François-Jean-Nicolas de, *Mémoires* (Paris, 1895).

Barthélemy, Edouard [ed.], *Les correspondants de la marquise de Balleroy* (Paris, 1883).

Beauvau, maréchal de, *Souvenirs* (Paris, 1872).

Belleval, Louis-René de, *Souvenirs d'un Chevau-léger* (Paris, 1866).

Bernadau, Pierre, *Histoire de Bordeaux* (Bordeaux, 1839).

Bernis, François-Joachim de Pierres, *Mémoires et lettres* (Paris, 1878).

Berthelé, Joseph, *Montpellier en 1768* (Montpellier, 1909).

Besenval, Pierre-Joseph-Victor, baron de, *Mémoires* (Paris, 1821).

Boisjourdain, Jacques-Claude de, *Mélanges historiques, politiques et satiriques* (Paris, 1807).

Bordeaux: *Archives municipales*, t.5–10 (Bordeaux, 1890–1913).

Bordeaux: *Bulletin de la société archéologique*, t. II.

Bordeaux: *Description historique* (Bordeaux, 1785).

Brancas, duchesse de, *Mémoires* (Paris, 1865).

Buvat, Jean, *Le journal de la régence* (Paris, 1865).

Campardon, Emile, *La cheminée de Mme. de la Pouplinière* (Paris, 1879).

Capelle, Catalogue du cabinet d'autographes de M. (Paris, 1849).

Capon, G. and Yves-Plessis, *La vie privée du Prince de Conty* (Paris, 1907).

Carnet historique et littéraire (Paris, 1898).

Carriera, Rosalba, *Journal* (Paris, 1865).

Casanova di Seingalt, Giacomo Girolamo, *Mémoires* (Paris, 1826).

Caylus, Marthe-Marguerite le Valois, comtesse de, *Souvenirs et correspondance* (Paris, 1881).

Celeste, Raymond [ed.], *Voyage du duc de Richelieu à Bordeaux, etc.* (Bordeaux, 1882).

Chamfort, Sebastien-Roch-Nicolas, *Oeuvres* (Paris, 1824–25).

Charavay, Jacques, *Catalogue* (Paris, 1855).

Charon, *Catalogue des autographes* (Paris, 1844–45).

Chesterfield, Philip Dormer Stanhope, Earl of, *Letters to His Son* (London, 1774).

Chicoyneau, François, *Journal de la maladie du roi* (Paris, 1745).

Cisternes, Raoul de, *La Campagne de Minorque* (Paris, 1899).

Collé, Charles, *Journal* (Paris, 1868).

Comminges, Bulletin de la Société des Etudes de, t. V, VII. XV.

Commission des archives diplomatiques, *Recueil des instructions données aux ambassadeurs*, t. I—*Autriche.*

Croÿ, Emmanuel, duc de, *Journal* (Paris, 1906).

Dangeau, Philippe de Courcillon, marquis de, *Journal* (Paris, 1854).

Delaunay, Paul, *Le monde médical parisien au XVIIIe. siècle* (Paris, 1906).

Destailleur, Hippolyte, *Recueil d'estampes relatives à l'ornamentation des appartements au XVIe., XVIIe. and XVIIIe. siècles* (*Paris*, 1858).

Detcheverry, Arnaud, *Histoire des théâtres de Bordeaux* (Bordeaux, 1860).

Dubois-Corneau, Robert, *Pâris de Montmartel* (Paris, 1917).

Dubuisson, Simon-Henri, *Lettres au marquis de Caumont* (Paris, 1882).

Ducéré, Edouard, *Dictionnaire topographique de Bayonne* (Bayonne, 1911–15).

Du Châtelet, Gabrielle-Emilie le Tonnelier de Breteuil, marquise, *Lettres* (Geneva, 1958).

Du Deffand, Marie de Vichy-Chamrond, marquise, *Lettres à Horace Walpole* (London, 1912).

Dufort de Cheverny, Jean-Nicolas, *Mémoires* (Paris, 1886).

Dugas de Bois-Saint-Just, *Paris, Versailles et les Provinces* (Paris, 1817).

Dupin, *Le portefeuille de Madame*, G. de Villeneuve-Gaibert [ed.] (Paris, 1884).

Espion anglais, L', t. II, VI.

Espion dévalisé, L'.

Feuille nécessaire, La (1759).

Filon, Charles-Auguste-Désiré, *L'ambassade de Choiseul à Vienne* (Paris, 1872).

Flassan, Gaetan de Raxis de, *Histoire de la diplomatie française* (Paris, 1811).

Fort Saint-Philippe, La siège de.

Fortia de Piles and Guys de Saint-Charles, *Souvenirs de deux anciens militaires* (Paris, 1813).

Frederick II (of Prussia), *Mémoires* (Paris, 1866).

Funck-Brentano, Frantz, *La Bastille des comédiens* (Paris, 1910).

Gassier, Emile, *Les cinq cents immortels* (Paris, 1887).

Gazette de la Régence, Jean Buvat Barthélemy [ed.] (Paris, 1887).

Gentleman's Magazine, Vol. 25 (1755), Vol. 27 (1757).

Gironde, Commission des monuments historique du département de la, t. II, VIII, X, XIV, XVI.

Gironde, archives historiques du département de la, t. I, II, XXIII, XXIV, XXV, XXVI, XXVII, XXVIII (Bordeaux, 1859–).

Grellet-Dumazeau, André, *La société bordelaise sous Louis XV* (Bordeaux, 1897).

Grimm, Friedrich-Melchior, baron von, *Correspondance* (Paris, 1877).

Griselle, Eugène [ed.], *Documents d'histoire* (Paris, 1910).

Guillaumin, Théodore-Albert, *Le parlement de Bordeaux sous Louis XV* (Bordeaux, 1878).

Guinodie, Raymond, *Histoire de Libourne* (Bordeaux, 1845).

Hénault, le président, *Mémoires* (Paris, 1911).

Hurtaut, Pierre-Thomas-Nicolas and Magny, *Dictionnaire historique de la ville de Paris et de ses environs* (Paris, 1779).

Iris de Guienne, L' (Bordeaux, 1763).

Journal de ce qui c'est fait pour la réception du roy (Metz, 1744).

Jullian, Camille, *Histoire de Bordeaux* (Bordeaux, 1895).

Kageneck, Lettres du baron de, Léouzon le Duc [ed.] (Paris, 1884).

Labat, *Le maréchal de Richelieu et les jurats de Bordeaux,* reprinted from *Les actes de l'académie des sciences, des belles-lettres et arts de Bordeaux,* 1903.

La Beaumelle, Laurent Angliviel de, *Mémoires pour servir à l'histoire de Mme. de Maintenon.*

Labrunie, Joseph, *Abrégé chronologique des antiquités d'Agen* (Agen, 1892).

Lambeau, Lucien, *La place royale* (Paris, 1906).

Lescure, M.F.A., *Les autographes et le goût des autographes en France et à l'étranger* (Paris, 1865).

Lévis, P.M.G. duc de, *Souvenirs et portraits* (Paris, 1815).

Lheritier, Michel, *La Révolution à Bordeaux* (Paris, 1942).

Ligne, C. J. E., prince de, *Mémoires* (Paris, 1827).

Luynes, Charles-Philippe d'Albert, duc de, *Mémoires* (Paris, 1827).

Magasin pittoresque, t. X (1842).

Marais, Matthieu, *Journal, Mémoires, Correspondance* (Paris, 1863).

Marmontel, Jean-François, *Mémoires* (Paris, 1891).

Marville, Claude-Henri de Feydeau de, *Lettres au comte de Maurepas* (Paris, 1901–1905).

Mary-Lafon, Jean-Bernard, *Le maréchal de Richelieu et Madame de Saint-Vincent* (Paris, 1863).

Masson, Pierre-Maurice, *Madame de Tencin* (Paris, 1909).

Maupassant, Jean de, *Abraham Gradis* (Bordeaux, 1917).
Maurepas, Recueil dit de (Leyden, 1865).
Montbarey, Alexandre-Marie-Léonor de Saint-Mauris, prince de, *Mémoires* (Versailles, 1826).
Moreau, Jacob-Nicolas, *Mes souvenirs* (Paris, 1901).
Musée d'Aquitaine, La, t. II.
Narbonne, Pierre, *Journal des règnes de Louis XIV et Louis XV* (Paris, 1860).
Nouvelle revue rétrospective, La (1893, 1894).
Nouvelles archives des missions scientifiques et littéraires, t. V (1893).
Nouvelles de la cour et de la ville (Paris, 1879).
Observateur anglais, L' (Pidansat de Mairobert), t. II, IV.
O'Reilly, Patrice-John, *Histoire de Bordeaux* (Paris, 1863).
Orléans, Madame la duchesse d', *Correspondance,* Jaegle [ed.] (Paris, 1880).
Ourry, E.T. Maurice, *Mémoires de Dazincourt* (Paris, 1822).
Pajol, le comte C.P.U., *Les guerres sous Louis XV* (Paris, 1880).
Papillon de la Ferté, Denis-Pierre-Jean, *Journal* (Paris, 1887).
Paris et de l'Ile de France, Bulletin de la société de l'histoire de (1880).
Piganiol de la Force, *Paris et ses environs* (Paris, 1765).
Piron, Alexis, *Oeuvres inédites* (Paris, 1859).
Piton, Camille, *Paris sous Louis XV* (Paris, 1906).
Poitou, Bulletin de la société des archives historiques du, t. XVI, XXXI, LIV.
Précis pour le sieur Bénaven, contre M. le maréchal duc de Richelieu (Paris, 1775).
Protestantisme français, Bulletin de la société de l'histoire du, t. IV, XXI, XXVI, XXVII, XXXII, XLVIII.
Remacle, Louis, *Voyage de Paris en 1782* (Vannes, 1900).
Réponse pour dame Julie de Villeneuve de Vence (Paris, 1776).
Résumé général pour Madame la présidente de Saint-Vincent (Paris, 1777).
Revue de l'Agénois, t. V (1878).
Revue de Paris, March 1912, July 1959.
Richelieu, Collection . . . de lettres du maréchal de (Paris, 1797).
Richelieu, Correspondance historique du maréchal de (avec M. Pâris-Duverney) (Paris, 1798).
Richelieu, Mémoires authentiques du maréchal de, A. de Boislisle [ed.] (Paris, 1918).

Richelieu, *Mémoires du maréchal de* [Jean-Louis Soulavie] (Paris, 1790–93).

Richelieu, *La vie privée du maréchal de* [usually attributed to Faur, but more probably by La Borde] (Paris, 1791).

Roque, *Histoire de la presqu'île de Gennevilliers* (Asnières, 1889).

Rulhières, Claude-Carloman de, *Anecdotes sur Richelieu* (Paris, 1890).

Saint-Amans, J.F. Boudon de, *Histoire . . . de Lot-et-Garonne* (Agen, 1836).

Saint-Beuve, Charles-Augustin, *Portraits Littéraires* (Paris, 1862).

Saint-Simon, Louis de Rouvroy, duc de, *Mémoires* (Paris, 1873).

Saunier, Charles, *Bordeaux* (Bordeaux, 1909).

Saxe, prince François-Xavier de, *Correspondance inédite* (Paris, 1874).

Sénac de Meilhan, Gabriel, *Portraits et caractères du XVIIIe siècle* (Paris, 1813).

Souffrain, Jean-Baptiste-Alexandre, *Essais . . . sur la ville de Libourne* (Bordeaux, 1806).

Soulé, François-Pierre, *Le duché de Fronsac* (Bordeaux, 1940).

Sourches, Louis-François du Bouchet, marquis de, *Mémoires* (Paris, 1882–93).

Stryienski, Casimir, *La mère des trois derniers Bourbons* (Paris, 1902).

Thiébault, Dieudonné, *Mémoires* (Paris, 1804).

Thomas, Fernand, *L'art décoratif à l'entrée du maréchal de Richelieu à Bordeaux* (Tarbes, 1919).

Tressan, Louis-Elisabeth de la Vergne, comte de, *Souvenirs* (Versailles, 1897).

Tricornot, Jean-Baptiste-René-Adrien, baron de, *Mémoires* (Besançon, 1894).

Valfons, Charles de Mathei, marquis de, *Souvenirs* (Paris, 1907).

Vaudreuil, François, *Le pavillon de Hanovre* (Paris, n.d.).

Villars, Louis-Hector, maréchal de, *Mémoires* (Paris, 1884–1907).

Voltaire: *Correspondence*, T. Besterman [ed.] (Geneva, 1953–).

Index